CROMWELL AND COMMUNISM

CROMWELL & COMMUNISM

SOCIALISM AND DEMOCRACY

IN THE GREAT

ENGLISH REVOLUTION

by

EDUARD BERNSTEIN

Translated by

H. J. STENNING

FRANK CASS & CO. LTD.
1966

Published by Frank Cass & Co. Ltd.,
10 Woburn Walk, London W.C.1
by arrangement with George Allen & Unwin Ltd.

First edition	1930
Reprinted	1963
Reprinted	1966

THIS BOOK HAS BEEN PRINTED BY OFFSET LITHO
BY TAYLOR GARNETT EVANS & CO., LTD.
AT WATFORD HERTS

CONTENTS

8 CROMWELL AND COMMUNISM

CHAPTER I

INTRODUCTION

ENGLAND revolted against absolute monarchy a century and a half earlier than did France, under conditions very dissimilar from those that marked the epoch of the great French Revolution. Nevertheless, important resemblances may be detected between the nature and the course of the two rebellions.

At the time of the Revolution England was on the whole more than one hundred years behind France in general development, and her social organization differed in essential points from that of France in 1789. Yet these differences were not all of the same kind, as they did not in all cases indicate backward social development. Only a remnant of the old feudal nobility was left in England; the title-deeds of most of the landed aristocrats were of recent date, and the majority of the estates were already being managed on commercial principles. There was a numerous free peasantry, whilst the middle class already represented a considerable economic force. In the latter class guild elements were still strongly represented. Its ways of living were somewhat coarse, and its mental outlook was narrow, at least when compared with that of Court circles. But intellectual limitation is by no means an impediment to vigorous action. A single-track mind is often the secret of political success. Lastly, the middle class and the bourgeois landowners in seventeenth-century England were confronted with a monarchy that fell far short of the brilliant absolutism of the Bourbons under Louis XIV.

Despite the differing social and political conditions of the two countries at the outbreak of their respective revolutions, and despite the different starting-points of these revolutions, a parallel can be traced both in the formal course which they assumed and the historical results which they achieved. The English Revolution, as it advanced, resembled the great French Revolution in outstripping the aims that were proclaimed at its commencement. During its course the various parties, and the different social classes behind them, came to the front, one after another, and played a leading part in the direction of events, and after a period of military dictatorship the English Revolution, like the French, came to a temporary conclusion in a restoration, which, again resembling the French, proved unable to restore the conditions that existed before the outbreak. Moreover, its last phase consisted in a weak repetition of the rebellion, viz., the Whig Revolution of 1688, which restored the initial political objects of the first revolt. Its Girondists were the Presbyterians; its Jacobins or its Mountain were the Independents; its Hébertists and Babeuvists were the Levellers, whilst Cromwell was a combination of Robespierre and Bonaparte, and John Lilburne the Leveller was Marat and Hébert rolled into one.

It goes without saying that these comparisons are only partially valid. The Levellers, for example, may be compared with the Hébertists only in so far as they constituted the party which, without ever itself being dominant, represented the most extreme element of the revolutionary movement. It was only at the height of its power that the Leveller movement produced a genuinely communistic offshoot in the sect or group of "true Levellers". This sect not only made an experiment in communistic self-help of remarkable originality, but left behind it a noteworthy sketch of communistic reconstruction which seems to have escaped the notice of historians of the English Revolution. In religious matters the majority of Levellers did not differ greatly from the mass of the Independents. Like the latter, they belonged to the Puritan school, but a minority of their leaders undoubtedly professed a rationalistic deism, if not definite atheism. If the personality around whom the Leveller movement grouped itself was in respect of erudition and literary power considerably inferior to Marat, yet "freeborn John"—as John Lilburne often calls himself in his pamphlets—may well be regarded in his strong democratic instincts, his courage, and his championship of plebeian interests as a prototype of the People's Friend. As to the *Père Duchesne*, Lilburne's pamphlets never bore the excessively vulgar character of Hébert's outbursts.

Middle-class historians, however, have been in the habit of treating Lilburne not a whit better than they treated the editor of the *Père Duchesne*. To Carlyle he was nothing but a noisy mischief-maker, and even William Godwin, in his *History of the English Commonwealth*, is frequently unjust to Lilburne.

Nevertheless, Godwin devotes so much attention to the activities of Lilburne and the Levellers that their effect on the course of the political struggle up to the inauguration of the Commonwealth may be gathered from his pages. And since Godwin's time historical investigation has been constantly bringing to light fresh material for this chapter of the Revolution.

Outstanding works dealing with this period are the late S. R. Gardiner's *History of the Great Civil War* and C. P. Gooch's *Democratic Ideas in the Seventeenth Century*. Since the first German edition of the present book appeared, Mr. Berens has published his study of *The Digger Movement*.

CHAPTER II

ENGLAND UP TO THE MIDDLE OF THE SEVENTEENTH CENTURY

1. ECONOMIC AND SOCIAL DEVELOPMENT

IN the seventeenth century England was still to a very large extent an agricultural country. About the middle of the century its population amounted to some 5,000,000, of which at least three-fourths lived on the country-side. With the exception of London, already grown very large, none of its towns was excessively populous. Towards the end of the century Gregory King estimated that a total population of 5½ millions was distributed in the following manner:

				Inhabitants.
London	..	..	..	530,000
Large and small towns	..	..	..	870,000
Villages and hamlets	..	..	..	4,110,000
Total	..	..	..	5,500,000

A similar proportion between London and the rest of the kingdom is given in William Petty's *Essays on Political Arithmetic*, published in 1687. Petty reckons the population of London and its suburbs at 690,000; that of the whole of England and Wales at 7,000,000. According to him, London had some half-million inhabitants about the middle of the seventeenth century, and, as he knew London during the revolutionary period, his reckoning is probably not very far out. Next to London, Petty takes Bristol as the "British emporium", and gives its population as 48,000. In fact, Bristol in the seventeenth century was an important staple town. It drove a flourishing trade with Spain and Portugal, and was the centre of the woollen manufacture in the south-west of England. Norwich, the centre of the woollen manufacture in the Eastern Counties, was Bristol's rival. These were the three most populous towns in England at that time.

Industry was on the whole in a somewhat backward state. In nearly all branches it had lagged behind that of the Continent. Well into the sixteenth century England produced the finest wool, but for long was content to work up the coarser types herself. The combing of the finer sorts was done abroad, especially in Flanders. The situation did not change until crowds of Flemish weavers were driven to England by the consequences of the religious wars in the Netherlands. A result of this immigration in the second half of the sixteenth century was the rise of the English wool-weaving trade, which at first flourished chiefly in Norfolk and certain neighbouring counties and later extended to the west, where we find it had assumed considerable dimensions at the period we are investigating.

It was not until the seventeenth century that the mineral wealth of England, with the exception of tin, began to be exploited to any considerable extent, although it did not play an important part in economic life at the period we are discussing. The value of coal for iron furnaces was beginning to be appreciated, but scores of years were to elapse before England became independent of the Continent as a source of supply for iron. According to Macpherson,[1] in 1720 England imported two-thirds of her crude iron from abroad.

According to Gregory King, there were living in England in 1688:

	Persons.
From agriculture	4,265,000
From trades and industries ..	240,000
From commerce	246,000

In this calculation domestic industry (production for household needs), still very important at that time, is not taken into account. Nor is there any indication of the many cases in which industrial and agricultural work was still carried on by the same people. It does not, therefore, give a reliable picture of production, although it reveals to how small an extent industry,

[1] *Annals of Commerce*, vol. iii. p. 114.

even at the end of the seventeenth century, had broken away from its elementary connection with domestic and agricultural work.

The population living by agriculture was subdivided into the classes of the great nobles, the landed gentry, the small peasants, the agricultural day labourers, and the great mass of paupers. The great nobility, even when of feudal origin, had already got rid of most of their feudal obligations, and managed their estates as seemed good to them. Part they placed under stewards and part they farmed out. The landed gentry consisted of the smaller landowners, the descendants of the purchasers of the confiscated feudal and monastic properties, farmers who had grown rich, and others. The numerous small peasants were partly freeholders, who were exposed to injury through the constant filching of common lands by the great, and copyholders, tenants at will, etc., who bore the brunt of the pressure exercised on farmers by greedy landlords. "The rents of the seventeenth century, small as they seem to us, began with competition rents, which rapidly slid into famine rents, by which I understand rents which leave the cultivator a bare maintenance, without the means of either improving or saving", writes Thorold Rogers. "There was, however", he adds, "in some parts of England, notably in the Eastern Counties, in the west and north, a by-industry of sufficient importance as to make the tenant-farmer comparatively indifferent to accretions of rent."[1]

This by-industry would be the wool and linen industry, which was carried on in most of the cottages of whole districts. But in Yorkshire and Lancashire the woollen industry was not so important in the seventeenth century as it was in East Anglia, where we should look for a class of small farmers enjoying some degree of independence.

It may appear surprising that in seventeenth-century England there should have been such a host of small peasants

[1] Thorold Rogers, *The Economic Interpretation of History*, pp. 174, 175.

and small tenants at will, in spite of the working of the land by capitalistic farmers, which began at the end of the fifteenth and increased during the sixteenth century, and in spite of the expropriation of peasants involved in converting arable into pasture land. But the agricultural revolution did not pursue an unbroken and unimpeded course. Under Henry VII and his successors various laws were passed designed to maintain a considerable peasantry, and while those laws were frequently a dead-letter when they collided with the land-hunger of the great nobles, they did prolong the process here and there. But there is another important circumstance, mentioned by Karl Marx, which may be regarded as the chief cause of the phenomenon. "England", writes Marx, "is at one time chiefly a cultivator of corn, at another chiefly a breeder of cattle, in alternate periods, and with these the extent of peasant cultivation fluctuates."[1] Thus during the religious wars in the Netherlands England ceased to sell her wool there, and the breeding of sheep stopped. On the other hand, weaving as a by-industry spread over the country, and, as shown above, averted the ruin of the small farmers by the rent-raising landlords.

The agricultural labourers lived under the ban of the famous Statute of Labourers of Elizabeth, the threefold aim of which is thus described by Thorold Rogers: "(1) to break up the combinations of labourers; (2) to supply the adequate machinery of control; and (3) by limiting the right of apprenticeship, to make the peasant labourer the residuum of all other labour, or, in other words, to forcibly increase the supply."[2]

As is well known, the Statute of Labourers prescribed a seven years' apprenticeship to any branch of industry, and, further, merchants and masters in certain trades could only take as apprentices the sons of freeholders of landed property of a fixed value. The wages of agricultural labourers and journeymen in different trades were fixed by the Justices of the Peace

[1] *Capital*, vol. i. p. 773.   [2] Ibid., p. 70.

at Easter of each year, and Thorold Rogers testifies that, in spite of threats of punishment, the wages actually paid were always higher than those fixed by the justices. On the other hand, W. A. S. Hewins, in his *English Trade and Finance, Chiefly in the Seventeenth Century*, adduces certain facts (pp. 82–159) pointing to the conclusion that, upon the whole, "the justices' wages were paid". W. Cunningham, in his work, *The Growth of English Industry and Commerce*, maintains, in opposition to Rogers, that in the time of James I the Statute was so altered that only the paying of less wages than those fixed by the Justices of the Peace was made penal, and not the paying of higher wages. If so, the effect on wages would scarcely have been unfavourable, so far as the law was observed at all. It is true that the Statute of Labourers of 1604 only refers to penalties for those who pay lower wages than are fixed. But the preamble to the law gives no indication that this new wording was intended to express a new principle. The sole aim of the Act is declared to be the extension of the law of Elizabeth to the clothmakers and others and the alteration of the rules of procedure in the fixing of wages.

According to Cunningham, the wage of the agricultural labourer of the time we are now considering was 6d. a day in summer and 4d. in winter, in addition to three meals, including butter, milk, cheese, and eggs or bacon. Having regard to differences in the purchasing power of money and the general standard of life, the agricultural labourer was probably better off than his posterity of three hundred years later.

Another fact mentioned by Thorold Rogers, of special interest for our subject, is that during the period of the Commonwealth, the legally fixed wages were higher than they were under the monarchy that preceded or the monarchy that followed the republic. In 1651 they were only 4¼d. below the wages actually paid; in 1655 only 2¼d.; but no sooner is the monarchy restored than the justices are up to their old tricks again and fix the wages at 3s. less than those actually paid. "The Puritans were perhaps stern men, but they had some sense of duty. The Cavaliers were perhaps polished, but appear to have had no virtue except what they called loyalty. I think if I had been an agricultural labourer in the seventeenth century I should have preferred the Puritan."[1] "So long as the republic lasted, the mass of the English people of all grades rose from the degradation into which they had sunk under the Tudors."[2] That the justices were suddenly affected by the sense of duty of the Puritans, of which Rogers speaks, may be ascribed to the greater influence which the struggle between King and Parliament had given to the working classes.

The general conditions of agricultural life prevented the development of a sharp class antagonism between the small peasant and the agricultural labourer. These classes resembled each other too closely in ways of life and labour (if we except those agricultural labourers who had been reduced to "vagabonds") for any serious conflicts to arise. A real class antagonism, in some phases sharply accentuated, existed only between small peasants, small farmers, and the agricultural labourers joining them, on the one hand, and the great landlords, particularly as the latter were mostly of recent origin, on the other hand.

The same considerations apply to handicrafts in town and country. The wages question being so completely settled by legal determination, there was scope only for minor individual adjustments. While conflict was not entirely absent, no employee thought for a moment of questioning the right of existence of the master as an established class or felt any solidarity with the employees of another trade. Moreover, owing to the long apprenticeship to the chief industries, the number of journeymen was very limited, a point to which we shall return later.

A stronger antagonism, however, existed between members of the handicraft industries, now developing into staple indus-

[1] Thorold Rogers, loc. cit., p. 44.   [2] Marx, loc. cit., p. 773 *n.*

B

tries and manufactures, and the merchants who dealt in their produce. As early as 1555 the weavers complained that "the rich and wealthy clothiers do many ways oppress them" by putting unapprenticed men to work on their own looms, by letting out looms on hire, and "some also by giving much less wages and hire for the weaving and workmanship of clothes than in times past they did". Thus the preamble of the "Act touching weavers" passed under the Catholic Mary, a law which, admitting the justice of the complaint just quoted, limits the number of looms to be owned by one person to two in the towns and one in the country, and forbids the hiring of looms. This law seems to have operated as a drag upon the development of manufacture, but eventually social forces proved too strong, and the vexatious law was in every way evaded, as is proved by the frequent and increasing complaints of the masters against the merchants. What we have to remember, for the purposes of our investigation, is that a sharp antagonism existed between the weavers and the merchants. And similar divergencies existed in other trades in which merchants had interposed themselves between producers and consumers. Great hostility was further evoked by the monopolies which governments, when in financial difficulties, sold or farmed out to the merchant trading companies. This last point brings us to the political conditions which existed at the beginning of the reign of Charles I.

2. POLITICAL AND RELIGIOUS CONDITIONS. KET'S INSURRECTION

Parliament in the time of Henry VII, and still more in that of Henry VIII, had become a tool in the hands of the King. Benevolences and duties belonging to feudal times were exacted on an immense scale; loans made to the King were again and again declared forfeit; decrees of the King had the force of laws; new crimes of high treason were created, and a special

Court was constituted for troublesome State criminals (the Star Chamber), to which was added, in the reign of Elizabeth, an exceptional Court, declared permanent in 1583 (the Court of High Commission), intended to deal with persons who denied the supremacy of the monarch for the time being over ecclesiastical affairs. This proclamation of the supremacy of the King over the Church was the culminating point of Henry VIII's "Reformation". Its objects were: (1) to put an end to the interference of the Pope in English affairs; (2) and, which is of far greater importance, as the Pope's influence in England had generally been very small, to convert the clergy into a tool of monarchical absolutism. And (3) after the declaration of the supremacy came the dissolution of the monasteries and the confiscation of their enormous wealth, which the spendthrift King made haste to squander. These methods of reformation, it will be apprehended, did not meet with the enthusiastic approval even of those who, otherwise, were hostile to the Romish Church, especially as Henry retained most of the dogmas and rites of that Church. Catholics and sincere Reformers alike were dissatisfied. There were frequent revolts, in which the country population took an active part, and which were successfully suppressed under Henry VIII and his son, Edward VI, but when the latter died in 1553 a victorious rebellion overthrew the Reformation leaders and established the Catholic Mary on the throne.

The revolt which has a special interest for us occurred in the reign of Edward VI, who succeeded his father in 1547 while yet a minor, and whose Government was at first carried on by his uncle, the Duke of Somerset, the Protector. In June 1549 the peasants of Devonshire rebelled and demanded the restoration of the ancient faith. They forced the priests to read the Mass in Latin, and besieged Exeter for a week. The revolt was then quelled by an army, composed mainly of mercenaries, led by Lord Russell. While this insurrection was of a religious character, the revolt of the agricultural population of Norfolk, under Robert Ket, which followed in the same month, wore a distinct political and social character, and was directed against the feudal aristocracy.

Ket's rebellion was not an isolated phenomenon. There was universal unrest among the agricultural population, and the flames burst forth now in one place and now in another. As early as 1537 there was a popular revolt in Yorkshire on behalf of the Catholic faith (The Pilgrimage of Grace), whilst in Walsingham (Norfolk) an insurrection against the "gentlemen" was prematurely discovered and its leaders executed. A woman, Elizabeth Wood of Aylsham (Norfolk), was reported to the Council of State to have said: "It was pitie that these Walsingham men was discovered, for we shall never have good worlde till we fall togither by the earys:

And with clubbes and clowted shone
Shall the dede be done,

for we had never good world since this Kynge rayned."

She is, says the report, a stiff-necked "ongracious" woman. Much stronger and more ominous sound the words reported of one John Walker from Griston: "If three or four good fellows wold ryde in the night with every man a belle, and cry in every town that they pass through: To Swaffham, to Swaffham! by the morning ther would be ten thousand assemblyd at the lest; and then one bold fellowe to stand forth and sey: Syres, now we be here assemblyd, you now how all the gentylmen in names be gone forth, and you now how little favour they bere to us pore men: let us therefore nowe go home to ther howsys, and ther shall we have harnesse, substance and vytayle. And as many as will not tirn to us, let us kyll them, ye, evyn ther chyldren in the cradelles, for yt were a good thinge if there were so many gentylmen in Norfolk as ther by whyt bulles."[1]

The great land thieves ignored these warnings. They relied

[1] Russell, *Ket's Rebellion in Norfolk*, p. 8.

upon Henry's Draconian edicts against all kinds of rebellion, and continued expelling peasants, raising rents, acquiring monastic property at ludicrous prices, and enclosing common lands or taking them for grazing lands.

Whatever his faults, Somerset, the guardian of Edward VI, seems to have sympathized with the poorer classes, for, soon after his assumption of the Protectorate, the harsh laws against the Lollards were repealed and a Bill to prevent the enclosing of land was introduced in Parliament. Neither House, however, would support it, and Somerset's initiative was ascribed to mere popularity-hunting. Later, Somerset was accused of having provoked the Ket insurrection by his clemency towards the country-people. Alexander Nevil, or Nevylle, the classic historian of the Ket rebellion, refers to these accusations in his work, *The Commotion in Norfolk*. "The Lord Protector had at that time lost himself in the love of the vulgar, by his severe proceeding against his brother; and in order to regain their love he caused a proclamation to be published in the beginning of May that all persons who had inclosed any lands that used to be common should lay them open again, before a fixed day, on a certain penalty for not doing so: this so much encouraged the commons in many parts of the realm that (not staying the time limited in the proclamation) they gathered together in tumultuous manner, pulled up the pales, flung down the banks, filled up the ditches, laying all such new enclosed lands open as they were before."[1] That the common people were troubled about the fate of Somerset's ambitious brother, Seymour, may well be doubted. Somerset had in fact arranged in 1548 for the appointment of a Commission to examine the legality of all enclosures that had been made since a given date, and to order the fences to be taken down in cases of doubtful legality. But as soon as they heard of the concession, the country-folk took the matter into their own hands, and began to "examine" the enclosures in their own

[1] P. 1 of the English edition published at Norwich in 1750.

way. Somerset is said, in May 1549, to have openly declared "he liked well the doings of the people, the covetousness of the gentlemen gave occasion to them to rise".[1] The authorities made but feeble efforts to put down the disturbances, while the Commission turned out to be a dead-letter. So in the summer of 1549 the peasants held numerous secret meetings, at which all kinds of diatribes were uttered against the ruling class. Nevylle imparts a somewhat rhetorical air to these speeches, but they probably bore a close resemblance to his report. Here is a specimen of these speeches: "We cannot any longer endure injuries so great and cruel; nor can we without being moved by it, behold the insolence of the nobility and gentry: we will sooner betake ourselves to arms, and mix heaven and earth in confusion, than submit to such atrocities. Since Nature has made the same provision for us as for them, and has given us also a soul and a body, we should like to know whether this is all we are to expect at her hands. Look at them and look at us: have we not all the same form? Are we not all born in the same way? Why, then, should their mode of life, why should their lot, be so vastly different from ours? We see plainly that matters are come to an extremity, and extremities we are determined to try. We will throw down hedges, fill up ditches, lay open the commons, and level to the ground whatever enclosures they have put up, no less shamefully than meanly." Before this it had been said: " . . . they have sucked the very blood out of our veins, and the marrow out of our bones. The Commons, which were left by our forefathers for the relief of ourselves and families, are taken from us: the lands which within the remembrance of our fathers were open, are now surrounded with hedges and ditches; and the pastures are enclosed, so that no one can go upon them".[2]

Open insurrection flared out at the beginning of July 1549. Robert Ket, an able and energetic man, of undoubted honesty

---

[1] Froude, vol. v. p. 168.   [2] Russell, *Life of Ket*, pp. 23, 24.

of purpose, aided by his brother William, endeavoured to transform the rabble into an army capable of resistance and of attack. He held his Council and his Court of Justice under a great oak, which he named the "Reform Oak". On Mousehold Hill, near Norwich, he pitched his camp, which soon numbered over ten thousand men, and grew day by day. He decreed that enclosures should be annulled, issued summonses and made requisitions "in the King's name". Moreover, he drew up a petition to the Government enumerating the complaints and the demands of the peasants, which the Mayor of Norwich and his predecessors were prevailed upon to sign along with Ket.

These demands are, on the whole, very moderate, and contain no communistic tendencies. In addition to the enclosing of the common land, the abuses singled out for attack are the dovecotes of the great, "those nests of robbers", a number of feudal exactions, and the raising of farm rents to the highest level. The rebels demanded that farm rents should be legally reduced to the level at which they stood in the first year of the reign of Henry VII. Very notable is the demand that *the priests shall be forbidden to buy land*, because it refutes the charge made at the time that the rising had been instigated by the priests.

This charge is supported by the Catholic historian, Lingard, who contends that the insurrection—like that in Devonshire—was aimed at the restoration of the old Catholic Church. It is true that the rapacity of the new landlords was unfavourably compared with the comparatively indulgent methods of the monasteries, but otherwise Lollard and Anabaptist teachings were much more evident in the insurrection than sympathy with Popery. Sir William Paget, Councillor of State, writes to Somerset on July 7th: "Look well whether youe have either lawe or religion at home, and I feare youe shall find neither. The use of the old religion is forbydden by a lawe, and the use of the newe ys not yet prunted in the stomackes of the eleven of twelve partes in the realm, what countenance soever men make outwardly to please them in whom they see the power restethe." Paget, one of the most notorious gorgers of Church property, urged a rapid march on the rebels, pointing to the German Peasant War as an example. Ket seems, on the whole, to have let religion remain a private matter. He looked after the clergymen who conducted divine service in his camp, but others, besides them, were allowed to preach, a privilege of which Matthew Parker, afterwards Archbishop of Canterbury, made use. In the same way, all kinds of people, foes as well as friends of the rising, were allowed to address the people from the Reform Oak.

The friends included various respectable citizens of Norwich, most of whom certainly turned out to be doubtful or even false friends at a later date. This was the case with T. Aldrich, one of the signatories to Ket's petition. On the other hand, the small handicraftsmen and workers of Norwich were wholly sympathetic to the rising. They frustrated various measures adopted by the citizens against the rebels, and rendered the latter valuable assistance in the collisions that occurred. Subsequently the citizens excused their temporary compliance with the rebels on the ground of the compulsion forced on them by the poorer classes of the town.[1]

We cannot here recount the details of the fighting, the defeat and overthrow of the first army sent against the rebels, under the Earl of Northampton. The first herald from the Protector offered, provided the rebels submitted, an inquiry into the complaints and the King's pardon for their offence against the authority of the law. Ket sent him back with the declaration that it was the habit of the King to pardon evil-doers, not innocent and righteous people. The peasants and their leaders had merited no punishment. Ket refused to lay down arms until definite concessions were made, for he well knew what little reliance was to be placed on general promises.

[1] Blomefield's *History of Norfolk*.

But even if Somerset had been willing to consent to this, the great men beside and behind him would not have yielded, and clamoured for an energetic suppression of the revolt, which was effected on August 28th by an army of German mercenaries under John Dudley, Earl of Warwick. At the last moment Ket seems to have shown himself a coward, but he may be forgiven for fleeing when he saw the battle was lost.

As "the people's judge" Ket had shown a humanity remarkable for his days. All prisoners and hostages taken by him, whose names are known, returned unharmed. But Ket and his brother William were hanged for high treason. On December 7th, shortly after Somerset had fallen from power and been cast into the Tower, Ket, who had been brought from London, where his trial had taken place, to Norwich some days earlier, was hanged from the top of the church tower of that town.

Warwick remained in Norwich a fortnight after the decisive battle and held a court of justice on the peasants taken prisoners. But severe as he was, the landlords clamoured for more bloodshed. Their thirst for vengeance demanded more and more victims, "whose entrails were torn from their bodies and burnt before their dying eyes", until at least Warwick said that if this slaughter continued, none would be left to plough the land, and to this argument the landlords yielded.

Somerset was beheaded on January 22, 1552. Warwick, who succeeded him as Lord Protector, and made himself Duke of Northumberland in the following year, also died on the scaffold, after the Catholic Mary ascended the throne. The policy pursued by her Government clearly showed that what the mass of the people wanted was not the reactionary measures of the Roman Catholic Church. The cruel decrees of her reign against all heretics had the effect of drawing the various Protestant sects closer to one another, so that when she died in 1558 the Catholic cause was as unpopular as it had been popular five years before.

In the reign of Elizabeth (1558–1603) the work of the Reformation was resumed and finished off, but not without provoking fresh rebellions. These were, however, suppressed with great cruelty, and the Catholic resistance was finally broken down. During this time resistance to the new State Church was growing up on the Protestant side, in the form of the Puritan opposition.

Who were the Puritans? The name connotes not merely a particular religious sect, but a complete religious and social tendency. It was first a collective name for all those for whom the Reformation or *purification* of the Church from Romish practices and Romish rules did not go far enough, and who connected with the purification of religion that of the morals of the body politic, and eventually it included a political tendency: resistance to absolutism in Church and State. Puritanism was not the movement of a single class. It had its adherents among the upper and lower nobility, among the clergy, the citizens, the handicraft workers, and the peasants. As a moral or social movement it accorded with the spirit of a time when, under the pressure of world commerce, it was becoming increasingly difficult to gain a livelihood, and when the habit of saving money was spreading. The natural economy of feudal times had been characterized by alternating scarcity and abundance, but with the rise of money and the growth of trade, the surplus that was not immediately consumed was turned into money. To consume more than was necessary, to squander what might be converted into money, now appeared as a social sin, and frugality and thrift became social virtues. Christian asceticism had been preached by the Lollard priests as a return to primitive Christianity, by way of protest against the mad luxury of the decayed Romish aristocracy. The peasants and artisans had welcomed the vaguely communistic teachings of the Lollards, because these teachings reinforced their own hostility towards the lords of Church and State. "The Lollard", writes Thorold Rogers, "was no doubt like the Puritan of two centuries later, sour, reserved, opinionative and stiff. But he saved money, all the more because he did not care to spend on priest and monk, friar or pardoner."[1] Lollardism was never completely suppressed, but continued to flourish among such classes as the weavers of the Eastern Counties. It must not be imagined that the weavers and peasants who gave heed to the gospel preached by the Lollards were in particularly indigent circumstances. On the contrary, in the fifteenth and sixteenth centuries, Norfolk, where the movement was strongest, was, as the various lists of taxes prove, one of the richest counties in England, although its natural resources were not very great. Thorold Rogers attributes the frugality of the population to the Lollard teachings, but we may fairly assume that the gospel of thrift met with approval among them, because it accorded with their economic situation.

It has been said that Lollardism was "the childhood of Puritanism". The circumstances and methods of the English Reformation contributed in no small degree to the general acceptance of its ascetic teaching. The elements in the population which were not Romish, but which rebelled against centralized, absolute rule in Church and State, were constrained, after the suppression of each rising, to seek refuge wholly in religious introspection, in moral self-discipline, and these habits were contracted by members of other classes whose social conditions did not otherwise foster asceticism. Calvinism, according to which every one of the elect was a chosen fighter for God, assured of salvation, found wide acceptance. This gospel, with its provision for Church government by the laity, reinforced the resistance of the discontented. Along with it, the Anabaptist propaganda, which had never been completely extinguished, made headway among the handicraftsmen and labourers. Of all the so-called Reformation Churches, Calvinism is the one that was most in harmony with the tendencies and needs of the rising citizen class of the towns and the middle-

[1] Loc. cit., pp. 79–80.

class landowners. According to Calvin, the Church should be linked up with the State, but as the lay element is strongly represented in the Church, it enforces the rigid Church discipline. The laity then consisted of the comfortable classes in town and country. In Geneva, its home, Calvinism had republican leanings, but in England and Germany monarchical absolutism was reaping the benefits of the anti-Romish movement. Where the classes in question were strong enough to resist absolutism, it was natural that they should look to Geneva as the model community for the true reformation of religion. Thus Calvinism rapidly became naturalized in the Netherlands, where resistance to the Spanish rule united the cream of the middle classes and the great nobles. Under somewhat similar conditions it spread through Bohemia and Hungary. It enrolled under its flag the Protestant traders and landowners of France. Calvin's political creed excluded alike princely absolutism and plebeian democracy, but between these two extremes it offered scope for compromise. Hence the most diverse varieties of Calvinism could fight together under one flag, so long as they were animated by a common hostility. Frederick Engels makes some suggestive remarks upon the connection between the Calvinist dogma of predestination and the contemporary situation of the middle classes. He writes:

"His predestination doctrine was the religious expression of the fact that in the commercial world of competition success or failure does not depend upon a man's activity or cleverness, but upon circumstances uncontrollable by him. It is not of him that willeth or of him that runneth, but of the mercy of unknown superior powers; and this was especially true at a period of economic revolution, when all old commercial routes and centres were replaced by new ones, when India and America were opened to the world, and when even the most sacred economic articles of faith—the value of gold and silver—began to totter and to break down. Calvin's Church constitution was thoroughly democratic and republican; and where the Kingdom of God was republicanized, could the kingdoms of this world remain subject to monarchs, bishops, and lords? While German Lutheranism became a willing tool in the hands of princes, Calvin founded a republic in Holland, and active republican parties in England, and, above all, Scotland.

"In Calvinism the second great bourgeois upheaval found its doctrine ready cut and dried. This upheaval took place in England. The middle class of the towns brought it on, and the yeomanry of the country districts fought it out. Curiously enough, in all of the three great bourgeois risings, the peasantry is just the class that, the victory once gained, is most surely ruined by the economic consequences of that victory. A hundred years after Cromwell the yeomanry of England had almost disappeared. Anyhow, had it not been for that yeomanry and for the *plebeian* element in the towns, the bourgeoisie would never have fought the matter out to the bitter end, and would never have brought Charles I to the scaffold. In order to secure even those conquests of the bourgeoisie that were ripe for gathering at the time, the revolution had to be carried considerably further—exactly as in 1793 in France and 1848 in Germany. This seems, in fact, to be one of the laws of evolution of bourgeois society."[1]

To be sure, during the reign of Elizabeth, Puritanism and its allied sects could only proselytize furtively, as her Government was too strong, too effective, and, we may add, too intelligent to provoke such a volume of discontent as was needed to enrol the mass of the population under the banner of Puritanism. Yet, even during her reign, the sect known as "Separatists" or Brownists, after the priest and teacher, Robert Browne, split off from the main body of the Calvinists. This sect stood for the complete independence of every con-

---

[1] Frederick Engels on "Historic Materialism," *Neue Zeit.*, 1892–93, vol. i. pp. 43, 44.

gregation of the godly. Browne, who lived for a year among
the Dutch fugitives in Norfolk and stayed in Holland for a
still longer time, was undoubtedly influenced by the Anabaptists.

Probably Brownism, from the outset, was strongly imbued
with democratic political tendencies. In any case, it engendered
the religion of the extreme political elements, who as an ecclesiastical organization called themselves "Independents". The
name signified the champions of independence for each con-
gregation, and came to denote a political party. The sect
began by preaching a return to primitive Christianity, the
re-establishment of the Kingdom of Christ. His spiritual
influence alone was sufficient to secure harmony and concord
among the congregations of the "saints", and rendered super-
fluous such coercive expedients as the organized Church
discipline of the Calvinists. The Independents rejected the
order of priesthood and everything that smacked of prelacy.
"The other sect, or faction rather", we read in the book *A
Brief Discovery of the False Church*, by Henry Barrowe, one
of the founders and martyrs of Independency, published in
1590, and referring to the orthodox Calvinists, "these Re-
formists, howsoever, for fashions sake, they give the People a
little liberty, to sweeten their mouths, and make them believe
that they should choose their own ministers; yet even in this
pretended choice do they cozen and beguile them also; leaving
them nothing but the smoky, windy title of election only;—
enjoining them to choose some University clerk; one of these
college-birds of their own brood; or else, comes a synod in
the neck of them, and annihilated the election, whatsoever
it be."[1]

Under James I the disintegrating tendencies in Church and
State were accentuated. Even in his first Parliament many
Puritans sat, and although, in accordance with custom, this

---

[1] Quoted in Benjamin Hanbury's *Historical Memorials Relating to the
Independents*, London, 1839, p. 47.

Parliament voted the King tonnage and poundage for life, it refused to discuss any further grants for the King's maintenance until it had inquired into the mandates and elections of its members. King and Parliament were thenceforward in ceaseless conflict, and while not venturing to the point of open resistance, Parliament refused to be intimidated by the King's threats and protested energetically against the violation of its rights. One of the most famous of these protests so angered the King that, in December 1621, he, with his own hand, tore the page on which it was written out of the journals of the House of Commons. He then dissolved Parliament and imprisoned certain of its members, among whom was John Pym, member for Tavistock, who subsequently headed the resistance to Charles I. Another member of the opposition in James' reign was Thomas Wentworth, member for York County, who afterwards became Earl of Stafford and the right-hand man of Charles I. He was destined to die on the scaffold for James' son.

James tried in every way to raise money: by forced loans, by traffic in titles and honours, by the sale of monopolies. The last Parliament he summoned (when war broke out with Spain), while granting the money for prosecuting the war, declared monopolies illegal, and accused James' Secretary to the Treasury, Earl Middlesex, of bribery. In 1625 James died, and bequeathed a troubled kingdom to his successor.

3. THE "UTOPIA" OF LORD CHANCELLOR BACON

One year after the death of James, his sometime Lord Chancellor, Francis Bacon, Baron Verulam and Viscount St. Albans, also died. Among his papers was the fragment of a Utopia, the *New Atlantis*, written in Latin. It is interesting to examine the social ideas of this cultured philosopher one hundred years after the appearance of More's *Utopia*.

The title of the work relates to the mythical Atlantis of

the ancients mentioned by Plato in *Timæus*. Just as the tradition of a great continent beyond the Pillars of Hercules almost suggested an early knowledge of the existence of America, so Bacon's *New Atlantis* has been supposed to hint at the existence of the Australian Continent.

Bacon's *New Atlantis* describes a model community engaged in scientific and technical pursuits rather than a social Utopia, and subsumes the technological speculations of the foremost thinker of his time. The social and moral side of the narrative is tedious and uninspiring compared with the bold swing of More's *Utopia*. "Bensalem", as the "New Atlantis" is called by its inhabitants, seems to be but little different from seventeenth-century Europe, and presents all the social categories of property, property distinctions, classes, priests, an official hierarchy, and a king who is both wise and absolute. The only touch of originality is an order of learned men devoted mainly to industrial experiments. The institute of these *savants*, "King Solomon's House", is a centre for the cultivation of useful knowledge, and one of the fathers of the order, in his enumeration of the directions, arrangements, and contrivances of the house, sketches the scientific Utopia of Bacon. The name Solomon was a compliment to James I, whose flatterers often compared him with the Jewish King.

A family festival attended by the narrator of the "New Atlantis" depicts a family resembling that of Bacon's time, but somewhat idealized and organized on patriarchal lines. We learn that in Bensalem rigid monogamy and the strictest chastity reign. Marriages contracted without parental consent, while not invalid, entailed partial disinheritance on the children. All of which was very reassuring to the comfortable classes of the period, for whose edification a corrective is administered to More. "I have read in a book of one of your men, of a feigned commonwealth", says a Jew (religious toleration being the rule in Bensalem) to the narrator, "where the married couple are permitted, before they contract, to see one another naked. This they (the inhabitants of the 'New Atlantis') dis-like; for they think it a scorn to give a refusal after so familiar knowledge, but because of many hidden defects in men and women's bodies, they have a more civil way." A friend or relation of one of the "high contracting parties" may see the other bathe.

In the "New Atlantis" of Bacon, the ardent advocate of the realistic and inductive method of inquiry, religion plays a much greater, much more obtrusive part than in the Utopia of the Catholic More.

In one respect only does Bacon's imagination soar, and that is in the enormous volume of the wealth of the "New Atlantis", the abundance of its means of enjoyment. The inmates of the House of Solomon do not pass their days in abstract speculation; they experiment, calculate, and produce. It is a Utopia with emphasis on the aspect of production, thus chiming in with the intellectual tendencies of the clearest thinkers amongst the middle class of the period, and presents no essential modifications in the modes of production and distribution. The description of Solomon's House begins: "The end of our foundation is the knowledge of causes, and secret motions of things; and the enlarging of the bounds of human empire, to the effecting of all things possible."

In an age of discoveries Bacon stands forth as the herald of an epoch of the great industrial inventions. This is indeed no small thing, but it involves a contracting of the social horizon, as individual utility is the immediate concern. This explains the paucity of ideas in all that relates to social organization as a whole. Bacon's Utopia reveals the progress which modern industrial doctrine had already made in his time.

CHAPTER III

EARLY YEARS OF CHARLES I's REIGN. JOHN LILBURNE'S
YOUTH AND FIRST PERSECUTIONS

A DETAILED description of the great English Revolution, its
immediate causes, and the vicissitudes through which it
passed, does not come within the purview of this book. No
movement, however, can be understood unless it be studied
in relation to contemporary events. It is therefore essential
to relate briefly such of the events as bear a close relation to
the subject of this work. Moreover, as the Leveller movement
was the fount of the extreme tendencies which manifested
themselves during the Revolution, and as this movement
clustered around the personality of John Lilburne, a bio-
graphical sketch of this remarkable man is clearly indicated
as our first task, the more so as up to a certain period the
chief phases of the Revolution are reflected in Lilburne's
personal activities and fate.

John Lilburne was born at Greenwich in 1615 or 1617, his
father being Richard Lilburne, an English gentleman, a
member of that important class of non-feudal landowners
which already set the tone of the House of Commons. It is
said of him that he was the last to decide a trial in England by
wager of battle, and John may have inherited his pugnacity
from his father. The family seat of the Lilburnes was in
Durham, in which place and in Newcastle John spent his
youth. Being a younger son,[1] John was obliged to earn a liveli-

---

[1] His elder brother, Robert Lilburne, held a high position in the Parliamentary Army and afterwards in the Commonwealth. He was a member of
the Extraordinary High Court of Justice that sentenced Charles to death
A younger brother of John, Henry Lilburne, also served in the Parliamentary Army, and, on Cromwell's recommendation, was made Governor
of Tynemouth Castle; but when the breach between Parliament and the
Army came to a head, he wavered in his allegiance to the Army, and was
preparing to surrender the castle to the Scotch Presbyterians hastening to
the assistance of Charles, when his own soldiers killed him during the
fight.

hood after leaving school, and in 1630 he came to London as apprentice to a great City merchant, the linendraper, Thomas Hewson.

The situation was already becoming critical. Charles was involved in a quarrel not only with the Commons, but also with the majority of the Lords. Even then the preponderating power rested with the Lower House, which represented a much greater aggregate of wealth than the House of Peers. According to Hume, the wealth then represented in the House of Commons was more than three times the volume represented in the House of Peers. The House of Lords then consisted of 97 lords temporal and 26 lords spiritual, while 90 county members, 4 university members, and over 400 members for towns and boroughs constituted the House of Commons. There are grounds for believing that the Puritans at that date were stronger than the High Tories, the moderate Churchmen, and the Roman Catholics put together.

In 1628, after two years of unconstitutional levying of taxes, imprisonment of persons refusing to pay them, and molestation of the King's opponents by billeting soldiers on them, Charles, whose foreign enterprises had come to grief, was obliged to summon Parliament. This Parliament compelled the King, who was in urgent need of money, to assent to the famous Petition of Right. The terms of this Petition were that no freeman should be compelled to pay any gifts, loans, benevolences, or taxes whatever that were not imposed by consent of Parliament; that no freeman could be arrested or kept in prison against the law; that soldiers and sailors were not to be billeted in private houses under compulsion; and that no more despotic tribunals were to be appointed. Not until he had signed the Petition of Right would Parliament vote Charles the money for the Spanish war that was still dragging on, whereupon Parliament was prorogued. Charles, however, interpreted the signature that had been extorted from him in quite another light than that in which Parliament had regarded it. He again proceeded to levy taxes that Parliament had not voted and to imprison those who refused to pay them. He had attracted the support of the able and strenuous Wentworth, up till then one of the leaders of the opposition, whilst Laud, an equally energetic priest, had his ear upon all ecclesiastical questions. Laud was known as a High Churchman, well disposed to the Catholics, and favouring the Catholic ritual. In Puritan circles his appointment was regarded as a fresh challenge, and when Parliament met again in 1629 the quarrel with the King was resumed. Numerous complaints gave voice to the dissatisfaction with the King's government, and open resistance was offered to the King's wish that the House should adjourn, the Speaker, who was intimidated by the King, being compelled to listen to the members' complaints. The King thereupon dissolved Parliament and arrested its nine leading members as rebels by way of example. Despite their appeal to their privileges as members of Parliament, the employment of devious legal expedients secured their condemnation by the judges of the Court of King's Bench to imprisonment until they submitted and paid a heavy fine. The heaviest penalty was inflicted on the ringleader, Sir John Eliot, who was thrown into the Tower. Declining to give even a formal submission, he died in 1632 from the effects of harsh treatment.

The dissolution of this, Charles' third, Parliament was followed by eleven years of absolute rule. Laud, Wentworth, and other renegades formed the King's Ministry, Buckingham having fallen under the knife of the fanatic Felton. Illegal taxes were levied, illegal monopolies farmed, illegal persecutions meted out, and illegal confiscations decreed. Wentworth went first to York, intending, as President of the Northern Council, to make a clean sweep—he signed his letters "Thorough"—of the Puritans of the Northern Counties, who were assuming a threatening attitude. But all his measures of repression only just averted an armed rising. For the time being the Puritans of the North, as elsewhere, confined themselves to legal resistance. They collected funds to send travelling preachers into the poorer districts, the City of London being a large contributor to such funds. Although Laud had the money so collected confiscated, there does not appear to have been any waning in the propaganda. The illegal imposts drove multitudes into the camp of the religious and political opposition. And other fiscal measures of the Government, justifiable enough in themselves, but regarded as unjust because of their illegal origin, had the same effect. This was particularly the case with ship money, a tax levied to defray the alleged expenses of protecting the coasts. At first Charles levied this tax on the maritime counties only, but later, in 1635, contrary to all precedent, he levied it on the inland counties. Servile judges pronounced the act legal, because the King could do no wrong, and John Hampden, who refused to pay ship money, was condemned and fined. The majority of people did not go as far as Hampden, but offered, in their own way, passive resistance, and the collection of ship money was attended with so many difficulties that the expenses quite swallowed up the proceeds.

Intense feeling was aroused when Laud was made Archbishop of Canterbury, and thus Primate of the State Church, in 1633. Laud's policy was to assimilate the ritual of the State Church more and more to that of Rome. It must be remembered that the Thirty Years War was then raging in Germany, and a Papist reaction in England would have been fatal to the Protestant cause throughout Europe. It was therefore to be expected that Laud's measures would meet with strenuous resistance. Although no Press in the modern sense of the word existed, the first regular newspapers, weekly news-sheets, appeared in 1640, so that the feelings of the Opposition found expression in pamphlets, for the most part printed in Holland. In Holland the Calvinists were in control, and Holland now became the land of freedom for their English co-believers.

Such was the general situation when John Lilburne entered upon his apprenticeship. His master was a Puritan of some renown. Even in Newcastle Lilburne had frequented the society of "men of light and leading", as he expressed it in one of his pamphlets. During his first years in London he read religious and historical books in his spare time, and while yet an apprentice took part in religious and political agitation. The apprentices of those days played no small part in the public life of London. History records a number of political demonstrations by apprentices of formidable aspect. On the other hand, the journeymen or labourers took no particular part in politics. The apprentices of the worshipful guilds, being the sons of gentlemen, were not unskilled in the use of arms.

When about twenty years of age, and while still an apprentice, Lilburne attracted the attention of the authorities owing to his activity in distributing prohibited literature that had been smuggled into the country from Holland, whither he was obliged to flee in order to avoid arrest. In "free" Holland he was not idle, but in December 1637 he returned to England, thinking that he had been forgotten in the meantime. No sooner had he arrived than he was lured into a trap through the treachery of a servant, probably suborned by one of his friends, the hot-presser J. Wharton, himself already in prison. According to Lilburne's own statement, the informer was in custody for the distribution of prohibited writings, and was induced to play the part of spy by the promise of his own liberty.

Lilburne's conduct in this his first trial is typical of the way in which he fought all his cases. He was the ideal of a fearless fighter for right. He was charged with having caused to be printed in the Dutch towns of Rotterdam and Delft various "scandalous" pamphlets and having them smuggled into England. After several weeks of imprisonment, Lilburne was brought before the Star Chamber, when he disputed the

accuracy of the statements relating to the various acts of which
he was accused and refused point-blank all further information,
contending that he was not called upon to be his own accuser.
He was sent back to prison. Ten or twelve days later he was
required to undergo a fresh examination before the Court of
the Star Chamber, but he was unshaken in his resolution not
to be deflected by a hair's-breadth from his legal position. He
was emphatic in refusing to comply with the formalities which
would have implied an admission of the legality of the proceedings of the Star Chamber. Neither by persuasion nor by
threats could he be induced to take the prescribed oath, which
would have laid on him the obligation to be his own accuser.
He returned to prison, and five weeks later, on February 9,
1638, he was brought to the bar of the high and mighty Court
itself, but with the same result. Neither the threats of the
Earl of Dorset nor the jeers of Archbishop Laud caused him
to recede an inch from his fundamental position. For three
days he was kept in strict custody for contempt. On February 12th he was condemned, together with Wharton, who
also refused to make any statement, to pay a fine of £500 and
to be imprisoned in the Fleet until he submitted to the jurisdiction of the Court. It was further ordered, "to the end that
others may be the more deterred from daring to attempt in the
like manner", that Lilburne should be publicly whipped and,
in company with the aged Wharton, placed in the pillory. On
April 18th this punishment was inflicted upon both of them
with the utmost severity. All the way from the Fleet Bridge—
now Ludgate Circus—to Westminster the three-thonged whip
fell hissing on the bare back of Lilburne. When his journey's
end was reached he was nearly in a swoon. Nevertheless, asked
if he was prepared to confess the error of his ways and avoid,
at least, the pillory—always attended with some physical torment—he had but one answer to make. He was not afraid for
the good cause he represented to suffer this additional torment.
The opening for his head being too low, he was obliged to

stand in the pillory with bent back; but there was no failure in courage, and he threw among the crowd three copies of the incriminated "libels", whose author, Dr. Bastwick, had in 1639, in company with the lawyer Prynne and the clergy-man Burton, suffered still crueller punishment. He explained to the people the illegality of the procedure adopted towards him, and denounced the cruelty of the bishops in such eloquent terms that the officers in attendance found it necessary to gag him. So for a further hour and a half he stood silent, his back on fire, his bare head exposed to the scorching rays of a noon sun. But when his time was up his first words were, "I am more than conqueror through Him that hath loved me." As punishment for these defiant words, the Star Chamber decreed that he should be rigidly confined, chained hand and foot, in the part of the prison allocated "to the lowest and worst criminals", and none of his friends was allowed to supply him with money. All this was literally carried out. Even the surgeon was only allowed to visit him once, and many com-plaints and bribes were needed before he was permitted, at his own cost, to replace the tight iron fetters on his hands and feet by looser gyves. In his cell, dirty and foul-smelling beyond measure, he suffered for a long time such agonies that again and again he thought himself at death's door. At last he wavered so far as to make an appeal to the Privy Council for somewhat better treatment. But when it was explained that this appeal could only be transmitted if he declared his readiness to submit, he at once withdrew it. So long as it was not proved to him that he was wrong, he answered, on no account would he give way, although he would much rather have gone to hang at Tyburn or burn at Smithfield than suffer the tortures of the prison.

But he had to bear them for more than another two years. His imprisonment would have lasted even longer but for the political revolution in the winter of 1640–41 that brought liberation at last to him and many of his companions in suffering.

It should here be mentioned that the harsh treatment of the religious sectarians caused the emigration of many weavers from Norfolk, Suffolk, and Yorkshire. Some of them went to the Netherlands, where they were received with open arms, just as one hundred years earlier England had welcomed the fugitives from Holland, who might have been the grandfathers and great-grandfathers of the very men and women now turning their backs on England. Nevertheless, enough were left behind to maintain the old traditions.

CHAPTER IV

PARLIAMENT AND THE MONARCHY

"THERE in the North the first shot rang." Charles I and Laud
had attempted to introduce into Scotland the episcopal policy
and the new semi-Catholic liturgy of the English State Church.
Since 1592 the Presbyterian Church had been the recognized
State Church of Scotland. Charles and Laud thought they
would be able to overcome the resistance of the Scotch by
methods at once gradual and harsh. But they were quickly
undeceived. In 1637 open rebellion broke out, A kind of
provisional Government was formed, in which were represented the four classes of nobles, gentry, burghers, clergy.
The National League and Covenant was proclaimed and
sworn to by the people everywhere. Unable at that time to
oppose the Covenanters with armed force, Charles was obliged
to enter into negotiations with them, which were protracted
for a considerable time. The King pursued delaying tactics,
but the Scotch remained immovable, and at last Charles had
no alternative but to raise a regular and effective army, for
which more money was required than his compulsory levies
and other financial devices brought him in. His trusted Wentworth, now Earl Strafford, held Ireland in subjection, partly
by force and partly by craft, and had assembled in that country
a docile Parliament. By Strafford's advice, Charles, after
eleven years of unconstitutional government, early in the
year 1640 summoned another English Parliament, which met
in London on April 13, 1640. The King expected an immediate vote of supplies for fighting the Scotch rebels gathered
together on the Border. But instead of doing so, Parliament
declared its intention of inquiring first of all into the legality
of the fiscal measures and political persecutions during the
past eleven years of Charles' government, whereupon Charles
angrily dissolved Parliament. On May 5th he sent the members
home again. Urged on by Strafford, who was of opinion that

the City would not be reasonable until a few fat aldermen had been hanged, the King once more tried to raise funds by enforced exactions of money. But the discontent that was thereby aroused was out of all proportion to the money collected. The attitude of the people of London and of the provinces became more and more threatening. The commotion was such that the King sent his wife, who was expecting her confinement, to Greenwich. And lastly, the Scotch, who had some time since come to an understanding with the leaders of the Opposition in England, crossed the border with a large army. The baffled King was obliged to retreat, and once more an English Parliament was summoned. The troops sent against the Scotch had practically refused to serve, and the four Northern Counties had been taken by the Scotch without any trouble.

After the failure of yet another attempt by Charles to play off the Lords against the Commons, in the autumn of 1640 the elections to the new Parliament took place. As may easily be imagined, these turned out more unfavourably to the King than all their predecessors. During the era of persecution the Opposition has mastered the art of agitation. There were not two members in the new Parliament unconditionally on the side of the King, and his avowed opponents were all the more numerous. The Opposition leaders had determined to take advantage of the precarious position in which Charles was placed to secure the rights of Parliament. As regards monarchical government, these stern Calvinists adhered to the Old Testament and the teaching of the books of Samuel and of the prophets rather than to the sentiment of "Render unto Cæsar the things that are Cæsar's" of the New Testament. They were willing to leave the Scotch unmolested in the counties they had seized until they had themselves settled their reckoning with the King. It is even said that John Hampden himself invited the Scotch leaders to enter the country. Popular songs hailed the Scotch as the saviours of the English people, and there was a universal readiness to co-operate even closer with the Scotch in case of need. Subsequent events proved the wisdom of keeping the Scotch in England as a reserve army. There were continuous conspiracies against Parliament by Royalist leaders of the troops, whilst Charles himself was watching for the moment when he could lay violent hands upon the stubborn representatives of the people.

Meanwhile concession after concession was extorted from Charles. He was forced to sacrifice his friend and counsellor, Strafford, who was impeached by Parliament, condemned, and on May 12, 1641, beheaded. The same fate overtook Archbishop Laud. Charles was obliged to assent to a law providing for the election of a new Parliament at latest three years after the dissolution of its predecessor, even if the King had failed to summon it; to a law which provided that Parliament could not be prorogued or dissolved without its own consent, and to laws which abolished the Star Chamber and Court of High Commission, and deprived the Privy Council of the King of the right to decree arrests and pass judicial sentences. Not until all these things had been secured in August 1641 was the Scotch army disbanded. The King then prepared to go to Scotland to negotiate with the Scottish Parliament, but in view of the distrust in which he was held, John Hampden and others accompanied him. Parliament prorogued itself for the time, intending to resume its work at the end of October. That work was not to end until accounts had been settled with the King and the bishops. A Bill to exclude bishops from the House of Lords, and another to abolish episcopacy altogether, had already been introduced into Parliament and read.

Parliament had, of course, not overlooked the victims of the persecutions by King and bishops. Among its very first acts was the liberation of Prynne, Bastwick, Burton, Lilburne, and others, who entered London to the pealing of bells and the acclamations of the populace. The member who took charge of Lilburne's petition for the wrong he had suffered was none other than Oliver Cromwell, whose speech in support was the first delivered in Parliament by the future Protector. On May 3, 1641, Lilburne took part in a great London demonstration, which was convened to protest against the resistance that the Lords and the King were offering to the proceedings against Strafford. The next day Lilburne was summoned to appear before the Lords owing to his action on this occasion, but these proceedings, like the resistance of Lords and King, broke down. On the other hand, on the self-same day Parliament, on Cromwell's motion, declared the punishment of Lilburne by the Star Chamber to be "illegal, and against the liberty of the subject; and also bloody, wicked, cruel, barbarous, and tyrannical", and further that Lilburne should be compensated for the pains and penalties illegally inflicted on him. It was the business of the Lords to assess the amount of compensation, and it took them nearly five years to reach a decision; but Lilburne received scarcely one-third of the sum of £2,000 which was finally agreed upon, and long before receiving this money he had been faced with the necessity of earning a livelihood. He became a brewer, but the times were "out of joint", and he was not able to carry on this business long.

In October 1641 Parliament met again, and one of its first acts was to draw up a great list of complaints—the "Grand Remonstrance"—which set forth in 206 paragraphs all the unconstitutional measures passed since the beginning of Charles' reign, and asked for security against their repetition. In addition, the action against the bishops was carried a stage farther. The bishops, for their part, had declared all laws passed during their absence from the House of Lords as unconstitutional. Huge popular demonstrations were held against the bishops. At one of these demonstrations, organized by the apprentices, the demonstrators were attacked by the King's soldiers and members of the Court faction. On the next day, December 28, 1641, armed apprentices proceeded to Whitehall by way of retaliation, and it is said that in the skirmish that ensued the nicknames "Roundheads" and "Cavaliers" were used for the first time. Lilburne, long since out of his apprenticeship, fought in the ranks of the apprentices and received a very painful wound.

The King attempted another stroke. Having failed to attract the support of John Pym, the leader of the Opposition, and whose house was the headquarters of the Opposition, by offering him the Chancellorship of the Exchequer, the King, on January 3, 1642, impeached of high treason Pym, John Hampden, three other members of the Commons, and one member of the House of Lords, Lord Kimbolton, afterwards Lord Manchester. In this case, conversely to that of Strafford, the accusation was supported in essential points by formal law, as, for example, in Article 4, when it was said that the accused "had traitorously invited and encouraged a foreign Power to invade the Kingdom". This referred to the Scotch, at that time still foreigners. But the whole question of high treason had been carried by events far outside the legal sphere. The attempt to arrest the members by surprise miscarried. When, on January 4th, the King, accompanied by his soldiers, entered Parliament, intending to seize the offending members, he found the birds, warned beforehand, flown. Although the King was listened to respectfully, as he left the House his ears were assailed with cries of "Privilege!" "Privilege!" A proclamation ordering the closing of the ports, in order to prevent the escape of the five members from the country, raised the excitement in London to fever heat. The citizens declared as one man for the Parliament, which, for greater security, had transferred its committee to the City. Threatening cries resounded in the King's ears as he drove abroad, and a paper thrown into the carriage by an ironmonger bore the ominous words, "To your tents, O Israel".

The words with which the rebellion against Rehoboam had started were flung to the son of the "British Solomon". Armed sailors, apprentices, and others in great numbers placed themselves at the disposal of Parliament. Feeling his position to be insecure in the capital, Charles left London on January 10th, not to see it again until seven years later as a prisoner.

Henceforth it was plain that the dispute admitted of no issue except the arbitrament of arms. The Queen departed to the Continent, to pawn the Crown jewels and raise money by loans in other ways; whilst the King moved about the country enlisting troops. The Parliamentarians also raised money and recruited an army, over which the Earl of Essex was placed as Commander-in-Chief. The cavalry was commanded by the Earl of Bedford, under whom Cromwell served as captain of a squadron (60) of horse. Lilburne, too, lost no time in offering to fight for the Parliament, and since, as a gentleman, he knew how to carry arms, he held a subordinate command in an infantry regiment. The Fleet passed over to the side of Parliament, and the London train bands were held in readiness.

Recruiting and other preparations went on all through the spring and summer, but in the autumn the parties came to blows. The first serious action between the King's seasoned soldiers and the people's army went against the latter. But in the second encounter, at Brentford, November 13–15, 1642, the fierce defence of the popular forces repelled the attack of the Cavaliers, and compelled the King to withdraw with his Loyalists to Oxford.

Lilburne had proved his mettle at the unlucky fight at Edgehill, where he was wounded. At Brentford he also distinguished himself by his great bravery, but he was struck down and carried off prisoner by the Loyalists. In Oxford he was tried and condemned to death for high treason, but the threat of Parliament, if he were executed, to shoot the Cavaliers they had taken, saved his life. He was, however, kept in prison a year and very badly treated. Not until September 1643 was he set free, in exchange for certain Royalist prisoners, after Parliament had threatened the King, who had ordered Lilburne's execution, that they would avenge his death doubly and trebly. An official post, carrying a salary of £1,000, was offered Lilburne, who refused it, and joined the army of the Eastern Counties which had been formed in the meantime. On the recommendation of Oliver Cromwell, who had been particularly active in organizing this army, Lilburne received a brevet as major of cavalry.

At the skirmish at Edgehill Cromwell had served with distinction, but after the unsuccessful issue of the fight he said to his cousin Hampden that an army made up for the most part of old tapsters and town apprentices would never succeed against an army of "men of honour". For success they must have men representing a still more lofty principle—"men of religion". The winter of 1642–43 was employed in reorganization. Unions of associated counties were formed to attend to the enrolment and drilling of the troops belonging to their district, but only the union of Eastern Counties, whose life and soul was Cromwell, had any vitality. The home of Lollardism, where sectarians of all kinds abounded, produced the nucleus of the Parliamentary Army, Cromwell's Ironsides, as they were later called. The increase of the sectarian element caused the withdrawal of the Presbyterian field chaplains, in whose place laymen, who felt moved by inspiration, undertook the preaching. Thus the Army itself fostered sectarianism and sectarian preaching.

To this eastern division of the Army Lilburne now belonged, and he distinguished himself so greatly on different occasions that in May 1644 he was appointed lieutenant-colonel of the dragoons commanded by Lord Manchester. In the beginning of June of the same year, at the battle of Wakefield, he was shot through the arm, but as early as July 2nd he was taking part again in a great fight, the famous victory of Marston Moor.

CHAPTER V

PARLIAMENT AND THE NATIONAL ARMY. PRESBY-
TERIANS, INDEPENDENTS, AND OTHER SECTS

ABOUT this time the antagonism, hitherto talent, between Presbyterians and Independents in the Parliamentary Army, as in Parliament itself, came to a head. The generals, who were adherents of the Presbyterians, wavered in their conduct of the war, holding steadily in view the possibility of a compromise with the King. Manchester neglected to follow up the advantage gained in the second battle of Newbury on October 27, 1644, so palpably that the angry Cromwell, who was coming into increasing military prominence, rode to London and accused him in Parliament of treachery, relying largely upon the evidence of Lilburne. Cromwell contented himself with driving Manchester out of the Army. With the assistance of his friends, he procured the passing of the so-called *Self-Denying Ordinance*, which enacted that any member of either House of Parliament who held a commission in the Army should resign. Thereupon Essex, Manchester, and others were constrained to resign from the Army, whilst Cromwell, after a short interval, was by general request appointed lieutenant-general of the reorganized "New Model" Army for an indefinite period. His services were indispensable in view of the King's preparations for a fresh attack. The chief command had been assigned to the brave, but politically unimportant, Fairfax.

From the New Model Army all unreliable elements were excluded. For the moment those soldiers whose views were more advanced than the views of their chiefs were not regarded as dangerous. The officers were obliged to sign the Covenant which Parliament, sorely pressed by the King, had in the autumn of 1643 made with the Scotch, who had thereupon despatched an army of 21,000 men. In this Covenant Episcopalianism was abjured, but the reference to Presbyterianism, which the Scotch desired to see introduced in England, was so ambiguous that the Covenant was signed by many people who objected to a rigidly centralized Church government. Only one man declined to salve his conscience by putting a convenient interpretation upon the wording in question, and he was Lilburne. All Cromwell's persuasive powers were vainly expended upon this fanatic for straight dealing. He sturdily refused to enter upon crooked courses, and returned to civil life in order to defend with his pen the cause of freedom of conscience.

In common with most of the advanced politicians, he had meanwhile transferred his allegiance from the Presbyterians to the Independents. Most Presbyterians were strangers to religious toleration, which they regarded as the "foremost means of the devil". The Scotch in particular regarded religious freedom as "the murder of souls".

Among Cromwell's letters there is one dated March 10, 1643, addressed to Major-General Crawford, a Scotsman already serving in the English Army. In this letter Cromwell writes very earnestly on behalf of an officer who had been suspended by Crawford. He says, among other things:

"Ay, but the man 'is an Anabaptist'. Are you sure of that? Admit he be, shall that render him incapable to serve the public? Sir, the State, in choosing men to serve it, takes no notice of their opinions; if they be willing faithfully to serve it—that satisfies."

The sentiment expressed in this letter was so novel that Lord Manchester used the letter against Cromwell in Parliament when accusing him of being a leader of sectarians. All sects were represented in Cromwell's Army, from bibliolaters to atheists. They formed the backbone of the Army. They were its bravest, most sacrificing, most democratic members, and for that reason gave the dictator Cromwell the most trouble at a later date, but for the time being Cromwell supported them.

Parliament was prepared to settle the matter, but it lacked

the necessary power, and the exhortations addressed to the
English Parliament from Scotland, to stamp out these abomina-
tions in the Army, remained without any practical effect.[1]
Cromwell, in his letters from the battlefield, always defended
the sectaries among his soldiers. "Sir, they are trusty, I beseech
you, in the name of God, not to discourage them", he writes
to the Speaker of the House of Commons after the battle of
Naseby. And again, after the storming of Bristol: "Presbyterians, Independents, all have here the same spirit of faith
and prayer, the same presence and answer; they agree here,
have no names of difference: pity it is it should be otherwise
anywhere!"[2]

Although the Presbyterians in London were unable to pass
from the rôle of persecuted to that of persecutor, as their
religion dictated, they were untiring in pulpit and pamphlet
denunciations of the sectaries. A "Great Assembly of Divines"
had been meeting in Westminster ever since 1643, deliberating
upon a common united Church of Scotland and England. In
this Assembly the Presbyterians had a great preponderance,
and it re-echoed to impassioned thunderings against the
"monstrous damnable doctrine of liberty of the conscience".
John Lilburne, in his pamphlets, derided this body as the
"Assembly of Dry-Vines". The Presbyterians, on their side,
constructed out of the letters of Lilburne's name the anagram,
"O I burn in hel(l)". And John Milton coined the phrase,
"New Presbyter is nothing but old Priest writ large".

It would be a fundamental mistake to detect in these Presbyterian sentiments nothing more than the voice of narrow
religious fanatics. They also express the feelings of prosperous
citizens, the wealthy City merchants being for the most part
Presbyterians. The most extreme social theories manifested

[1] E.g., in an address to the English Parliament from the Scottish in 1645
it is said: "The Parliament of this kingdom is persuaded that the piety and
wisdom of the honourable houses will never admit toleration of any sects
or schisms contrary to our solemn league and covenant."
[2] Letters of June 14 and September 14, 1645.

themselves at that time in a religious form. Consequently the majority of ccmfortable citizens would be unconsciously biased in favour of that form of religion which was most acceptable to the existing order, and the religion that met this requirement was in those days Presbyterian Puritanism. In his *History of the Great Civil War*[1] Gardiner writes: "It is no matter for surprise that the City was tenaciously Presbyterian. The fear of ecclesiastical tyranny which was so strong on the benches of the House of Commons had no terrors for the merchants and tradesmen of the City. By filling the elderships those very merchants and tradesmen constituted the Church for purposes of jurisdiction. Whatever ecclesiastical tyranny there was would be exercised by themselves." This divergency between the Parliamentary representatives of the middle classes and those classes themselves is a characteristic phenomenon that persists throughout modern history. Among members of Parliaments ideologies of all kinds work a modifying, and even a distorting, influence upon the class character of the representation, but they are generally effaced and lost among the masses that are represented. The change in the relations between the City and Cromwell forms one of the most instructive chapters of the English Revolution.

"Independent" was as yet an indeterminate concept. It connoted those persons who, on various grounds, were opposed to any form of religious absolutism or centralized religious authority, just as at a later stage of political development "Liberal" and "Radical" are collective names for persons whose sole bond of union is their opposition to certain institutions, and who are likely to part company when other issues arise. Thus in the next chapter we shall have to relate political splits among the Independents. The extent of the differences in religio-social views may be gathered from the number of sects designated as "independent". There were the Anabaptists, with strong communistic tendencies; the Familists, dominated

[1] Vol. iii. pp. 78, 79.

by Anabaptist ideas; the Fifth Monarchy Men, who aimed at the establishment of a monarchy of Christ, as foreshadowed in the book of Daniel, to succeed the four great world monarchies, in which there would be no earthly rulers; the Antinomians, who were even more anarchical in their opposition to all written religious and moral law, holding that the internal illumination by the spirit of the Gospel was a sufficient guide for all conduct and reaching very revolutionary conclusions; and the Ranters, among whom were extremists alleged to profess free love and kindred extravagances.

It does not come within our scope to describe in detail all the sects that appeared in that fermenting age. Those that play a part in our history will be considered as occasion demands. For the moment it is sufficient to note the popularity among the people of the Chiliastic sects, which expected the advent of a millennial, communistic kingdom of God on earth.[1]

The denunciations of the Presbyterians were aimed particularly at these sects. They were anathematized by the Presbyterian special London Council, Sion College, and a Presbyterian light of the Church, Th. Edwards, in 1646, published a work called *Gangræna*, full of fulminations against them. Many of the sects, as, for example, the Antinomians, held the same fundamental dogmas as the Presbyterians, but they differed as regards the practical application of these dogmas, and this was the question at issue.

The idea that the interests of property forbid any serious

---

[1] This subject is exhaustively discussed in Hermann Weingarten's *Die Revolutionskirchen Englands*, Leipzig, 1868. Weingarten writes: "We see the Independents advancing in two directions: in the religious, through the sectarian fermentation, which culminated in Quakerism, and in the political, whose first incidental form was the Leveller movement, but whose fundamental ideas have passed as driving forces into the political life of modern times." Masson, in his *Life and Times of John Milton*, vol. iii. pp. 142–59, gives a very clear summary of the sects in the early days of the Revolution. In vol. v. (pp. 15 et seq.) of the same work is a description of the sects under the Protectorate. Robert Barclay, in his *Inner Life of the Religious Societies of the Commonwealth*, gives much information bearing on this subject, although his standpoint is narrow.

interference with the centralized State Church was at that time plainly expressed by a poet, Edmund Waller, famous for his elegant verses and almost more elegant apostasies. On May 27, 1641, the House of Commons proceeded to discuss a resolution to abolish the episcopate, when Waller, a nephew of John Hampden and still a partisan of Parliament, said it would be a good thing to clip the bishops' horns and claws. They might, perhaps, go even a little farther, but to abolish the episcopacy altogether would entail very serious risks. That the masses were against episcopacy seemed to Waller, as he avowed, an argument in its favour, "for I look upon episcopacy as a counterscarp, or outwork; which, if it be taken by this assault of the people, and, withal, this mystery once revealed, 'that we must deny them nothing when they ask it thus in troops', we may, in the next place, have as hard a task to defend our property, as we have lately had to recover it from the Prerogative. If, by multiplying hands and petitions, they prevail for an equality in things ecclesiastical, the next demand perhaps may be *Lex Agraria*, the like equality in things temporal."

Waller proceeds to refer to the history of ancient Rome, in which the decline of the Republic coincided with the assumption of power by the masses. The power to demand a law (*legem rogare*) quickly became the power to make a law (*legem ferre*), and once the legions discovered that they could make anyone they pleased dictator, they refused to allow the Senate to have any more voice in the matter. If it should be objected that the episcopacy was not that which had been laid down in the Holy Scriptures, Waller was not prepared to dispute this, "but I am confident that, whenever an equal division of lands and goods shall be desired, there will be as many places in Scripture found out, which seem to favour that, as there are now alleged against the prelacy or preferment of the Church. And, as for abuses, when you are now in the remonstrance told what this and that poor man hath suffered by the bishops, you may be presented with a thousand instances of poor men that have received hard measure from their landlords; and of worldly goods abused, to the injury of others, and the disadvantage of the owners."

The House of Commons ought therefore by a resolution to reform the episcopate, but not to abolish it, so as to restore peace to men's minds. Waller had given utterance to the thoughts of many. In May 1646 delegates from more than two thousand inhabitants of Buckinghamshire and Hertfordshire appeared at the bar of the House to petition for the removal of the tithes. Their demand met with no support, and they were sent home with the paternal injunction that they did not understand either the law of God or the law of man. They had better betake themselves off and obey both. "Some of the members observed that tenants who wanted to be quit of tithes would soon want to be quit of rent. Nine-tenths were due to the landlord on the same ground that one-tenth was due to the minister."[1] Such authentic utterances as these throw interesting sidelights on the history of the Revolution.

We resume our narration of events.

Prynne, Lilburne's quondam teacher and leader, had published a pamphlet steeped in the Presbyterian spirit of persecution described above. In answer to this pamphlet Lilburne in January 1645 published an open letter, in which he defended the sectaries and vigorously opposed the tyrannical spirit of the Presbyterians. This letter was declared by Parliament, under pressure from Prynne, to be "scurrilous, libellous, and seditious", and a prosecution was started against Lilburne. When, in a second pamphlet, he denounced these proceedings, he was arrested by a resolution of Parliament in July 1645. In Parliament and among the big City merchants the Presbyterian influence prevailed, but Lilburne had strenuously opposed the granting of monopolies to the great merchants, which was as much in vogue as ever, and he was too popular

[1] Gardiner, *History of the Great Civil War*, vol. iii. p. 124.

with the great mass of the citizens for summary treatment to be meted out to him. A deputation of citizens called the attention of Parliament to Lilburne's services "against the oppression and tyranny of the prelates and Court parasites", and were assured that he should receive a fair trial and be allowed proper maintenance in the meantime. The deputation was not satisfied with this, and some of the more eager spirits seem to have planned an assault on the prison, an idea which Lilburne decisively vetoed as soon as he heard of it. When October arrived, in which month the trial was to be held, Parliament ordered his release, in answer to a new petition and in view of his long preliminary detention. The House was now in a somewhat difficult position. True, it had nothing further to fear from the King, who, after the battle of Naseby, had abandoned all thoughts of victory and had again resorted to negotiations. But Cromwell's Army, almost to a man, supported the Independents, on whose side were also large numbers of the people of London; and unless these inconvenient and pressing men, who desired reform "root and branch", could be mastered, the fruits of victory threatened to be lost. Thus these "advanced" men were regarded, to an increasing degree, as the foe.

Lilburne did not long enjoy his recovered freedom. Of his attitude towards the parliamentary majority there could be no doubt. A few days before his liberation he had published two violent pamphlets against them, the titles of which sufficiently indicate their purport. The first is called: "England's Birthright justified against all arbitrary usurpation, whether regal or parliamentary, or under what vizor soever; with divers queries, observations, and grievances of the people, declaring this Parliament's present proceedings to be directly contrary to those fundamental principles whereby their actions were at first justified against the King." The main title of the second is: "England's Lamentable Slavery, proceeding from the arbitrary will, severity and fulness of Parliaments, covetousness, ambition and variability of priest, and simplicity, carelessness and cowardliness of people." On regaining his freedom, Lilburne became a regular attendant at the meetings of the London Independents, which were held in City taverns, and at these meetings the aristocratic character of the Lower House was already a standing topic. The general conditions of election to the Commons, both in town and country, had gradually worsened as time went on. At the period now under consideration, the suffrage, which had become of great moment, was restricted in many towns to the members of corporations, and even to their officers only, and, in the counties, to a minority of landowners. Those excluded from the vote, by tradition rather than by original enactments, felt that they were unjustly treated. Moreover, serious anomalies had grown up in connection with the size of the places represented. Towns and boroughs that had remained stationary, or had fallen behind the great centres of commerce, had the same representation as the most important commercial centres in the kingdom.

Composed almost exclusively of members of the wealthy classes in town and country, Parliament had abolished a great many institutions and impositions that were obnoxious to it, but had taken no great heed of the grievances of the lower middle and the working classes. It had cancelled the monopolies granted by the King, and had even taken the step of expelling those of its members who held such monopolies, but the privileges of the great trading companies were left intact. Feudal obligations, like the royal right to dispose of *wardships* —a right "oppressing to all the considerable families", according to Hume—or such duties as *knight service*, were either expressly abolished or fell into desuetude, after practically all the prerogatives of the King had ceased to exist. But the game laws, tithes, etc., by which the small tenants and other "inconsiderable" families were grievously oppressed, remained, as we have seen, "unconsidered", all petitions against them notwithstanding.

At this time the House of Lords gave its decision that the proceedings of the Star Chamber against Lilburne were illegal, and that he must be compensated for the wrong he had suffered. In consequence probably of this decision, he married the same winter, and set up his own establishment, but he was again arrested on April 14, 1646. There was one Edward King, a Presbyterian colonel, whom Lilburne—and not Lilburne alone—had accused of playing into the hands of the Royalists on several occasions by traitorous delays, but, owing to his parliamentary influence, no action had been taken against him. This man complained of Lilburne on the ground of malicious slander, and caused him to be put under preliminary arrest.

Out of this affair grew a whole string of actions and persecutions aimed at Lilburne, of which we can here only mention the most important. Lilburne exposed the illegality of the proceedings against him in his appeals to the judicial and parliamentary authorities, and asked for redress. In one of his addresses, "The Just Man's Justification", he refers to what he designates as the treachery of the ex-general, Lord Manchester, who had in the meantime become the Speaker of the House of Lords. Instead of the anticipated legal protection, Lilburne received a summons to appear before the Lords to justify his attacks. Repeatedly brought before them, he steadfastly refused to answer them, or in any way to acknowledge their authority, holding that they possessed no jurisdiction over him in criminal matters. He appealed from them "as encroachers and usurping judges" to his "competent, proper and legal triers and judges, the Commons of England assembled in Parliament". But before the Commons could reach a decision, he was, on July 10th, condemned by the Lords to a fine of £2,000, the loss of the right ever to hold any official position, and seven years' imprisonment in the Tower. On the whole, his treatment in the Tower was tolerable. In this respect, at least, the new regime was better than the old, although the prisoners were exposed to scandalous exploitation by the officials.

Even in prison, however, Lilburne was not quiet. He and his friends were tireless in their efforts to prevail upon Parliament to intervene, and they succeeded to the extent that at the end of 1647 Lilburne was liberated on bail. He used his freedom to promote all kinds of agitations, in the course of which he journeyed to places where certain divisions of the Army, in which he had many friends, were quartered. The object of these journeys will transpire later. Early in 1648 he was denounced by a hostile minister for speaking at a meeting in Shoreditch, which had resolved upon the distribution of 30,000 copies of the leaflet, undoubtedly his, *The Earnest Petition of many Freeborn People of this Nation*. As a consequence Lilburne was informed that he had forfeited his permit, and must return to the Tower.

This petition is one of the most remarkable documents of the English Revolution. In fact, the organization of petitions was one of the chief means of propaganda at that time, and a study of these petitions is indispensable to an understanding of contemporary history. In March 1647 the House of Commons is described in a petition promoted by Lilburne as "the highest authority in the nation". This was such an audacious assertion of the sovereignty of the elected representatives of the people that Parliament on May 29th, by 94 votes to 86, ordered the pamphlet to be burnt by the common executioner, because it "called in question the existing constitution". Besides its strictures on the constitution, the pamphlet attacked tithes, trade monopolies, and the whole judicial system, and demanded in energetic language its radical reform both in principle and procedure.

On their side, Lilburne's friends and adherents among the London public were not idle. Petition after petition in his favour was presented. Finally, on August 1, 1648, again "ten thousand citizens of London, men and women", petitioned that

Lilburne be set free or have a legal trial. This time they succeeded in prevailing upon Lords and Commons to liberate Lilburne and cancel the fine decreed against him. But there was a special reason for this act of compliance with the popular will.

CHAPTER VI

THE LEVELLERS *VERSUS* THE "GENTLEMEN' INDEPENDENTS

IN the meantime important differences had revealed themselves in the relations of the parliamentary parties to one another, to the King, and to the Army. In some cases antagonisms had become more marked, in others there had been a certain measure of reconciliation.

In the spring of 1646 Charles I had fled to the Scotch camp, but the Scotch surrendered him to his adversaries in England in return for the payment of subsidies due to them. He was at first sent to the castle of Holdenby or Holmby, in Northamptonshire, whence he tried to play off Parliament and Army alternately one against the other. The Army was the organized democracy of the country, the bulk of it consisting of yeomen and artisans. After the withdrawal of the Presbyterian generals, its leaders consisted partly of men promoted from the ranks, partly of the more radical members of the possessing classes. And although differences between the latter and the bulk of the Army had already arisen, both sides had for the time being a common interest as against the Parliament, in which the landowners and the great burgher interests predominated. Now that the King had been reduced to military impotence, the majority of the Parliamentarians soon lost their enthusiasm for their own victorious Army, with whose whims they were too well acquainted, and to whom nearly a year's pay was owing. They sought to lessen its influence by disbanding some of the regiments and distributing the rest in different places. But the leaders and the soldiers realized the meaning of this intention, and answered the move by constituting themselves into an independent force. The soldiers created for their own purposes a completely democratic institution, the "agitators". This name, first met with in an address to Fairfax dated May 29, 1647, had been interpreted by

Carlyle and others after him as a misspelt reading of "adjutators", quite inaccurately, however. The word derives from "agitate", to lead affairs, and had originally the same significance as the word "delegate" has to-day.[1] In any case, the "agitators" were rather agitators in the modern meaning of the word than merely "adjutators" of the higher officers. They were the agents of the common soldiers. As such, under the influence of Lilburne, who was in constant contact with them, they exercised the greatest influence on the trend of events, and often brought matters to a head.

The officers and the general staff had perforce to recognize this new institution. It was agreed that each regiment should elect two "agitators", who were only to be chosen from the rank and file of the non-commissioned officers. These "agitators", with the two officers appointed for each regiment, were to constitute the "Council of the Army". All kinds of negotiations proceeded between this Council and the Parliament, but as they did not achieve the desired result, a great convention of the Army was held on Newmarket Heath on June 4, 1647, when a manifesto was drawn up, declaring that the Army was no troop of mercenaries, hired for the service of arbitrary power, but literally "free commoners of England drawn together and continued in arms in judgment and conscience for defence of their own and the people's rights and liberties", and that they, officers and soldiers alike, pledged themselves by their signatures not "willingly to disband nor divide, nor suffer ourselves" to be disbanded or divided until security was forthcoming that "we as private men, or other the free-born people of England, shall not remain subject to the like oppression, injury, or abuse, as has been attempted".

Six days later, on Triploe Heath, near Cambridge, there was a still greater demonstration, 21,000 men being present. From the general staff down to the rank and file they were determined to resist all attempts at cajolery, and they fell

[1] Cf. Gardiner, loc. cit., vol. iii. p. 243 et seq.

back upon St. Albans, nearer and nearer to the Metropolis. The Parliament made answer by a proclamation that those who left the Army should receive their arrears of pay and their fare, either to America or to the garrison in Ireland, as each man might wish. A "committee of safety" was appointed, which approached the leaders of the City militia, in order to organize an armed resistance to the Army. With the tacit consent of the City Presbyterians, the City apprentices, with a number of discharged soldiers (Reformadoes), sailors, and others, broke into Parliament. on July 26th, prevented the admission of the Independent members, and extorted from the Presbyterian majority a vote hostile to the Army. Thereupon the Army occupied London on August 7, 1647, "in order to protect the Parliament", and eleven Presbyterian members who had made themselves conspicuous with resolutions and measures against the Army were expelled from Parliament, and eight of them went into exile. Then, on August 20th, Cromwell, his hand on his sword, carried a resolution in Parliament that annulled all the resolutions passed during the time the House had been terrorized, and placed responsibility for the public turmoil on those members of the House who had taken part in the sittings in question and had connived at the terrorism or had endeavoured to carry out the resolutions that were then passed. This caused yet more of the Presbyterian Hotspurs to remain away from the sittings for some time, so that in the House the balance inclined more and more to the side of the Independents.[1]

[1] Cromwell had attended various sittings of Parliament, and himself witnessed the attacks made on the Army by the Presbyterian majority. "These men will never leave till the Army pull them out by the ears", he once whispered to his neighbour, Edmund Ludlow. It must not be forgotten that Parliament was asserting the right to sit as long as it pleased. Under the circumstances, it was only natural that the Army, which had won the victory for the Parliament, should resent the latter's tendency to assume personal power. A circular addressed to Parliament on July 10, 1647, signed by Cromwell, Fairfax, and eleven other representatives of the Army, was studiously moderate in tone, and conceded to the Presbyterian majority in Parliament more than was wise, but the latter wanted to be

The Army then withdrew to Putney to watch further developments. So far all had gone well. With this preliminary victory over Parliament, however, the opposition of the Independents within the Army began to assume a different form. In the early days of June the King had been carried from Holmby Castle to Newmarket by a troop of dragoons, led by Ensign Joyce, an "agitator" in Colonel Whalley's regiment. Joyce is said to have been a tailor by trade, and he was an enthusiastic Anabaptist. It was suspected that this was done by secret orders from Cromwell, who, however, protested that he had given no instructions of the kind. His protest appears to have been justified to this extent, that he only agreed that it was wise to secure at once the person of the King by sending to Holmby a number of trustworthy soldiers, to prevent Charles being carried off by the Scotch, who were no longer reliable. But the "agitators" considered that the safest plan was to have the King actually in the hands of the Army, and, on their own admission, exceeded their orders. In any case, what was done was not undone. When the Army was drawing nearer and nearer to London, the King's quarters also were transferred nearer and nearer to London, and finally

absolute masters of the situation, and thus provoked the expulsion of the eleven.

There were good reasons for the sudden partisanship by the apprentices of the parliamentary majority. The apprentices had presented petitions for the restoration of the opportunities for recreations, games, etc., which they had lost by the Puritan regime. Parliament made some concession to the sentiment expressed in these petitions on the 8th to the 11th of July, 1647, when it enacted that every second Tuesday in the month should, after the despatch of all necessary work, be a holiday for all scholars at school, apprentices, and servants (including the labourers). Quite obviously the sole object of this decree was to purchase the temporary support of the "apprentices", and this object was achieved. The City apprentices proved themselves true Pretorian guards so long as they were able, with the tacit approval of the City militia, to demonstrate against the parliamentary minority, but neither they nor the City militia nor the hurriedly enrolled deserters from the Army were capable of offering serious resistance to the seasoned regiments of the Army advancing on London. The whole attempt at armed resistance was a grotesque failure, and City and Parliament gave in without a shot being fired.

Hampton Court was assigned to Charles as a residence. But instead of the intrigues ceasing, now they began in good earnest. After the expulsion and withdrawal of the chief Presbyterian stalwarts, the Independents and the Presbyterians in Parliament were nearly equal in numbers, a large number of Royalists having left Westminster as early as 1644, when Charles I summoned an opposition Parliament at Oxford. But the Presbyterians were now eager to make a compromise with the King. This caused the Independent leaders of the Army, on their part, to traffic with the King, to prevent the Presbyterians stealing a march on them. Charles exploited this situation to the best of his abilities. An adept in double-dealing, conscious of Divine Right, he shrank from no species of dissembling that promised results. He sought to hold in check the various parties dealing with him by half-promises which he retracted the next moment. He did not scruple to treat one day with Cromwell and his son-in-law, Ireton, the next day with the Scotch and English Presbyterians, and the day after, behind the backs of all these, with the Irish Catholics, in order, as occasion arose, to play them off one against the other. He held high state at Hampton Court, treated the thousands of London citizens and others who made pilgrimage to him with an exquisite courtesy, and consequently saw his stock rising day by day.

Upon all this the soldiers and the rest of the more revolutionary members of the Army looked with an increasing bitterness. Was it for this that they had fought in numberless battles against the foreign mercenaries of the King? They had sacrificed their property and shed their blood in the fight against him, and now their leaders were bandying courtesies with him and allowing him, the conquered, to usurp the position and the honours of a conqueror. They saw no more than their leaders saw the real character of the tactics of the King, but it was plain to them to what result these intrigues were leading. They saw that their leaders were playing their

E

cards very badly, and, either through want of resolution or through ambition, were getting perilously near the betrayal of their cause. In a pamphlet, to which we shall revert, Lilburne writes: "At which time also it's very remarkable with how much height of state they (the generals) observed the King at Hampton Court, visiting him themselves, and permitting thousands of people daily to visit him, to kiss his hand, and to be healed by him, whereby his party in the City and everywhere were exceedingly animated, his agents being as familiar at the headquarters as at the Court."[1] The nicknames "gentlemen independents" and "grandees" of the Army began to be used, in distinction to the "honest nounsubstantive soldiers", as the peasants and the artisans in the Army called themselves, while the "grandees", on their side, reproached the soldiers and their leaders, the "agitators", with being destructive "levellers".

"In the Army, his Majesty's real purpose becoming now apparent, there has arisen a very terrible 'Levelling Party', a class of men demanding punishment not only of Delinquents, and Deceptive Persons who have involved this Nation in blood, but of the 'Chief Delinquent': minor Delinquents getting punished, how should the Chief Delinquent go free? A class of men dreadfully in earnest; to whom a King's Cloak is no impenetrable screen; who within the King's Cloak discern that there is a Man accountable to a God!"[2]

[1] *The Second Part of England's New Chains Discovered*, p. 7.
[2] Carlyle, *Oliver Cromwell's Letters and Speeches*, note on Letter 44. In Letter 79, dated November 25, 1648, Cromwell himself mentions the Levellers for the first time. The letter is to his friend, Colonel Robert Hammond, and is intended to silence his scruples in respect to the King. In it Cromwell makes the following characteristic avowal: "Dost thou not think this fear of the Levellers (of whom there is no fear) 'that they would destroy Nobility', etc., has caused some to take up corruption, and find it lawful to make this ruining hypocritical agreement on one part? [The reference is to the compromise of the Presbyterians with the King whilst Cromwell was in the North.] Hath not this biased even some good men? I will not say the thing they fear will come upon them; but if it do, they will themselves bring it upon themselves. Have not some of our friends by their passive principle . . . been occasioned to overlook what is just and honest,

At length the dissension became so marked that a large number of the officers themselves avowed their dissatisfaction with this policy of protracted negotiations and backstairs intrigues. The "agitators" met and drew up a democratic republican manifesto, which they called "Agreement of the People, upon Grounds of Common Right, for uniting of all unprejudiced people therein", and henceforth the watchword of all Levellers is the carrying out of an "agreement of the people". This "Agreement of the People" contains in germ almost all the political demands that are elaborated in the remarkable manifesto of the Levellers published under the same title in the spring of 1649, which we shall consider in the next chapter. Parliament declared it to be seditious and its authors liable to punishment. The same fate befell a second pamphlet issued by the "agitators," *The Case of the Army*, which censured among other things the scandalous waste of the confiscated Church land, etc., by Parliament. The general staff, although attacked no less severely by the authors than the Parliamentary majority, began to negotiate with them. It could not make short work of the Levellers, as several of the higher officers openly sympathized with them. Among these sympathizers were Colonels Rainsborough and Pride, who were themselves of plebeian origin. On the other hand, Cromwell could not declare unequivocally for the abolition of the King's prerogative, so long as he was himself negotiating with the King. In a word, the negotiations, known as the "Conferences of Putney", proved abortive. The dissensions and mutual mistrust increased, and, at last, the "agitators" threatened extreme measures on their own account.[1]

and to think the people of God may have as much or more good the one way than the other? Good by this Man—against whom the Lord hath witnessed and whom thou knowest! Is this so in their hearts; or is it reasoned, forced in?" It will be seen later why Cromwell then declared that there was "no fear" of the Levellers, provided an energetic policy were pursued.

[1] Major John Wildman, an officer siding with the Levellers, published at the end of 1647 a pamphlet, under the anagram pseudonym of John Lawmind. It was called *Putney Projects, or the Old Serpent in a New Form,* and

The atmosphere became uncomfortable to the King. Ostensibly because he heard that the Levellers were preparing a plot against his life, he left Hampton Court secretly on the night of November 11, 1647, in a fog, and went to the Isle of Wight, where he was confined in Carisbrooke Castle by Colonel Hammond, mentioned above, the Governor of the Island. In the opinion of the Levellers, the general staff—the "grandees" of the Army—and Cromwell in particular—connived at the King's flight, to enable them to pursue their negotiations with him unhampered. Cromwell's letters at this time, however, lend no support to this suspicion. Yet a general feeling of mistrust existed, in which even some of the higher officers shared, and from the "agitators" and soldiers came repeated threats of rebellion to compel consideration for the "Agreement of the People". Lilburne, who was then in the enjoyment of comparative freedom, if not solely responsible for the "Agreement", was certainly one of its authors. He

described what was going on from the standpoint of the revolutionary wing of the Army. Bitter as are its attacks upon Cromwell, yet this pamphlet shows that the charge made against Cromwell by the Presbyterians, and repeated in most histories, that he was then in collusion with the radical agitators, was quite unfounded.

Most interesting light is thrown on these transactions by the Clarke Papers. They are the minutes of an officer who acted as secretary to the Council of the Army. Of particular interest is the report (vol. i. pp. 226–363) of a conference of the Army Council held at Putney Church, under the presidency of Cromwell, on October 28th and 29th. To this conference the Levellers and the radical agitators had been invited, and the "Agreement" drawn up by the Levellers was discussed. Cromwell was ready with opportunist arguments against the "Agreement". While it certainly contained a number of excellent things, other people might come and draw up a programme, and others and yet others, and this might lead to great confusion. "Would it not make England like the Switzerland country, one canton against another, and one country against another?" It was doubtful whether the country was yet ripe for all this. The conference must weigh the consequences of all this, and be clear as to the ways and means of attaining these objects. "There will be very great mountains in the way of this." On the second day the suffrage was discussed. The various "agitators" and also some of the radical officers championed universal suffrage, but Cromwell and the majority of the officers maintained that it was very risky to give the vote to those who had neither possession nor "position" in the country, and therefore not "a permanent fixed interest in it".

was assiduous in fostering this feeling in the Army, where his influence was very great. His pamphlets were eagerly read by the soldiers, and, as is noted in a report in the spring of 1647 to the Lords, "quoted by them as statute laws".[1] Another document, quoted by Gardiner,[2] says the whole Army was "one Lilburne throughout, and more likely to give than to receive laws".[3] Whole regiments were won over to the cause. Unreliable "agitators" were removed and replaced by men whose radical views were undoubted. All this did not, of course, escape the notice of Cromwell, to whom it was, indeed, reported by certain intermediaries that Lilburne and another Leveller, the Major John Wildman mentioned above, desired his removal as a traitor. He now perceived that measures would have to be taken to cope with this agitation. He had hesitated long enough to call Charles personally to account, probably because he still shrank from this extreme step, and, moreover, had not the requisite legal means, but the Army were clamouring loudly for "justice", and the revolt of a large section of the Army would inflict the gravest injury on him and his party. Without the Army, they were a helpless minority in Parliament, where, despite the expulsion of the Presbyterian leaders, they had been defeated again on October 13th by three votes on the question of a State establishment of Presbyterianism. A letter of Charles, intercepted by him and Ireton in October, had, on the other hand, revealed to him what the King's real thoughts were concerning him. The time had come for action, and action was taken. Three meetings of the different regiments were convened. The first was held on November 15th in Corkbush Field, near Ware in Hertfordshire. To this first meeting, it is said, those regiments were purposely summoned

[1] Gardiner, vol. iii. p. 237.
[2] Loc. cit., p. 245.
[3] "For he hath continuously his sword in one hand, and one of Lilburne's Epistles in the other, which hee takes to bee the ballance that must weigh all men in this world, and in the world to come." From *The Agitator Anatomized, or the Character of an Agitator*, a Royalist work published in March 1648.

that had kept themselves comparatively quiet. If they proved pliable, it was to be expected that their example would not be without effect on the more rebellious. And this calculation, as things turned out, proved accurate. Cromwell's dominating energy as leader of the Army did the rest.

A majority of the soldiers and many officers at Ware wore in their hats, to indicate their opinions, copies of the Agreement with the motto "England's Freedom—Soldiers' Right". Besides the regiments still responsive to discipline, there were present Robert Lilburne's cavalry and Thomas Harrison's infantry, which were animated by a very rebellious spirit, and also prominent Levellers from other regiments. John Lilburne, Colonel Rainsborough, one of the bravest of the Army leaders, who had particularly distinguished himself at the storming of Bristol, Major Scott and other republicans rode from division to division and exhorted the soldiers to stand firm, the cause of freedom being at stake. Loud shouts of all kinds were raised, which boded but little good to Cromwell. He, however, proved equal to the occasion. Along with Fairfax and others of the general staff, he rode along the front, at first of the more moderate regiments. A remonstrance was read containing a refutation of the complaints of the "agitators", and impressing on the soldiers the necessity of the whole Army standing together if their demands, which the generals endorsed, were to be realized. The general tenor of the declaration and the promises it held forth were received by the soldiers with great applause, and they promised to maintain discipline. Then they proceeded to Harrison's regiment, which also listened quietly to the remonstrance and were induced to remove from their hats the emblems mentioned above, on the ground that they were "seditious". With Lilburne's cavalry it was another matter. They received Cromwell and Fairfax with defiant shouts, and as Fairfax read the remonstrance they interrupted him with bitter taunts. Then Cromwell rode forward. "Take those papers from your hats!" "No, no!" they shouted back.

But Cromwell did not see the necessity of any further parley. Followed by other officers he rode among the rioters, some of whom were nonplussed, while others were afraid to offer any effective resistance to the man who had led them in so many victorious fights. With his own hands he tore out the emblems and arrested as mutineers fourteen soldiers who had been specially refractory. A court martial was held and sentence of death passed on three of the accused. They drew lots, and two were set free, but the third, Richard Arnold, suffered the death penalty. As to Major Scott and Captain Bray, who had stood up for the mutineers and stigmatized the execution of Arnold as a violation of the Petition of Right, by which courts martial were abolished, warrants were issued against them by Parliament.

Thus the first attempt at a revolt was suppressed. The two other meetings were held without any incident. The soldiers who sympathized with the Levellers were induced, on the plea of the need for unity against the common foe, to make their submission. The discontent, however, was only suppressed, not removed. Arnold's memory, as that of a martyr to the cause of right, was cherished, and at every later dispute the demand was again raised for expiation for that "innocently shed blood". The flames were glowing beneath the ashes, to burst out fiercely again at the first opportunity.

Cromwell, for his part, had acted under dire necessity. The Presbyterians in and out of Parliament could not be held in check by an undisciplined Army. To them and to the Royalists, who were constantly recruiting new forces, the Army had to present a united front. For this reason during the next few months Cromwell introduced various modifications in the organization of the Army, designed to weed out the unreliable and excessively unruly elements. On the other hand, he and his friends carried in Parliament a resolution that no more addresses should be moved to the King, and that no member of either House should hold any commerce with the King without the permission of Parliament. Yet their situation was the reverse of comfortable. Everywhere was ferment. "A King not to be bargained with; kept in Carisbrooke, the centre of all factious hopes, of world-wide intrigues: that is one element. A great Royalist Party, subdued with difficulty, and ready at all moments to rise again: that is another. A great Presbyterian Party, at the head of which is London City, 'the Pursebearer of the Cause', highly dissatisfied at the course things had taken, and looking desperately round for new combinations and a new struggle: reckon that for a third element. Add lastly a headlong Mutineer, Republican, or Levelling Party; and consider that there is a working House of Commons which counts about Seventy, divided in pretty equal halves too—the rest waiting what will come of it. Come of it and of the Scotch Army advancing towards it."

This is the picture drawn by Carlyle of the state of affairs, and it is, in the main, accurate, although it should be added that this situation imposed on Cromwell the policy which the "headlong mutineer, etc., party" wanted to pursue. Cromwell did his utmost to effect a union between the anti-Royalist elements. He attached to himself the foremost men of the Parliament and of the Army. He attended, with some of them, a meeting in the City, in order to win over the City Fathers. But no understanding was reached. The right wing Presbyterians were relying on their friends in Scotland, where a Presbyterian-Royalist party had gained the upper hand and assembled an army of forty thousand to invade England. In April 1648, on the very day after Cromwell's visit to the City meeting, a great rising of the "apprentices" took place, which was only suppressed on the third day. "God and King Charles" was the slogan of the rebellious sons of citizens, with whom artisans and day labourers allied themselves.[1] But this was

[1] The years 1646–51 were dear years, 1648 being the worst, according to Thorold Rogers.

only the beginning. In May the fires of rebellion broke out in
all directions. In Kent, Essex, and Wales the adherents of
the King rose, and the Marquis of Hamilton, leader of the
Monarchist Presbyterians in Scotland, marched with an army
of forty thousand men into England. But the Independent
generals and their army soon showed that they were masters
of the situation. The leaders held a conference at Windsor.
After they had strengthened themselves with prayer during a
whole day,[1] they determined that, once the risings and the
invasion were disposed of, Charles Stuart, "that man of
blood", should be brought to an account for all the blood
he had shed and the mischief he had done to his utmost "against
the Lord's cause and People in these poor Nations". And this
resolution, which was, of course, not concealed from the
troops, seems to have restored harmony between them and
their leaders. It was resolved to march against the enemies
of "God's cause". Fairfax undertook Essex and Kent; Cromwell went first against Wales and afterwards against the Scotch.
Whilst Cromwell was still engaged in the North, the Presbyterians in London lifted their head again. This was about the
time of Lilburne's liberation, mentioned in the preceding
chapter, and six weeks thereafter a vote of Parliament granted
to him as compensation certain confiscated lands of much higher
value than the cash award at first proposed.

It will be appreciated that "honest John", as the *Mercurius
Pragmaticus*, a paper hostile to Cromwell, called Lilburne in
those days, was loath to earn these favours from the Presbyterian
members of Parliament, hitherto so hostile to him, by con-

[1] General Adjutant Allen, an Anabaptist and Fifth Monarchy man and
formerly an "agitator", published in 1659 a full description of this prayer
meeting and the subsequent council of war. "A gracious hand of the Lord",
says he, made them conscious "that those cursed carnal Conferences, our
own conceited wisdom, our fears, and want of faith had prompted us, the
year before, to entertain with the King and his Party" had been "a depar-
ture from the Lord" and had "provoked Him to depart from us". As a
consequence of this "illumination from on high", the resolution referred
to in the text was passed.

tinuing and intensifying his attacks on Cromwell.[1] He was anything but the revengeful personage portrayed by nearly all historians. Almost as soon as he was out of prison he wrote a letter to Cromwell and despatched it to him by Captain Edward Sexby, formerly one of the "agitators". In this letter he held out to Cromwell the hand of reconciliation, and soon after, on a journey to the North he sought out Cromwell in his very camp. In this letter the following passage is noteworthy: "Although, if I prosecuted or desired revenge for an hard and almost starving imprisonment,[2] I could have had of late the choice of twenty opportunities to have paid you to the purpose, I scorn it, especially when you are low, and this assure yourself, that if ever my hand be upon you, it shall be when you are in your full glory, if then you shall decline from the righteous way of Truth and Justice, which, if you will fixedly and impartially prosecute, I am, yours, to the last drop of my heart's blood (for all your late severe hand towards me), John Lilburne."

This letter, dated "Westminster, August 3, 1648, the second day after my liberation", is printed with others in the work *Lieutenant Colonel Lilburne Revived*, which appeared in 1653. I am not disposed to agree with Gardiner's estimation of it as

[1] Among those most eager for Lilburne's release, for example, was Sir John Maynard, who had been compelled a year before to quit Parliament at the behest of the Army. In the article referred to above from the *Mercurius Pragmaticus* it is written: "Now then, seeing Honest John is getting loose, 'twill not be long ere Mr. Speaker and Noll Cromwell be both brought to the stake; for he means to have a bout with them to some purpose, I can tell you."

[2] In the autumn of 1647 Cromwell had moved in the House of Commons that the Commission which had inquired into Lilburne's complaints about his illegal condemnation by the Lords should also investigate the precedents for this action. It may remain an open question whether his motive was to avoid an open challenge to the Lords or to prevent Lilburne's premature release. Suffice it to say that Lilburne regarded Cromwell as responsible for the prolongation of his imprisonment. He was prompted to this belief because Cromwell, a few days before the sitting of the House of Commons, had visited Lilburne in prison and promised him his support, upon which Lilburne had pledged himself to abandon politics and go to America once he had shown that the Lords had no right over a commoner.

an expression of "amusing self-sufficiency", as it indicates that Lilburne was in close touch with the situation from day to day. Cromwell's brilliant victories in the second half of August 1648 had restored his ascendancy. Had he been defeated, or had the campaign lasted longer even, Cromwell and the advanced democrats would have found themselves in a critical position. In any case, it was not good policy to exploit Cromwell's precarious position for futile acts of revenge. Wisdom dictated that he should be induced to make concessions to the Levellers. And this policy proved successful. Lilburne could not be persuaded by Cromwell to enter the Army again, but, after his return to London, he arranged with his political friends to send Cromwell a message, stating that the latter was expected to help the good cause to victory and to understand "the principles of a just government. The war cannot be justified upon any other account than the defence of the people's right unto that just government, and their freedom under it." This letter prompted Cromwell to instruct his friends in London to enter into negotiation with the Levellers.

Cromwell and the Levellers had equal need of each other. At this time Parliament was again briskly negotiating with the King, and the arrangements with him referred to above were made, according to which Parliament was to control the Army and its officers for the next twenty years, and the Presbyterian Church was to be made a State Church for a probationary period of three years. The dictatorship of a Parliament having a Presbyterian majority was as obnoxious to Cromwell as it was to the Levellers, although for different reasons. Whereas Cromwell's opposition was largely determined by his personal interests and enmities, the Levellers were actuated by doctrinal antipathy. After the Levellers had made a gesture of reconciliation, Cromwell had good reasons for writing to Colonel Hammond that it was not they that were to be feared, but the irresolute men working for compromise with the King. He probably reflected that once the question of the

King was settled, the recalcitrant soldiers could be held in check by energetic measures. The Ware mutiny had been easily quelled.

For the moment, however, the Army was to be relied upon. On October 29th the popular Colonel Rainsborough had been assassinated under treacherous circumstances, and this cowardly murder served to strengthen the demand for strong measures against the man primarily responsible for all this bloodshed. On November 20th a new remonstrance was sent to Parliament from the headquarters of the Army at St. Albans by Colonel Ewer, demanding that the "chief delinquent" should be brought to justice. Whilst Parliament was still discussing whether this disrespectful remonstrance should be "taken into consideration", this same Colonel Ewer, by order of the general staff of the Army, brought the King from Newport to Hurst Castle, where he was most rigorously guarded. One of the two companions allowed him was James Harrington, later on the author of *Oceana*.

CHAPTER VII

THE STRUGGLE FOR DEMOCRACY AND THE
LEVELLERS' "AGREEMENT OF THE PEOPLE"

BEFORE the happening of the events last mentioned, however, Cromwell's followers had reached an agreement with the Levellers as to the terms upon which they could co-operate for the time being. This understanding was not achieved without difficulty, as Lilburne and his friends had learnt the lesson of Ware too well to place themselves, even provisionally, in the hands of the "gentlemen" without guarantees. The "gentlemen" were now all zealous for the purification, if not the dissolution, of Parliament, and were nearly unanimous for the execution of the King. But Lilburne and the Levellers desired assurances respecting the subsequent course of events before they would assist in these immediate measures. They clearly perceived that a mere victory of the Army conferred no durable benefits on the people, and Lilburne made this position perfectly plain to the "gentlemen".

He summarizes his opinion of the negotiations in a report whose authenticity in this respect has not been questioned: "It's true I look upon the King as an evil man in his actions, and divers of his party as bad; but the Army hath cozened us the last year, fallen from all their promises and declarations, and therefore cannot rationally any more be trusted by us without good cautions and security. In which regard, although we should judge the King as arrant a tyrant as ye suppose him, or could imagine him to be, and the Parliament as bad as ye could make them; yet, there being no other balancing power in the Kingdom against the Army but the King and Parliament, it is our interest to keep up one tyrant to balance another till we certain know what that tyrant that pretended fairest would give us as our freedoms, that so we might have something to rest upon, and not suffer the Army (so much as in us lay) to devolve all the government of the Kingdom into

their wills and swords (which were two things we, nor no
rational man, could like) and leave no persons nor power to be
a counterbalance against them. And if we should do this,
our slavery for the future might probably be greater than our
first; and therefore do I press hard for an Agreement amongst
the People first, utterly disclaiming the thoughts of the other
till this be done. And this is not only my opinion, but I believe
it to be the unanimous opinion of all my friends with whom I
most constantly converse."[1]

This plain speaking, which sounds a note destined to recur
frequently in the history of English democracy, was clearly
not at all to the taste of the partisans of the "grandees". First,
on account of the outspoken distrust of them, which they
contended was quite unwarranted. They were, as Lilburne
writes, "most desperately choleric" about this. And secondly,
because these further negotiations would consume precious
time. But the Levellers declined to be intimidated either by
protests or asseverations. More experienced than the soldiers
who supported them, they stood firm until a compromise was
effected, by which four chosen representatives of each side
should discuss together the chief points of the signed "Agreement". The selection of the commission led to an angry dispute. Besides Lilburne himself, an elderly merchant named
William Walwyn was chosen as one of the Leveller members.
One of the "gentlemen" Independents, John Price, objected to
him, which provoked Lilburne to answer that Walwyn had
more honour and honesty in his little finger than his opponent
had in his whole body, and that he would rather resign his
place on the Committee than serve on it without Walwyn.
This incident, which, after much discussion, was smoothed
over by both Walwyn and Price retiring, is interesting, inasmuch
as in a work published shortly afterwards Walwyn is attacked
as an extreme communist and atheist, while in the official

[1] Quoted in John Lilburne's *The Legal Fundamental Liberties of the People
of England Revived, Asserted, and Vindicated.*

publications of the Levellers, many of which are signed by Walwyn with other co-signatories, the proposals put forward relate solely to political matters. The work in question was by one William Kiffin, a renegade Independent, who subsequently became a man of great wealth. We shall discuss this work in detail at a later stage of our inquiry. For the present, it is sufficient to say that it does not accuse Walwyn of a single shady transaction, but only of holding and propagating with great cleverness atheistic and communistic theories, so that it could only have been those opinions which led to Walwyn's rejection.

The Committee, reduced in number to six, on November 15th agreed upon the following points: A Committee formed of representatives of the Army and delegates of the "Well-meaning" or "Well-affected"[1] in the country, to meet at the Army's headquarters to formulate a scheme for "the foundations of a just government"; this scheme was then to be submitted to and voted upon by all the Well-affected.[2]

The constitution thus created, provided it came into force, was to take precedence of all other laws, in other words, to form that "paramount law" of the land demanded by the "agitators" and Levellers a year before, and to be signed, with all its provisions governing the authority of Parliament, etc., by *all* members on the day of their election. To avoid confusion, the Levellers waived their demand for the immediate dissolution of Parliament, contained in a petition, called their "masculine" petition, presented by them on September 11, 1648. But a definite date for dissolution was to be fixed, and the "Agreement" itself was to be embodied in the Remonstrance of the Army which was then being drawn up.

[1] These names played in the English Revolution the part played in the French by the word "patriot". They were commonly used for the adherents of the people's cause. The Royalists and their supporters were generally called "Malignants" by the opponents.

[2] This is the first appearance in modern history of the idea of applying *direct legislation* to a great State question. The French Revolution, at its zenith, as is well known, brought forward a similar proposal.

At the Army headquarters, which were shortly transferred from St. Albans to Windsor, a declaration assenting to these stipulations was made, but the Remonstrance presented to Parliament on November 20th by Major Ewer demanded only that all negotiations with the King should be broken off, and that the prime movers in the recent disturbances, both individually and collectively, and therefore including the King, should be brought to justice.

The Remonstrance further demanded the dissolution of the present Parliament and the election of a new one, as well as a decision that henceforth no king who had not been elected by the people should be recognized. The Levellers perceived that this was only in partial agreement with their demands, and contained much that was not to their taste. For the present they did not openly oppose it. They went to Windsor, in order to ascertain the feelings of the "grandees" of the Army, who appeared to be in a conciliatory frame of mind. But once the parties began to discuss the future constitution, serious differences of opinion revealed themselves. Ireton, for example, wanted to reserve to Parliament the right to pass bills of attainder when reasons of State demanded them, which meant that, in certain circumstances, Parliament might pass sentences in opposition to law. But Lilburne, fanatical legalist as he was, and cherishing a rooted distrust of all ruling powers, was strongly opposed to this suggestion, and this Parliamentary privilege was gradually abolished in the course of centuries. Ireton wanted religious tolerance limited to certain forms of Protestant worship, but the Levellers championed the most complete freedom of conscience. Finally, the Levellers made a new proposal. The members of Parliament siding with the Independents, the Army, and "we whom they nickname Levellers", should each choose four representatives, who should conjointly draw up an "Agreement", which should be absolutely binding on all concerned. In his efforts to unite all factions not absolutely Royalist, Lilburne went so far as to

propose to assign four seats on the Committee to the Presbyterians, if they were disposed to accept them. The "grandees"
made no difficulties; some, like Colonel Harrison, because they
really believed in union—others in order to gain time. The
place of meeting in London had already been arranged, and
to London they went. Each party chose its representatives,
the Levellers selecting, in addition to Lilburne and Walwyn,
a certain Maximilian Petty and John Wildman. Petty is not
to be confused with his more famous contemporary, Sir
William Petty, to whom he was not even related, although
both of them belonged to James Harrington's "Rota Club",
of which Wildman was also a member. Wildman seems to have
done his best to live up to his name. He was a democrat and
radical of very impulsive nature. In 1654 he was elected to
Cromwell's first Parliament, but refused to acknowledge the
constitution of the Protectorate as final. In February 1655 he
was arrested at Exton at the very moment he was dictating to
his secretary "A Declaration of the free and well-affected
People of England now in Arms against the Tyrant Oliver
Cromwell". A "stirring man; very flamy and very fuliginous",
writes Carlyle of him; "perhaps, since Freeborn John was
sealed up in Jersey, the noisiest man in England". Gardiner
speaks of him and Lilburne as "men of transparent honesty".
Cromwell contented himself with shutting Wildman up in
Chepstow Castle. After the Restoration, Wildman, out of
hostility to Clarendon, became embroiled with the Duke of
Buckingham, whose ministry introduced a measure of toleration. In 1683 he was in the so-called Rye House Plot, but
received timely warning and fled to Holland. Finally he took
part in the "glorious revolution" of 1688 which placed William
of Orange on the throne of England. Among a collection of
memoirs, pamphlets, etc., in connection with that event,
which was published in 1705, is a "Memorial from the English
Protestants to their Highnesses the Prince and Princess of
Orange, concerning their Grievances and the Birth of the

pretended Prince of Wales", to which, in the index, is affixed
the note "Said to be written by Major Wildman", so that the
fiery republican ended as a monarchical Whig, albeit after
forty years of constant disappointment.

Among the delegates of the Independent Parliamentarians
may be mentioned one Thomas Scott, not to be confounded
with Scott the regicide (peppery Scott), who was hanged
after the Restoration. There was also Henry Marten or Martyn,
who escaped the same fate on the score of his former efforts
to obtain pardon for the Royalists, although he had not been
slow in calling for the execution of Charles, on the ground
that it was better for one family to suffer than the whole
country. Marten was a witty and clear-headed man, like Scott
a thorough republican, and in religious questions extremely
advanced. By general testimony Marten is credited with
unusual generosity. He desired religious toleration to be
extended to the Roman Catholics. A republican when others
dared not dream of an alternative to the monarchy, he carried
a proposal in Cromwell's Parliament that the laws against
those who refused to recognize the new order should not be
enforced against women. It was enough, he declared in Parliament, to hunt the bull. They ought not to want to hunt the
cow also. Carlyle writes of Marten: "A tight little fellow, though
of somewhat loose life: his witty words pierce yet, as light
arrows, through the thick oblivious torpor of the generations;
testifying to us very clearly, Here was a right hard-headed,
stout-hearted little man, full of sharp fire and cheerful light;
sworn foe of cant in all its figures; an indomitable little Roman
pagan, if no better."

The "grandees" of the Army choose amongst others Ireton
and Sir William Constable as their representatives. Amongst
the delegates of the citizen Independents we meet the names
of Colonel White, Dan Taylor, and "Master Price the
Scrivener".

In the meantime Parliament resolved on November 30th

not to consider the Remonstrance of the Army, and stigmatized as an "insolent and unseemly letter" a communication from Fairfax, demanding payment of the arrears due to the Army, failing which the Army would take the money where they could get it. To this the Army Council replied that the Parliament had betrayed the trust of the people, and therefore the Army would "appeal" from its authority "unto the extraordinary judgment of God and good people". The day after it was known that the Remonstrance had been rejected, the Army had, on the proposal of Major Goffe, united in prayer that God would enlighten them and show them the right way, and when the Levellers arrived at Windsor for the discussions, they found the Army on the point of marching to London. The fruits of the enlightenment which their prayers brought these pious men were the purging of Parliament and the execution of Charles I. The Levellers were not too pleased with the turn that events had taken, but their objections were in vain, and the Army chiefs resolved that the situation demanded an immediate settlement of the question between the Army and the Parliament. On December 2nd the Army marched to London and took possession of Whitehall, St. James' and other places of importance. The discussions with the Levellers were at first carried on in London, but were not allowed to interfere with the active steps that were being taken. On the morning of December 5th, after a long and heated debate, Parliament agreed to a declaration that the removal of the King had been effected without its knowledge and consent, and a few hours later carried by 129 votes to 83 a resolution that the conditions laid down by the King at Newport should form the basis of a settlement of the difficulty. This was a bold defiance of the Army, but Parliament was without the means to enforce its views. Against the Army Parliament was powerless. It had the City bourgeoisie on its side, but the City had made no attempt at resistance when, in the summer of 1647, the Army had first seized London, although the train

---

bands and some regular troops had been specially drilled in readiness for the emergency. In his *History of the Civil War*, written in dialogue form, Hobbes shows plainly his anger at the City's weakness. Referring to the events of August 1647, he writes:

"B. It is strange that the Mayor and Aldermen, having such an army, should so quickly yield. A. To me it would have been strange if they had done otherwise. For I consider the most part of rich subjects, that have made themselves so by craft and trade, as men that never look upon anything but their present profit; and who, to everything not lying in their way, are in a manner blind, being amazed at the very thought of plundering" (*Behemoth*). While this may be a characteristic of shopkeepers grown prosperous, it should be remembered that the City Fathers did not have the undivided support of the town. It is certain that many small shopkeepers, with their dependents, sympathized with the Army, and various outlying places, notably Southwark, where the Levellers had many friends, received the Army with open arms.[1]

The Army and those Independents who supported it had no alternative but to answer Parliament's decision by a *coup d'état*, which took the form of Pride's Purge, as a result of which only hard and fast Independents were left in Parlia-

[1] Hobbes is particularly annoyed because the City, as a whole, supported the Rebellion for a long time. The work from which quotation has been made, even more than his *Leviathan*, reveals the narrow-minded champion of aristocratic absolutism. Thus he castigates the "Little Parliament" for making marriage a civil act. The Puritan democrats who were in the majority in that Parliament were more liberal in Church matters, and more advanced in secular questions than their opponents, the enlightened statesmen and philosophers. The reforms, civic, ecclesiastical and legal, which they initiated were in the main highly credible to them, and as, for example, their decision to codify civil law, anticipate the most famous enactments of the Convention of 1793. After an existence of six months, the "Little Parliament" was dissolved, amid the rejoicings of the classes and the castes, the lawyers, whose interests and privileges had been in jeopardy, celebrating the event by a huge drinking bout in the Temple. See *Exact Relation of the Transactions of the Late Parliament*, London, 1654, printed in Somer's Tracts, vol. vi. pp. 266–284.

ment. This Parliament was nicknamed by its opponents the "Rump Parliament".

A few days later the mixed commission of Levellers and Independents had prepared the new "Agreement", which the Levellers were anxious should be signed at once by the general staff of the Army, the soldiers and members of Parliament, and then sent round the country for the signatures of all the Well-affected. With this purpose in view, Lilburne had the Agreement printed, but already difficulties were arising with the general staff. The question of the limits of religious tolerance was again discussed at great length, and in view of what has been said respecting the nature of the different sects, it will be understood why the middle-class elements sought to draw a line beyond which toleration should not extend. On December 21st a compromise was made, that all Christian sects which did not disturb the public peace should not be interfered with by the State, Roman Catholics and episcopal State Churchmen excepted; but that in all "natural", that is secular, matters the decision should rest with Parliament. In those exceptional cases which the "grandees" demanded should be punished by State tribunals instead of the ordinary Courts, a compromise was reached, whereby these cases were limited to acts committed by State officials in contravention of their duty. But the stumbling-block was the dissolution of Parliament. Throughout Cromwell was against the idea of fixing an early date for this, and although upon this point he was in a minority on the Council of Officers, events turned out in accordance with his anticipations. He succeeded in imposing his views that the revised "Agreement" should not be sent forthwith to Parliament for signature and subsequent circulation, but should be further considered, and that so much of the "Agreement" be circulated as Parliament should deem fit.

When Lilburne and his friends perceived that this was to be the end of the matter, they retired, with bitter reproaches, from the conferences about the middle of January 1649.

They were so far right that Parliament on January 20th shelved the "Agreement" of the officers by declaring that it would "take it into consideration as soon as the necessity of the present weighty and urgent affairs would permit", and with this the officers were satisfied.

It must, however, be admitted that Cromwell was right and that the time for the dissolution of Parliament had not arrived. The elements hostile to the Independents and the Army were too numerous to risk the experiment of a new election. Even in such counties as Norfolk and Suffolk, most of the middle class and the gentry were opposed to the Independents and the Army, and these classes constituted a difficult problem for Cromwell, as they set the example in most of the counties, and, like the peasants, were anxious to get rid of the military burden. It was necessary to placate them, and the extreme demands of the Levellers did not assist this object. Gardiner ascribes the revulsion of feeling in the Eastern Counties and other places directly to the increase of "fanaticism", that is, radicalism, which had driven the possessing and business classes into the ranks of the Presbyterians and Royalists.[1] Where Lilburne and his friends saw nothing but malevolence, falsehood, and self-seeking in Cromwell, there was, together with his ambition and class prejudices, a strong inclination to shape his conduct according to the possibilities of the moment. He was the practical politician *par excellence*; the Levellers were the ideologues of the movement. They started from abstract political theories, and accordingly saw facts through the spectacles of these theories; but Cromwell, whose whole being was alien from abstract thinking, saw things as they really were at any given moment better than they. In a word, he was far superior to the Levellers as a practical politician, although they deserve the credit of having in the course of this revolution championed with vigour the political interests of the contemporary and the future working class. So long as

[1] Loc. cit., vol. iii. p. 175.

the fight was against the forces of the old regime, the Levellers could and, in fact, did show the way again and again, but the moment these old forces were vanquished and the new forces proceeded to arrange matters after their fashion, the suppression of the Levellers became a political necessity. The hour of the class for which they fought had not yet struck.

The first edition of the new Agreement of the Levellers was followed on May 1, 1649, by a second edition, which was again issued from the Tower, wherein Lilburne and his friends were once more incarcerated. Here it is fitting to pause in the record of events in order to discuss these important documents, which anticipate in many respects the "Contrat Social".

According to the Agreement, which had been printed not only as a pamphlet but also as a manifesto that could be exhibited as a placard, the supreme authority of the nation should be vested in a representative body of four hundred members, and "all men of age" and not in receipt of wages or alms should, "according to natural right", be eligible to vote for or sit as members of this assembly. Wage-earners in town and country were thus excluded from the suffrage. It should be borne in mind that the workers of that period formed an undeveloped and socially insignificant class, and an industrial proletariat in the modern sense of the word did not exist. The journeymen in the handicrafts were usually in the transition stage between apprentice and master. To extend the suffrage to the agricultural labourers would, in the then circumstances, have strengthened the reactionary party.

It is interesting to note that during the debates between Cromwell and the Levellers universal suffrage was condemned on the ground that it would lead to anarchy, and in a Cromwellian newspaper the Levellers were called "these Switzerizing anarchists".

The Agreement advocated annual Parliaments, the members of which were not to be eligible to sit in the two succeeding Parliaments. Salaried State officials were not to be eligible, and lawyers sitting in Parliament were not to practise. No coercive laws respecting religion should be enacted, and there should be no religious tests. Each parish should elect its own minister, but no one should be compelled to contribute towards his maintenance. A conscientious objection to military or naval service should be respected. All tolls, taxes, and tithes should be abolished within a short fixed period, and be replaced by a direct tax on every pound's worth of real and personal estate. In his pamphlet, *England's New Chains Discovered*, which is by way of a commentary on the Agreement, Lilburne is plain-spoken on the subject of indirect taxes. The Levellers, states this pamphlet, had "resolved to take away all known and burdensome grievances", of which the pamphlet enumerated "Tythes, that great oppression of the counties, Industry and hindrance of tillage; excise and customs, those secret thieves and robbers, drainers of the poor and middle sort of people, and the greatest obstructors of trade, surmounting all the prejudices of ship money, patents and projects before this Parliament. Also to take away all monopolizing companies of merchants, the hindrances and decayers of clothing and cloth-working, dying and the like useful professions. . . . They have also in mind to provide work and comfortable maintenance for all sorts of poor, aged, and impotent people." All privileges were to be cancelled, and a national militia was to take the place of the standing Army, the decision as to war resting with Parliament. Each county should select its own officials; the laws were to be printed in English, and all complaints and prosecutions to be dealt with only by a sworn jury of twelve citizens of the district. Measures should be taken to ensure work and decent maintenance to the poor, the aged, and the sick.

The demands set out above constitute a remarkable programme for the time in which it was formulated. It was the more formidable in that it shunned all communist-Utopian speculations, which found champions enough in the camp of

the Levellers. Communism made no appeal to the town population, which did not yet possess an industrial proletariat. At
the most, communistic proposals might have attracted the
rural workers at certain times. In fact, there is no instance
during the Great Rebellion of an independent class movement
of the town workers, although during the zenith of the movement there were several attempts at agrarian communist
risings.

In some historical works the Levellers are depicted as religious sectarians, who exceeded the Puritans in fanaticism, but
the Agreement does not support this suggestion. It postulates
a greater measure of religious toleration than was conceded by
any other parties of the time. Certainly the writings of individual Levellers contain numerous texts from the Bible, but
this is not remarkable in a time when the Bible was the only
book that had great weight with the mass of the people. Moreover, these texts never relate to religious dogmas. On the other
hand, the Levellers were frequently accused by their contemporaries and opponents of atheism, and there is proof of the
existence of a widespread rationalism or deism in their ranks.
There is, in any case, good ground for the statement of other
historians that the Levellers originally called themselves
rationalists to mark that they recognized the authority of reason
alone.

CHAPTER VIII

ATHEISTIC AND COMMUNISTIC TENDENCIES IN THE LEVELLERS' MOVEMENT

WE have referred to Henry Marten as a "heathen". But notwithstanding all his friendship for the Levellers, Marten was never one of them.

As a representative of advanced rationalism among the Levellers, special mention should be made of Richard Overton, who, with W. Walwyn and T. Prince, frequently figures in company with Lilburne as signatory of their political pamphlets. We have seen that he was mentioned for his profane sentiments in the pamphlet against Walwyn, as a subject of natural detestation, and in his case we are in a better position, than in Walwyn's, to determine the justice of the accusations brought against him. He wrote a small pamphlet on the immortality of the soul, which gives full information on this matter, and it is interesting to recognize in Overton the first representative of the school of thought which combined systematic rationalism, or even materialism, with political and social radicalism in England. He forms in this respect a characteristic pendant to Hobbes, his contemporary, who grafted upon the stem of philosophical materialism the doctrine of political absolutism and State religion. But the philosophic radical representative of the interests of the lower classes has passed into oblivion, mainly because, after the Revolution, social radicalism for a long time manifested itself in religious movements only. It is therefore very difficult to discover any exact particulars as to his personality. Godwin assumed, erroneously,[1] that Richard Overton was a brother of Robert Overton, the friend of Milton (and the republican partisan of Cromwell before he became Lord Protector and Dictator); but all that Professor D. Masson, Milton's biographer, knows about him is that he was "a printer and assiduous publisher

[1] *History of the Commonwealth*, vol. iv p. 280.

of pamphlets". At any rate he was an indefatigable Leveller, and we shall again meet with him in that capacity later on.

The first edition of Overton's pamphlet appeared anonymously in 1643. Amsterdam is named on the title page as the place of publication, but there is good reason to believe that it was printed in London. At that time the Presbyterians were still predominant, and a manifesto of their conclave against contemporary unbelief and heresy attacks this pamphlet: "The chief representative of the tremendous doctrine of materialism, or the Denial of the Immortality of the soul, is 'R.O.' ", the anonymous author of the tract on *Man's Mortality*—the title of the first edition.

The title of the completely revised second edition, which appeared twelve years later, in 1655, in London, reads as follows: "Man wholly mortal, or a Treatise wherein 'tis proved, both Theologically and Philosophically, that as whole man sinned, so whole man died; contrary to that common distinction of Soul and Body; and that the present going of the Soul into heaven or hell is a mere fiction: And that at the Resurrection is the beginning of our immortality; and then actual condemnation and Salvation and not before. With Doubts and Objections answered and resolved, both by Scripture and Reason; discovering the multitude of Blasphemies and Absurdities that arise from the Fancie of the Soul."

As will be seen from the title, a last concession is made to the supernatural idea; a resurrection at the end of time is admitted. But Godwin is hardly wrong in concluding, from the fact that Overton treats this subject quite superficially, that he maintains the doctrine of the Resurrection simply for the purpose of forestalling the charge of propagating crass atheism. It has no connection whatever with the argument on the main question.[1]

[1] There is a connection only in so far as it is shown that the existence of a soul without a body being impossible, there could be no Purgatory or the

The "theological" ground for this main argument consists in a number of Biblical texts cited by Overton, referring to a complete perishing after death, while he declares that other texts which apparently imply the contrary are based on false readings or misinterpretations of the original text. Thus, on the title page, verse 19 of the third chapter of Ecclesiastes: "For that which befalleth the sons of men befalleth beasts; even one thing befalleth them: as the one dieth, so dieth the other; yea, they have all one breath; so that a man hath no pre-eminence above a beast: for all is vanity."

The "philosophical" proof is of an entirely different nature. It is thoroughly *scientific*, as far as this was possible in those times. From the development of the psychical activity in the developing human being—ascending from the infant to the adult man, descending thence to the age of second childhood, and modified in the sick—Overton demonstrates the impossibility of the separation of soul and body. He compares man with animals, and shows from many examples that nearly all of his mental capacities are likewise found in animals, merely differing in degree, and in not being in the latter combined in equal fullness. If, therefore, the human soul can survive the decay of the body, the soul of the animal also must be immortal. With keen logic he demonstrates, from pathological conditions, etc., that if the soul is something independent of the body, man ought to have, not one soul, but a large number. Most categorical are his statements as to corporality in general: "The form", he writes, "is the form of the matter, and matter is the matter of the form; neither of themselves, but each with

like, where disembodied souls were supposed to pass after death. No other immortality of the soul than by the raising up of the whole man is possible, and until this happened the whole man that died, soul as well as body, is dead. "On the whole, were it not for the appended concession of a Resurrection, or New Creation, and an Immortality somehow to ensue thence, the doctrine of the Tract might be described as out-and-out Materialism. Possibly, in spite of the concession, this is what the author meant to drive at" (Masson, *Life of Milton*, vol. iii. p. 157).

the other, and both together make one Being."[1] In another place he writes: "All that is created is material; for that which is not material, is nothing".[2] Overton quotes, in support of his views, many passages from Greek and Roman classics, which suggests that he was an uncommonly well-read man. From the quotations given the reader will scarcely be surprised to learn that this publication made considerable stir; in fact, the author appears to have given great offence to his pious fellow-citizens, while on the other hand his work seems to have had a highly stimulative effect on unprejudiced spirits; thus, for instance, Masson considers it probable that Milton arrived at his views on death through Overton.

As regards Walwyn, Overton's associate, no independent writings by him, on religious and political questions, are extant. A reply from his pen to Kiffin's pamphlet is on strictly defensive lines. It repudiates, in general terms, the charge of irreligion and of revolutionary communism, so that nothing definite can be gathered from it in any direction. The same may be said of a publication which appeared under the initials "H. B.", *The Charity of Churchmen*, whose author, a certain Doctor Brook, declares that he feels bound to stand up for Walwyn, who was confined within prison walls. The conversations quoted by Kiffin had certainly taken place, but Walwyn's utterances had been exaggerated by Kiffin in a partisan spirit. As both apologies appeared at the time when Walwyn was confined in the Tower awaiting his trial, not much weight is to be attached to this mode of refutation. All that can be inferred from them is that Kiffin's charges may possibly have been exaggerated in certain respects, but in substance were not mere fabrications. On the contrary, persons are named who are said to have been present during the conversations in question.

As we are not so much concerned with the precise phraseology as with the general tendency of these conversations, we will now

---

[1] Second Edition, p. 10.   [2] P. 21.

consider how Walwyn is alleged to have endeavoured to corrupt the young people who frequented his house.

It is said that he questioned the young men: "How can you prove that the Bible is God's Word?" "What better proof have you for the divine authorship of the Bible than the Turk has for his Koran?"

He is said to have taken the young people on Sundays to the various churches, one after another, to let them hear how the preachers of the one inveighed against those of the other, pointing out to them the contradictions and absurdities in the sermons, and after having thus prejudiced them against religion in general, representing "the great mysteries of life and salvation through Jesus Christ as well as the doctrines of justification through His death, resurrection, sanctification, and condemnation by His spirit as mere fancies, as ridiculous, nonsensical, vapid, and empty conceptions", to have embarked upon a criticism of the various political and social systems.

He was specifically accused of having said to some pupils that there was "more wit in Lucian's dialogues than in the whole Bible", that the Proverbs and Psalms were composed by kings, solely for their own ends, that the Song of Songs was a poem written by Solomon about one of his whores, that hell is nothing but the bad conscience of evil men in this life, and that it was inconceivable that God should torment men throughout all eternity for a short period of sinful life. King David and the patriarch Jacob had been a couple of sly foxes and cunning knaves. It was absurd to engage in continuous prayer, and the only true religion consisted in helping the poor. The Protestant priests were most of them greedy fellows; even the Catholics had not been as bad as they were to the poor. He could not blame the Irish for their rebellion, they were right in demanding liberty for themselves. It is laid to Walwyn's charge, as a particularly heinous offence, that he even defended suicide, whereby a friend of his wife, who suffered from an incurable disease, had actually been encouraged to kill herself.

So much for Walwyn's "soul-destroying" atheism. Now for his communism.

The associate of Lilburne, whom Freeborn John so warmly defended, is said to have expressed himself as follows concerning the *"disproportion and inequality of the distribution of the things of this life"*:

"What an inequitable thing it is for one man to have thousands and another want bread! The pleasure of God is that all men should have enough, and not that one man should abound in this world's goods, spending it upon lusts, and another man (of far better deserts and far more useful to the commonwealth) not to be worth twopence." . . . He wishes that "there was neither pale, hedge, nor ditch in the whole nation", and says that "the world shall never be well until all things be common". It would not by any means be "such difficulty as men make it to be to alter the course of the world in this thing; a very few diligent and valiant spirits may turn the world upside down if they observe the seasons and shall with life and courage engage accordingly". To the objection that this would upset all and every Government, he answered: "There would then be less need of Government; for then there would be no thieves, no covetous persons, no deceiving and abuse of one another, and so no need of Government. If any difference do fall out, take a cobbler from his seat, or any other tradesman that is an honest and just man, and let him hear the case and determine the same, and then betake himself to his work again."

Have not these sentiments a decidedly modern ring about them?

However, Walwyn's views have been preserved for us by his opponents, and, like Overton's treatise—of which the first edition appeared before the outbreak, and the second after the suppression of the Leveller movement—have no direct connection with this movement itself. As party leaders, Walwyn and Overton, as well as Lilburne, appear to have confined themselves mainly to political matters and to have treated religion as a strictly "private affair".

But the movement itself was not exclusively concerned with political questions. The masses, as a rule, will not be inspired with enthusiasm for political reforms unless these appear to them a means for improving their own material position; and the Leveller movement was no exception to this rule. As long as it was confined to portions of the Army and of the London populace, its political character was uppermost, but when it spread into the country, it at once assumed the character of a "social-democratic agitation".

A striking illustration of this, and of how it was customary for the Bible to be quoted on every occasion and for meanings to be read into the text, is supplied by a pamphlet written by a Leveller and entitled "*Light Shining in Buckinghamshire*, or the discovery of the main ground, original cause of all the slavery in the world, but chiefly in England, presented by way of Declaration of many of the well-affected in the country, to all the poor oppressed countrymen of England, and also to the consideration of the present army under the conduct of Lord Fairfax", 1648. The motto of this pamphlet runs as follows: "Arise, O God, judge Thou the earth", and at the very commencement it says: "All that which is called Magistracie is from the king's Patent, and his is from the devil; for the king's predecessor, the outlandish bastard *William*, came to be king by conquest and murther; now murtherers are, saith Jesus, the devil's children, for, saith He, the devil was a murtherer from the beginning and he abode not in the truth; now kings are utterly against the truth and persecutors of the saints, for, saith Jesus, they shall bring you before kings, so that Kings are enemies unto the Kingdom of Christ".[1]

The argument is as bold as the quotations, but it shows how

[1] P. 3.

it was sought to prove everything from the Bible. The pamphlet goes on to say: "And, therefore, those called the Levellers, their principles to free all alike out of slavery, are most just and honest in reference to the matter of freedom, for it is *the end of redemption by Jesus to restore all things*."[1] Who required a king at all? is a question put by the unnamed author, who then proceeds to show that it is *the rich, the nobility, the priests, and the "horseleech" lawyers* who require the protection and countenance of a king, but not the real people. He adds that what "honest people" desire is:

1. "A just portion for each man to live, so that none need to beg or steal for want, but everyone may live comfortably."

2. "A just rule for each man to go by, which rule is to be found in Scripture."

3. Equal rights for all.

4. Government by "Judges called Elders" elected by the people.

5. A commonwealth after the pattern of the Bible. "Now in Israel, if a man were poor, then a publicke maintenance and stocke was to be provided to raise him again. So would all Bishops' lands, Forrest lands, and Crown lands, do in our land, which the apostate Parliament-men give one to another, and to maintain the needlesse thing called a king, and every seven years the whole land was to the poor, the fatherless, widows and strangers, and at every crop a portion allowed them. *Mark this, poor people, what the Levellers would do for you*."[2]

The rest of this remarkable pamphlet constitutes a keen and apposite criticism of the situation and political constitution in England, and in conclusion there appears in leaded type the ominous verse from the twelfth chapter of the first book of Kings: "What portion have we in David? Neither have we inheritance in the son of Jesse: to your tents, O Israel."

The little pamphlet must have been received very favour-

---

[1] P. 6. [2] P. 6.

ably, as three months after a sequel appeared, entitled *More of the light shining in Buckinghamshire*. It describes how the people had been robbed of their natural inheritance and enslaved by the Norman conquest, and subsequently by the usurpations of the lords, by illegal enclosure of lands and similar means. The remedy was not to revert to the state of things preceding the Norman conquest, but to build up a state of true equality and justice, and do away with all kinds of kings and vice-kings. A third pamphlet was promised to show how this could be done.

But no such pamphlet seems to have appeared, or at least not under the same title. However, we shall soon see that the author, or the group to which he belonged, had worked out elaborate schemes in support of their proposals. First of all, we would mention two features which the pamphlets referred to have in common with quite a number of pamphlets issued at that period.

The first and more general characteristic is the extremely hostile language used towards the monarchy, the nobility, the Church, and the rich class, but particularly towards the lawyers. No epithet seems too strong to be used against them— the most common, recurring in innumerable writings, is "these caterpillars of society". It seems that they were bitterly hated by a large part of the population, and evidently not without good cause, inasmuch as they were the ready tools of the great land-robbers, ever prepared to give legal sanction to their acts of spoliation, while turning a deaf ear to the cry of the robbed and oppressed without means to pay.[1] And how jealously did they, as a caste, guard their privileges, the right to fleece as they pleased those seeking justice. We have already mentioned that not the least important reason for the collapse

---

[1] "Would it not be a notable booty for the soldiers", we read in the last quoted pamphlet, "when so many cheating lawyers are together at the Term, to drive them out, or else strip their long-tailed gowns over their ears? O soldiers, you could never do a better piece of service than to put down the lawyers."

of Barebone's Parliament was that it designed to replace the tangle of statute law by a codified system of law and thus clip the nails of the legal profession. When questioned in Parliament, about that time, by Edm. Ludlow, one of the republican generals, Cromwell named as one of the obstacles to a drastic reform the resistance of the lawyers, "the sons of Zeruiah". "As soon as we speak of improving the laws they cry out that we propose to destroy property."[1] Even Cromwell dared not incur the enmity of bigots.

The second popular slogan of the period is the denunciation of existing property as the fruit of "Norman law", which was merely the law of a conqueror. There is extant a whole literature of popular pamphlets, which are variations on this subject, and which of course are chiefly written by Levellers or other extreme Independents.[2] But abolition of the "Norman law", as urged in these pamphlets, meant abolition or, at least, revision of the existing *conditions of property*—the word *property* being chiefly or exclusively understood to mean landed property. The English Levellers, without having studied Brissot and Proudhon, came to the conclusion that the land belonged by right to the nation, and regarded landlordism as "robbery".

It was chiefly literature based on these premises that championed the cause of the landless and the expropriated in this Revolution, which, historically considered, was a revolution of the possessing classes: a struggle for the emancipation of proprietors—landholders—from the surviving remnants of feudal burdens on the land. But this was not all. When once society had been aroused, other elements came to the surface and formulated comprehensive proposals for social reform; side by side with the revolutionary socialists of the time we also find "State Socialists" or Social Reformers.

[1] Edm. Ludlow, *Memoirs*, vol. ii. pp. 46–51.
[2] Three such pamphlets against the "Norman law" are reproduced in the *Harleian Miscellany*, vol. vi. p. 36 ff., vol. viii. pp. 94 ff., and vol. ix. pp. 90 ff. The name of the author is John Hare.

We may consider as such, for instance, P. Chamberlen, physician, an Independent of French extraction, who in 1649 published a pamphlet entitled *The Poor Man's Advocate*, in which a most remarkable proposal was made for solving the social question of the period. It bears the sub-title "A Samaritan England" and its motto is "Bonum quo communius eo melius". The author advocates *the nationalization of all land that had hitherto been Crown or Church land, or other forfeited land, as the* PATRIMONY OF THE POOR. All these estates and other public property should be thrown together into a great national "Stock", as a treasure for the poor, and administered on communistic lines, by an organization having a thoroughly democratic constitution and accessible to all, and for the chief direction of which a responsible supervisor was to be appointed. Otherwise, Chamberlen proposes to leave society as it is, except that all restrictions on industry and commerce are to be removed, all articles of food and raw materials are to be admitted into the country duty-free, and similarly, all manufactured products are to be exported free, and no duties are to be levied except on the exports of the former and the imports of the latter. As the reader is no doubt aware, the last mentioned proposals were the demands of the more radical mercantilism which was then coming to the fore. But Chamberlen does not stop there. "Provide for the poor and they will provide for you, crush the poor and they will crush you", is the warning which he addressed to the politicians. He combats the assertion that the poor (meaning not actual mendicants only, but the poorer classes generally) can be brought to reason by hunger and coercive laws only, and that they become lazy if protected against extreme want, and insolent and rebellious if not kept down by force. The economical policy which was carried through in France, half a generation later, by Colbert, is outlined in this pamphlet in every point, except that it is chiefly directed here to the semi-communistic institution of a national "stock". This national "stock" was to

be used to build roads and canals, create manufactures, introduce improved machinery, establish schools and technical
institutes for the instruction of the people; in short, it was to
serve as a lever for raising, together with the situation of the
lower classes, the general level of culture in the country.
Chamberlen does not confine himself to mere general indica-
tions, but proceeds at once to calculate the financial probabili-
ties of his project, which is in every way an interesting example
of the mighty impetus which the Revolution had given to the
minds of men. Although the author was not himself a Leveller,
and is never mentioned in connection with Levellers, he
nevertheless appears to have been closely allied with them.

His treatise was published by Giles Calvert, who published
most of the Levellers' pamphlets, and whose name figures
as that of a co-editor on the title page of the third edition of
the Levellers' *Agreement of the People*, which appeared on
July 23, 1649. Perhaps it would not be altogether erroneous to
regard it as an endeavour to provide a sociological supplement
to the "Agreement", which, as regards the main question with
which it deals, merely lays down a general principle.

Other writings that may be referred to in this connection
are some of the tracts of Samuel Hartlib, or Hartlieb, a learned
Protestant German Pole, whose parents, under the pressure
of Jesuitical dominion, had migrated from Poland to West
Prussia. Hartlieb went to England about 1630, and became
active as a diplomat and as the promoter of all kinds of movements that aimed at the common weal. He made translations
into English of various writings of Comenius, the famous
pedagogue of the Bohemian Brethren (1592–1671), besides
himself writing various essays on education. Keenly interested
in the better cultivation of the soil, he established a small
model farm and published popular works on agriculture as
practised in Flanders, bee-keeping, fruit-growing, etc. In
recognition of his merits, the "Long Parliament" granted him
in 1646 a pension of £100 sterling, which in the following year

was raised to £300. But Hartlieb's boundless liberality, which extended to numerous Protestant and sectarian refugees, and which had exhausted his own property, still kept him poor, and when towards the end of the Republic the payment of the pension fell into arrears, the plight of this unselfish man became deplorable. Though afflicted with a painful disease (calculus), he literally had to beg in order to procure the barest necessaries of life for himself and his family. The restored monarchy was still less eager to pay Hartlieb the arrears of his pension, and he died in extreme want in 1662. He had maintained relations with the most eminent men in England. Milton dedicated to him an essay on Education, and a similar tribute was paid by William Petty, whose talent Hartlieb had been quick to recognize. The great Comenius wrote that he did not know of anyone who equalled Hartlieb in the extent of his knowledge.

Hartlieb's first original work is his treatise, conceived in a Utopian form, on the State as a promoter of industry, entitled: "A description of the famous Kingdom of Macaria; showing its excellent government, wherein the Inhabitants live in great Prosperity, Health and Happiness; the King obeyed, the Nobles honoured, and all good men respected. An example to other nations. In a Dialogue between a Scholar and a Traveller."[1]

The book is dedicated to Parliament, and Hartlieb observes that he has set forth his ideas in a fiction as "a more mannerly way", following the example of Sir Thomas More and Bacon. But *Macaria* (the word is Greek and signifies "Place of Bliss") is written with a severely practical aim. It does not describe an imaginary society, but presents definite institutions and laws—in sufficiently general terms to admit of their being readily applied to the conditions of that time. Briefly summarized, they amount to this, that the State should control and promote production, and that property should entail the discharge

[1] London, 1641 (reprinted in vol. i of the *Harleian Miscellany*, pp. 580 ff.).

of certain obligations, under penalty of its forfeiture to the community. The government of Macaria consists of five departments ("Councils of State"), composed of the most competent citizens, devoted to agriculture, fishery, commerce and trade on land, maritime commerce, and the colonies ("new Plantations") respectively. Of course these officers are represented as fulfilling their tasks in a most exemplary manner, stimulating progress and improvement in every direction. Consequently there is general prosperity, science flourishes, the poorer members of society are provided for in the best possible way, etc. The fundamental idea is that the State should be an economic institution. Hartlieb held fast to this idea throughout his whole life; "Macaria" figures in his letters almost to the very last.[1]

However, in those later days he coupled the "Macaria" project with another scheme, viz., the formation of an association of lovers of physical sciences, which were then totally neglected at the Universities. This plan was realized before Hartlieb's death by the foundation of the "Royal Society". But Hartlieb could not succeed in gaining influential support for his other project. Even the suggestion to make a small commencement in the chief branch of production, i.e. agriculture, was coldly received, as he found to his chagrin, when, after having published several works on improvements in the cultivation of the soil, he brought out, in 1651, an *Essay for Advancement of Husbandry-Learning or Propositions for the Erecting of a Colledge of Husbandry*.

Notwithstanding the sensible and practical arguments used by Hartlieb in recommending this proposal, nearly two hundred years elapsed before it was realized in England. We mention this essay because its sub-title, which recurs in many other writings of Hartlieb's, foreshadows the title of John Bellers' proposal, which will be dealt with hereafter. Hartlieb's agri-

[1] In 1659, to his great mortification, a diffuse and bombastic parody of *Macaria*, entitled *Olbia* (The Happy One), was published in his name, without his knowledge or authority, which served to mystify even some of his friends.

cultural essays and proposals have been highly commended in works of modern agriculturists.

Another of Hartlieb's suggestions was the compilation of a State "Book of Addresses" for traffic in goods, employment registry, etc., where inventories and registers should be kept of all goods, persons, offices, and situations, etc., and where any desired information should be given to all applicants, to the rich against payment of a penny or twopence, "but to the poor all shall be supplied gratis". Hartlieb also advocated the free interchange of all inventions—in which respect he himself set the example—and finally there is extant "an opinion" by him on a project for a land (agricultural) bank. Although these proposals are all in harmony with the nascent capitalist system, the idea is stressed that inventions which tend to increase production are bound to improve the situation of the poorer classes, and that the State should step in where the capabilities of the individual do not suffice to realize this object.

But the literature of the time did not always stop short at proposals compatible with the existing order, and this brings us to the communistic sect of the "True Levellers", as they first called themselves in a spirit of revolutionary defiance, or "diggers", as the people and contemporary writers nicknamed them.

CHAPTER IX

THE "TRUE" LEVELLERS AND THEIR PRACTICAL COMMUNISM

On Sunday, April 8, 1649, while Lilburne and other leaders of the Levellers were again confined in the Tower, there suddenly appeared, near Cobham, in the County of Surrey, a number of men, armed with spades, who commenced to dig up uncultivated land at the side of St. George's Hill, with the intention of growing corn and other produce. They explained to the country-people in the neighbourhood that as yet they were few, but their number would soon increase to four thousand. They proposed to "open and present the state of community to the sons of men", and to prove that it was "an indeniable equity that the common people ought to dig, plow, plant, and dwell upon the Commons without hiring them or paying rent to any". After they had worked for a week, erected tents, and also prepared land on a second hill for sowing—their number having increased to forty and still continuing to increase—some were driven away and some arrested, about the middle of the following week, by two troops of horse. Their leaders, William Everard and Gerrard Winstanley (the first-named being a Leveller who had left or been dismissed the Army), were brought before General Fairfax, when Everard declared that he, like most people who were called Saxons or the like, belonged to the race of the Jews.[1]

He said "that all liberties of the people had been lost by the coming of William the Conqueror; and that ever since then, the people of God had lived under tyranny and oppression worse than that of our forefathers under the Egyptians. But now the time of deliverance was at hand; and God would

[1] This, of course, is to be taken in the sense of God's people or perpetuators of the Jewish theocracy. Similar phrases are met with in the case of many religious-communistic sects of the sixteenth and seventeenth centuries. The Münster Anabaptists also called themselves Israelites.

bring His people out of this slavery and restore them to their
freedom in enjoying the fruits and benefits of the Earth.
And that there lately had appeared to him, Everard, a vision,
which bade him 'Arise and dig and plough the Earth, and
receive the fruits thereof.' That their intent is to restore the
Creation to its former condition. That as God had promised
to make the barren land fruitful, so now what they did was
*to restore the ancient Community of enjoying the Fruits of the
Earth*, and to distribute the benefits thereof to the poor and
needy, feed the hungry and clothe the naked. That they intended not to meddle with any man's property, nor to break
down pales or fences", as they were accused of doing, "but only
to meddle with what is common and untilled, and to make it
fruitful for the use of man". For those who would join them
and work, there would be meat and drink and clothes, "which
is all that is necessary to the life of man". They considered
the present freeholders "their elder brethren that had received
their portion first, even were it unjustly and by force or other
evil means. But though being younger brethren, they saw
not why they should be debarred from all participation in the
common heritage, and die while there was an abundance of
common land lying untilled." The time would soon come
when they "would have absorbed all the poor, workless, and
oppressed, into their ranks, and from shiftless vagabondage
brought them into good citizenship". Yea, the time would
come when even the present freeholders, the perpetuators of
the Norman tyranny, would pull down their fences, give up
their landed property, and willingly join their community,
thus ending all tyranny and slavery and establishing God's
kingdom on earth.

For the rest, Everard declared "that they will not defend
themselves by arms, but will submit unto authority, and wait
till the promised opportunity be offered which they conceived
to be at hand. And that as their forefathers lived in tents, so
it would be suitable to their condition now to live in the same."

"While they were before the General they stood with their hats on, and being demanded the reasons thereof, they said, 'Because he was but their fellow-creature.' Being asked the meaning of that phrase, 'Give honour to whom honour is due', they said, 'Your mouth shall be stopped that puts such questions.' "[1]

They were condemned to pay fines which, for those times, were excessive, and as they could not pay, distress was levied on their goods. But they were not so easily induced to abandon their cause; again and again they attempted anew to carry their idea into practice, only to be forcibly dispersed again. They also published pamphlets defending their ideas and protesting against the treatment they had received. These pamphlets are couched in somewhat mystical phraseology, which manifestly serves as a cloak to conceal the revolutionary designs of the authors.

As an example we may mention a pamphlet entitled, "The true Leveller standard advanced or The state of community opened and prepared to the sons of men by William Everard, Gerrard Winstanley (here follow 13 names) beginning to plant and manure the waste land upon George Hill, in the Parish of Walton, in the County of Surrey, London 1649." It opens with a sentence which savours of the eighteenth century: "In the beginning of time *the great Creator Reason made the earth to be a common treasury*."

It proceeds to state that through violence and usurpation, slavery and oppression first came into the world, and that this was the true Adam, the father of original sin. In a spirit of popular interpretation it adds: "But this coming in of bondage is called A-dam, because this ruling and teaching power without, doth *dam* the spirit of Peace and Liberty."

It proceeds to relate a vision, but the words ascribed to the heavenly apparition betray its mundane purpose: "Work

[1] Communicated, *inter alia*, in B. Whitlocke's *Memorials of the English Affairs from the Reign of Charles I to the Restoration*, p. 384.

together, eat bread together, declare this all abroad," are the words alleged to have been addressed to the person to whom it appeared (Everard), and "Israel shall neither take hire nor give hire".[1]

But the voice is not satisfied with its denunciation of rent. It goes on to say: "Whosoever laboureth the earth for any person or persons that are lifted up to rule over others and doth not look upon themselves as equal as others in the creation: the hand of the Lord shall be upon that labourer: I, the Lord, have spoken it and I will do it."[2] No plainer language could be used to stir up revolt against the landlords or provoke a strike of agricultural labourers and threaten "black-legs" with the wrath of God, manifesting itself by the hands of "God's people".

But the "true Levellers" were disappointed in their hopes. With the suppression of the first attempt to arouse agricultural labourers, by a singular "propaganda by deed", before they had secured as many hundreds of adherents as they had hoped to gain thousands, their fate was sealed, more especially as actual rack-rents did not come into vogue until after the Restoration, and as the wages of agricultural labourers had not yet reached their lowest level. Moreover, and this was probably the decisive factor, the most energetic members of the peasantry were serving in the Army, where meanwhile a crushing blow had been inflicted on the Levellers.

Nevertheless they did not refrain from repetitions of the experiment, which of course were equally futile. In vol. xlii of the *Calendar of State Papers* there is a copy of a letter from Gerrard Winstanley and John Palmer, on behalf of their associates, to the Council of State of the Commonwealth, wherein they protest against the attacks of a priest named Platt and

---

[1] In view of this celestial "no rent" manifesto, we may recall the sudden rise of rents in the seventeenth century, the years from 1647 to 1650 being years of scarcity, which in some cases nearly amounted to famine (cf. Th. Rogers, *History of Agriculture and Prices*).
[2] P. 18.

others to the effect "that we and others called 'diggers' are
riotous, will not be ruled by the justices, have seized a house
and put four guns into it, and are 'Cavaliers', and wait for an
opportunity to bring in the prince (Charles II), on which
you sent soldiers to beat us. These reports are untrue. We
are peaceable men, do not resist our enemies, but pray God
to quiet their hearts, and we desire to conquer them by love".

It then goes on, very appositely:

"We plough and dig, that the impoverished poor may get a
comfortable livelihood and think that we have a right to do it
by virtue of the conquest over the late king who had William
the Conqueror's title to the land. . . . But if the Norman
power is still upheld we have lost by sticking to the Parliament.

"We joined them, relying on their promises of freedom of
land, and claim freedom to enjoy the common lands, bought
by our money and blood. We claim it by equality in the contest.
Parliament and Army said they acted *for the whole nation;
you gentry have your enclosures free, and we claim a freedom in
the common land.*

"There is waste land enough and to spare. We only desire
leave to work and enjoy the fruits of our labour. If this is
denied we must raise collections for the poor out of your
estates; but many are proud, and desperate, and will rob and
steal rather than take charity, and many are ashamed to beg;
but if the land were granted there would not be a beggar or idle
person.

"England could then support itself, and is a stain to religion
for land to be waste and yet many to starve.

"If you grant the land we shall rejoice in you and the Army
protecting our work, and serve you at will."

This letter supplies in simple words a good criticism of the
English Revolution from the standpoint of the proletarian of
the period. Carlyle, notwithstanding the supercilious manner
in which he does so, is quite right when representing the
Levellers and their followers as saying to themselves in 1649:

"God's enemies having been fought down, chief Delinquents all punished, and the Godly Party made triumphant, why does not some Millennium arrive?" The question whether farmers, peasants and labourers should have laid down their lives for nothing was quite natural and justified, and no less justified was the remark, in the letter referred to: "if the Norman power" (the traditional distribution of property) "is still upheld we have lost by sticking to the Parliament". In fact, the labouring agricultural population, as a class, was destined to lose by the Revolution, at least for the time being; their exploiters were emancipated, but the exploitation was intensified. They had not realized this at the outset, when the struggle with the King was represented as a fight for God's justice against priestcraft, and for liberty against tyranny, or for "eternal justice", as Carlyle says. How were the poor country-people to know that "eternal justice" in the seventeenth century meant the overthrow of divine right and the enthronement of the right of property?

The document from which we have just quoted is the last manifestation of collective action on the part of the "true Levellers". Neither in the class whose cause they championed nor in the existing social conditions did they find a foothold for their movement. Those of them who were reluctant to abandon their agitation to improve social conditions had no alternative but to join allied movements which found more favour. And this in fact was what eventually happened, as we shall see hereafter.

The second volume of the "Clarke" papers contains some information about the "diggers". The last-quoted letter addressed by Winstanley to the Council of State is here shown to bear the date December 8, 1649, whilst in the *Calendar of State Papers* it is erroneously dated 1653. As appears from another letter emanating from some of the "diggers", reproduced in the "Clarke" papers,[1] the event related in Win-

[1] Vol. ii. pp. 215–217.

stanley's letter occurred on November 28, 1649. A notable
feature in the last-mentioned letter is the complaint of the
writers that the landlords, at whose instigation Commonwealth
soldiers were pulling down the "diggers'" house, were Royalists.
They say: "But if you inquire into the business you will finde
that the Gentlemen that sett the souldgers on are enemyes
to you, for some of the chiefe had hands in the Kentish rising
against the Parliament." The signatories, seven in number,
request, on behalf of their fellows, that the soldiers should be
called to account, in order "that the country may know that
you had noe hand in such an unrighteous and cruell act".
However, the Council of State was probably more concerned
to placate the middle class by enforcing law and order.

The same volume from which we take this letter also contains a "Digger's Song", found among the "Clarke" manu-
scripts. We cannot refrain from reproducing here at least a
few verses of this communistic song, which most probably
was sung to some popular tune:

> You noble Diggers all, stand up now, stand up now,
> You noble Diggers all, stand up now;
> The waste Land to maintain, seeing Cavaliers by name
> Your digging does disdaine, and persons all defame.
> Stand up now, stand up now.

Aristocracy, gentry, lawyers, and clergy are handled in turn:

> With spades, and hoes, and plowes, stand up now, etc.
> Your Freedom to uphold, seeing Cavaliers are bold
> To kill you if they could, and rights from you to hold.
> Stand up now, diggers all.

The Cavaliers would pull down houses and terrorize the
poor people, but "the gentry must come down" and the poor
men must "bear the crown". Despotism is the Cavaliers' law,
and they do not consider it a sin to starve poor people, but:

> The gentry is all round, on each side they are found;
> Their wisdom is so profound to cheat us from our ground.

The lawyers come next. They advise how the poor are to be imprisoned, and devise all sorts of madness—"the devil in them lies". Nor are the clergy forgotten:

> The Clergy they come in, and say it is a sin
> That we should now begin, our freedom for to win.

They want their tithes and the lawyers want their fees, hence both approve of grinding the faces of the poor. Therefore the next verse bids them rise "'Gainst lawyers and 'gainst priests", who are both tyrants and oath-breakers. They intimidate the poor by sheer force. But they cannot appeal to any vision which has bidden them to uphold such a law. The last verse but one attacks the Cavaliers who have revealed themselves as foes "By verses not in prose to please the singing boyes". In fact, the Royalists deluged the country with songs and poems of every kind.[1] The last verse advocates a peaceful course:

> To conquer them by love, come in now, come in now.
> To conquer them by love, come in now;
> To conquer them by love, as it does you behove,
> For he is king above, no power is like to love,
> Glory hear Diggers all.

While this ballad is only remarkable for its sentiments, another communistic song of those days has some poetical merit. We subjoin three verses of it in the orthography of the original:

> The Poore long
> Have suffered wrong,
> By the gentry of this Nation,
> The Clergy they
> Have bore a great sway
> By their base insultation.

---

[1] See the collection published after the Restoration under the title, *Rump, or an Exact Collection of the Choycest Poems and Songs Relating to the Late Times*, where two satirical poems on the Levellers are given.

But they shall
Lye levell with all
They have corrupted our Fountains;
And then we shall see
Brave Community
When Vallies lye levell with Mountains.

.   .   .   .   .

The time is nigh
That this mystery
Shall be no more obscure,
And then we shall see
Such community
As shall alwayes indure
The Rich and Poore
Shall love each other
Respecting of Persons shall fall,
The Father alone
That sits in his throne
Shall be honoured of all.

The glorious Hate,
Which I do relate,
Unspeakable comfort shall bring,
The corn will be greene
And the Flowers seene
Our Store-houses they will be fill'd.
The Birds will rejoyce
With a merry voice
All things shall yield sweet increase.
Then let us all sing
And joy in our King
Which causeth all sorrowes to cease.

From "A mite cast into the common Treasury, or, Queries propounded (for all men to consider of) by him who desireth to advance the work of public community". The author of this little publication, which appeared on December 18, 1649, signs himself as Robert Coster. The "Queries" which he propounds are kept throughout in the spirit of the "diggers", and most skilfully and sarcastically formulated. He first asks whether it is not true that certain passages in the Bible praise community of goods and condemn the domination of men

H

over men. Next he asks in "Query 3": "Wether particular propriety was not brought into the roome of publick Community by Murther and Theft; and accordingly have been upheld and maintained?" And "wether such naked shameless doings do not lie lurking under fig-leave clothing, such as Sabboth, Fasting and Thanksgiving dayes, Doctrines, Formes and Worships?"

The fourth Query asks, among other things, whether it is not true that the strongest title in the landlord's title-deed is "Take him, jayler!" The sixth and last Query is as to whether "it would not prove an Inlet to Liberty and Freedom, if poor men which want Imployment, and others which work for little wages, would go to digging and manuring the Commons, and waste places of the Earth; considering the effects that this would produce". And these effects, according to the author, would be threefold: (1) "If Men would do as aforesaid, rather than to go with Cap in hand, and bended knee, to Gentlemen and Farmers, begging and intreating to work with them for 8d. or 10d. a day . . . if poor men would not go in such a slavish posture, but do as aforesaid, then rich Farmers would be weary of renting so much Land of the Lords of the Manor." (2) If the Lords of Manors could not let out their lands by parcels their income from rent ("those great baggs of money") would be reduced, and consequently (3) "down would fall Lordliness of their spirits", and then "there might be an acknowledging of one another to be fellow creatures".

The "mad diggers" would seem to have had some knowledge of political economy.

But before the "diggers" abandoned their agitation, so far as its aims were of an economic nature, Gerrard Winstanley, their intellectual leader, wrote a pamphlet which unfolded the real principles and ultimate aims of the agitation without any attempt at concealment. This last independent work issuing from the "true Levellers" is also an important and interesting document in the history of Socialism. Dropping all mysticism and paraphrase, the author propounds a complete social system based on communistic principles, a Utopia, which unmistakably suggests some acquaintance with More's *Utopia*. As the outcome and expression of a propaganda conducted among the labourers, and by reason of its democratic and revolutionary tendencies, it calls for fuller treatment.

CHAPTER X

THE COMMUNISTIC UTOPIA OF GERRARD WINSTANLEY

WHEN the "True Levellers" commenced their agitation with spade and hoe, William Everard appears to have figured as their chief leader, although Winstanley always appears side by side with him. The latter, however, is the author, among other publications, of the Utopia of the True Levellers.

It is entitled *The Law of Freedom on a Platform, or True Magistracy Restored*, London, 1651–1652, Giles Calvert, wherein the author sets forth what "kingly government" and what "commonwealth government" mean. "Humbly presented to Oliver Cromwell . . . and to all Englishmen my brethren whether in church fellowship or not in church fellowship, both sorts walking as they conceive according to the order of the Gospel, and from them to all the nations of the world."

A motto in verse calls for the speedy realization of the principles of the new doctrine.

> In thee, O England, is the Law arising up to shine,
> If thou receive and practise it, the crown it will be thine.
> If thou reject, and still remain a froward Son to be,
> Another hand will it receive, and take the crown from thee.

The work itself is prefaced by an address to Cromwell, which entreats him, who had now risen to the first place in the realm, to change not only the names but also the realities of existing institutions. Upon him had been conferred the high honour of becoming the head of a nation that had cast out an oppressive Pharaoh. But the despotic power exercised and represented by the late tyrant was still subsisting. Land and freedom had still to be bestowed upon those who had risked their person and their purse for it. Not Cromwell as an individual nor he and his officers had conquered the King, who had only been vanquished with the aid of the common people, who had either rendered personal assistance or worked at home for the sustenance of the Army. Consequently all should share equally in the fruits of the victory. Cromwell had two courses open to him: either to make over the land to the people, and thus deserve the honour bestowed on him, or simply to assent to a transfer of political power, by which he would compromise his honour and wisdom. He would either fall or prepare the way for a heavier bondage than that which had hitherto obtained. After this almost prophetic introduction, Winstanley enumerates the grievances from which the people suffer. They are as follows:

1. That the influence of the clergy on the people continued.

2. That many priests were enemies of liberty, many being even adherents of the King's cause.

3. That the tithes still continued in force, and pressed heavily on the people.

4. That justice was still administered by the judges with the old capricious severity.

5. That the laws were still the old, anti-popular ones. They had simply changed the name of "King's Law" for that of "Law of the Commonwealth".

6. That the economic evils were very great. In the country the "Lords of the Manor" still oppressed their brethren after their old fashion, exacted fines and other feudal imposts from them, and drove them from the common land if they did not pay rent. In parishes with common land, the wealthy landlords—"the rich Norman Freeholders" as well as the new gentry who are said to be even "more covetous" than the old landlords—would "overstock the commons with sheep and cattle", so that the poorer peasants and labourers could scarcely manage to keep a cow. In the assessment of taxes, the influence exerted by the great led to the most shameful injustice. In the towns, on the other hand, the people were oppressed by high octrois, market dues, and the like.

This is followed by a drastic onslaught upon the titles to the existing landed property, from which we extract the following sentences:

"But you will say, is not the land your brothers'? And you cannot take away another man's right by claiming a share therein with him. I answer: It is his either by creation right or by right of conquest. If by creation right he call the earth his and not mine, then it is mine as well as his; for the spirit of the whole creation who made both is no respecter of persons. And if by conquest he calls the earth his and not mine, it must be either by the conquest of the Kings over the Commoners or by the conquest of the Commoners over the Kings."

"If he claims the earth to be his from the King's conquest, the Kings are beaten and cast out and that title is undone."

"If he claim the title to the earth to be his from the conquest of the Commoners over the Kings, then I have the title to the land as well as my brother", for *all* had helped to carry on the war.[1]

The sufferings of the people had prompted Winstanley to devise this plan, on the basis of which just conditions should be restored. He had no intention at first of publishing it, but in the end the fire that burnt within him drove him to do so. Possibly not all that he proposed might be correct, but Cromwell might do like the bees which draw the honey from the flowers and leave the rest. "Though this Platform be like a peece of Timber rough hewd, yet the discreet workman may take it, and frame a handsome building out of it."

Cromwell might perhaps inquire how priests and proprietors and the great landlords were to be provided for, if the former were deprived of their tithes and the latter of the services hitherto rendered to them. But when these duties and tithes were imposed no one had troubled about the poverty of the people. And the plight of the lords and priests would not be a serious matter; as members of the free society to

[1] Pp. 9–10.

THE COMMUNISTIC UTOPIA OF WINSTANLEY 119

be created, they would have equal right to the common property with their fellow-citizens and need therefore suffer no
want.

In this new society an end would, above all, have to be put
to *trading*, to "buying and selling". Winstanley describes the
commencement of trading as the "fall" of the human race.

"Is not buying and selling a righteous law? No, it is the
law of the conqueror, but not righteous law of creation: how
can that be righteous which is a cheat? For is not this a common
practice when he (who) has a bad horse or cow, or any bad
commodity, he will send it to the market, to cheat some simple
plain-hearted man or other, and when he come home will
laugh at his neighbour's hurt, and much more? *When mankind
began to buy and sell, then he did fall from his innocency; for
then he began to oppress and cozen one another of their creation
birthright*. As, for example, if the land belong to three persons
and two of them buy and sell the earth, and the third give
no consent, his right is taken from him and his posterity is
engaged in a war."

Thus, he continues, Crown and Church lands, instead of
being set apart for common use, were now being sold to land-
grabbing officers of the Army and speculators of all kinds,
"to the scandal of poor people. This buying and selling did
bring in, and still does bring in, discontent and wars which
have plagued mankind sufficiently for so doing. And the
nations of the world will never learn to beat their swords into
plowshares and their spears into pruning-hooks, and leave off
warring, until this cheating device of buying and selling be
cast out among the rubbish of kingly powers."[1]

Winstanley proceeds to discuss the questions connected
with his scheme of the future. He asks: "But shall not one
man be richer than another?"

And his answer is:

"There is no need of that. For riches make men vain-

[1] P 12.

glorious, proud, and to oppress their brethren, and are the occasions of war."

He shows, and in this he anticipates the arguments of the nineteenth-century socialists, that great private riches are impossible without exploitation.

"No man can be rich but he must be rich either by his own labours, or by the labour of other men helping him. If a man have no help from his neighbour, he shall never gather an estate of hundreds and thousands a year. And if other men help him to work, then are those riches his neighbours' as well as his, for they be the fruits of other men's labours as well as his own. But all rich men live at ease, feeding and clothing themselves by the labours of other men, not by their own, which is their shame and not their Nobility, for it is a more blessed thing to give than to receive. But rich men receive all they have from the labourers' hand, and what they give, they give away other men's labours, not their own."

But inequality might exist as regards titles and honours. "As a man goes through offices he rises to titles of Honour, till he comes to the highest Nobility, to be a faithful commonwealth man in a Parliament House. Likewise he who findes out any secret in *Nature*, shall have a Title of Honour given him, though he be a young man. But no man shall have any Title of Honour till he win it by industry, or come to it by age, or office-bearing. Every man that is above sixty years of age shall have respect as a man of Honour by all others that are younger, as is shewed hereafter."

He next asks:

"Shall every man count his Neighbour's house as his own, and live together as one Family?"

His answer is:

"No. Though the Earth and Storehouses be common to every Family, yet every Family shall live apart as they do; and every man's house, wife, children, and furniture for ornament of his house, or anything which he has fetched from the Storehouses, or provided for the necessary use of his Family, is all a property to that Family, for the Peace thereof." Whoever offends against this shall be punished "*as an enemy of the Commonwealth Government*".

Will there be any lawyers?[1]

The reply is in the negative, and the reason is stated briefly and tersely:

"There is no buying and selling."

For the rest, the law shall be its own "Counsel"—its wording shall be so clear as to require no interpretation. "The foes of contention, Simeon and Levi, must not bear Rule in a free commonwealth."

So far the preface. The first chapter of the treatise itself discusses the meaning of liberty, which does not, as many have imagined, consist in the free use of trading, as this is "a Freedom under the Will of a conqueror".[2]

Nor does it consist in liberty of religion, as "this is an unsettled Freedom", nor in the "Freedom to have community with all Women", or in the "elder brother" being the Landlord and the "younger" being made to serve him. "All these, and such like, are Freedoms: but they lead to Bondage, and are not the true *Foundation-Freedom* which settles a commonwealth in Peace. *True Commonwealth Freedom lies in the free Enjoyment of the Earth.* True *Freedom* lies where a man receives his nourishment and preservation. . ˜. . A man had better to have no body, than to have no food for it; therefore this restraining of the Earth from brethren to brethren, is oppression and Bondage."

"I speak now in relation between the Oppressor and the

---

[1] The reader will remember what has been said above as to the hatred against lawyers.

[2] Compare with this the following sentence of the Communist Manifesto: "By freedom is meant, under the present bourgeois conditions of production, free trade, free selling and buying. But if selling and buying disappears, free selling and buying disappears also." (Karl Marx and Fred. Engels, *The Manifesto of the Communist Party*, p. 18.) With Winstanley, the "law of the conqueror" means "bourgeois" right of property.

Oppressed; the inward bondages I meddle not with in this place, though I am assured that if it be rightly searched into, the inward bondages of the minde, as covetousness, pride, hypocrisie, envy, sorrow, fears, desperation, and madness, are all occasioned by the outward bondage, that one sort of people lay upon another."[1]

Winstanley again refers to the Normans as the enslavers of England, to the laws introduced by them, and the State clergy who defend these laws. He says:

"Their work was to persuade the multitude of people to let William the Conqueror alone have possession and government of the Earth and to call it his and theirs, and so not to rebel against him. Then do the Ministers prepare War against the common man and will make no Covenant of Peace with him till they have their Reason blinded, so as to believe every Doctrine they preach and never question any thing saying, *The Doctrine of Faith must not be tried by Reason.* No, for if it be, their Mystery of Iniquity will be discovered and they would lose their Tythes."

"Therefore no marvell, that the National Clergy of England and Scotland who are the Thything Priests and Lords of blinded men's spirits, held so close to their master the King, for, say they, *if the people must not work for us and give us Thythes, but we must work for ourselves as they do our Freedom is lost.* Yes, but this is but the cry of an Egyptian Task-master who counts other men's freedom his bondage."

"If the earth could be enjoyed as . . . it may by this Platform I have offered then", pursued Winstanley, "man need not act so hypocritically as the Clergy do and others to get a living. . . . *The glory of Israel's Commonwealth is this, They had no beggar amongst them.*"

The first chapter concludes with an appeal to the communistic spirit of the Mosaic law and a protest against the aspersion that the projected Commonwealth would mean

[1] Pp. 17, 18.

general idleness, abolition of marriage ties, and lawlessness. The second and third chapters discuss the meaning of Government in general and define what is "kingly" and what "commonwealth" Government. We will only quote a few of the more significant sentences.

"The original Root of magistracy is common Preservation, and it rose up first in a private Family: for suppose there were but one Family in the World as is conceived[1] Father Adam's Family wherein were many persons, Adam was the first Governor or officer. He was the most wise in contriving, the most strong for labour and so the fittest to be chief Governor. For this is the Golden Rule: Let the wise help the foolish, and let the strong help the weak."

The objection which might be raised, that Adam was not subject to any law, but was an autocrat, free to exercise his own will, is anticipated by Winstanley, who points out that the law of necessity was then paramount, and it indicated Adam as the head of the family so clearly that all parties concerned would readily submit to him. Necessity chose him as the head on behalf of the children.

Winstanley contends that while necessity imposes some form of government, it does not sanction despotic rule.

"*All Officers in a true Magistracie of the Commonwealth are to be chosen Officers.*"

"*All Officers in a Commonwealth are to be chosen new ones every year.*" When publique Officers remain long, they will degenerate. "Great Offices in a Land and Army have changed the disposition of many sweet spirited men. Nature tells us, *That if water stand long, it corrupts*, whereas running water keeps sweet and is fit for common use."

The definite exposition of the organization of the true commonwealth commences with the fourth chapter. As the title suggests, it is elaborated in the form of a platform, or as we should say nowadays, in "articles" or "clauses". Beginning

---

[1] The hypothetical form used in this instance is very characteristic.

with a list of the various offices, it proceeds to explain the functions and duties of each class of officials, and where appropriate, describes certain of the social institutions. The fifth chapter is devoted to problems of education, both academic and commercial, whilst the sixth chapter expounds several special laws of the true commonwealth as opposed to the "kingly" laws.

In view of the industrial conditions under which the author lived, the economic basis of the new society is mainly small-scale production, each individual being at liberty to produce in his own home. At the same time the community maintains public workshops, where any boys may be trained who do not elect to learn their father's domestic trade, or that of any other master. The *exchange of products*, on the other hand, is effected according to the principles of mutuality. Each individual delivers what he has produced into the common "storehouse", from which he draws whatever he requires either for his private use or for manufacturing purposes. There are two kinds of storehouses, viz., those for products in bulk, such as corn, wool, and raw products of all kinds, and those for the various products of manufacture. The *delivery of finished goods* into the storehouse, and *the drafts from the store*, are TOTALLY INDEPENDENT AND SEPARATE TRANSACTIONS, NO CALCULATION OR SETTLEMENT OF ACCOUNTS BEING MADE. The risk of a disparity between production and consumption is obviated in the following manner: Each able-bodied member of the community is expected to supply a certain quantity of work. If he habitually supplies less than his quota, he is first to be privately (!) reminded of his duty by the overseer for his trade, and if such admonition proves without effect, he is to be called to account by the community. This would suffice in most cases, but failing this, and then only, punishment will be resorted to. Similar rules apply as regards excessive drafts of stores, or waste and destruction of material and tools and implements. *Education is to be general*, the children are to be educated together *in public schools*, and *work is to be compulsory up to forty years of age*. Every pupil shall receive scientific and trade instruction, but there shall not be any purely academic section "who set themselves up above their brethren". Anyone over forty years of age may spend his time as he chooses, as a teacher, in trade, agriculture, etc., or he may stand for election as overseer or the like.

The following are the various "offices":

1. In the family, the *father*.

2. In the town, city, or parish, the *peacemaker*, four different kinds of *overseers* (the overseers to preserve peace —a kind of assistant to the "peacemaker"—the overseers for trades, the overseers of the common storehouses, and the general overseers), *soldiers*, *taskmasters*, and *executioners*.

3. In the counties: one *Judge* for each, the *Peacemakers* of every town within that circuit, the *overseers* and the *soldiers*.

These together are to form the *County Senate* or the *Judges Court*, and to sit alternately in the various divisions of the county.

4. For the whole country, a *Parliament*, a *Commonwealth*, a *Ministry*, a *Postmaster*, and *an Army*.

Men over sixty years automatically become overseers of the general welfare (observance of laws, etc.). Otherwise, all officers, including soldiers, who in time of peace are to act as constables, are to be elected annually. The duties of the majority of officers and official bodies are apparent from their titles, and therefore require no further explanation except the "postmasters" and the "ministers" of the commonwealth.

The *Postmasters* are entrusted to conduct the *Intelligence Service*. They are to collect, in each locality, reports of remarkable events (phenomena, discoveries, accidents, etc.), and forward them to the capital, where monthly reports are compiled, and printed in the form of books, which are forwarded to the various local postmasters, who are to bring the contents to the knowledge of the members of the community.

The *ministers of the commonwealth* are to ensure the due observance of the weekly day of rest, when they are to convene meetings of the members of the community, at which three kinds of discourses are to be held, viz., (*a*) Communication of the contents of the reports received by the postmasters on *the affairs of the country*; (*b*) Readings of sections of the *Law of the Land*, so that this may again and again be impressed on the minds of the citizens; (*c*) lectures and discussions on subjects from the *history* of their own or other countries, *arts* and *sciences*, *natural history*, the *nature of man*, etc. *No one is to propound phantastic theories*, but only to relate what he has himself ascertained by *study* and *observation*.[1] Moreover, the lectures are *not always to be held in the English language*, but sometimes in a *foreign* language also, so that the citizens of the English commonwealth may be able to learn of their neighbours and gain their respect and love.

"But saith the zealous but ignorant Professor, *this is a low and carnal ministry indeed*, this leads man to know nothing but the knowledge of the earth, and the secrets of nature, but we are to look after spiritual and heavenly things. I answer, to know the secrets of nature, is to know the works of God within the creation, is to know God Himself, for God dwells in every visible work or body."

Then follows a remarkable onslaught upon what Winstanley calls "The Divining Doctrine", and this argument is not surpassed as a dialectical performance by the anti-clerical literature of the French Revolution. Winstanley expatiates upon the contradictions between theory and practice, of the spiritualistic priesthood. He shows how metaphysical doctrine stultifies the people, in many instances driving them to madness, and finally declares quite bluntly: "Thirdly, this Doctrine is made *a cloke of policy* by the subtil elder Brother

---

[1] "And everyone who speaks of any Herb, Plant, Art, or Nature of mankind, is required to speak nothing by imagination, but what he hath found out by his own industry and observation in tryal" (p. 57).

to cheat his simple younger Brother of the Freedoms of the Earth."[1] Here follows, by way of illustration, a dialogue, which concludes with the "elder" brother (the rich man) saying to the "younger" (the poor man), who is unwilling to believe that the unequal distribution of goods is in accordance with the intentions of the Creator: "What, will you be an Atheist, and a factious man, will you not believe God?" thus intimidating him who is "weak in spirit", and has "not a grounded knowledge of the Creation, nor of himself", "so that this divining spiritual doctrine is a cheat; for while men are gazing up to Heaven, imagining after a happiness, or fearing a Hell after they are dead, their eyes are put out, that they see not what is their birthrights, and what is to be done by them here on Earth while they are living: THIS IS THE FILTHY DREAMER AND THE CLOUD WITHOUT RAIN".[2]

Another interesting feature is the reason given by Winstanley for rejecting all "knowledge of the scholars". As we have already observed, he did not adopt this attitude out of hostility to learning. On the one hand, the restriction of education to the acquirement of practical knowledge reflects the similarly limited empiricism taught by Bacon, but on the other hand Winstanley's opposition to the so-called pure or theoretical knowledge, "the knowledge of the scholars", was

[1] By "elder brother" he always means, as we have seen, the ruling and proprietary class.
[2] P. 62. Imagery taken from the Epistle of St. Jude, 8 and 12. We cannot forbear quoting a few more passages showing how Winstanley anticipated most of the arguments of the deistic and sensualistic writers who came after him.

"If a man should go to imagine what God is beyond the Creation, or what he will be in a spiritual demonstration after man is dead, he doth as the proverb saith, build castles in the air, or tell us of a world beyond the moon, and beyond the sun, merely to blind the Reason of Man.

"We appeal to your self in this question, what other knowledge have you of God, but what you have within the circle of the Creation? . . . For to reach God beyond the Creation, or to know what He will be to a man, after the man is dead, if any otherwise, than to scatter him into his essences of fire, water, earth and air, of which he is compounded, is a knowledge beyond the low capacity of man to attain to while he lives in his compounded body" (p. 58).

prompted by the anti-democratic attitude of the Universities and professional scholars. Popular champions could not but distrust learning which imbued its representatives with contempt for the working classes and made them the sycophants of despotic rulers. We must also bear in mind the status and character of contemporary schools of philosophy and their close connection with orthodox theology. We need only refer to the dissertations of Hobbes, the materialist, on the "Kingdom of God", "Christian Government", etc., in his *Leviathan*, which appeared in the same year as the work we are discussing.

Passing over the regulations for the improvement of agriculture, industry, etc., which, although interesting in themselves, do not constitute an advance upon contemporary proposals, we will briefly discuss in conclusion a few regulations governing *elections*, *matrimonial relations*, and *punishments*.

Every male over twenty years of age is an elector, save those who, at the time of the election, are undergoing punishments inflicted by a judge. Every male of forty is eligible for office, but promising younger men may also be eligible.

Marriage is entirely free. "Every man and woman shall have the free liberty to marry whom they love, if they can obtain the love and liking of that party whom they would marry."

The common storehouses to serve for their mutual dowry, "as free to one as to another". If a man has relations with a maid and begets a child he is bound to marry her. Rape committed on a woman is punished by death—"it is robbery of a woman's bodily Freedom". Attempted abduction of the wife of another man is punished by public reprimand for the first offence, by twelve months' loss of liberty on the second occasion. "Loss of Liberty" means forced labour for the commonwealth, or servitude in a family. Marriages are contracted by mutual declaration before the overseers of the district and in the presence of witnesses, and two years after the appearance of this proposal a resolution in favour of civil marriage was passed in Barebone's Parliament.

The severest punishment is reserved for buying and selling. Whoever tries to induce anyone else to buy anything of him or sell it to him is to be punished with twelve months' loss of liberty. Whoever actually sells land, or the fruits thereof, is to be punished with death. Whoever calls the ground his own and not his brother's will be sentenced to twelve months' forced labour and will have his words branded on his forehead.

No one shall hire labour, or let himself out for labour on hire. Whoever requires assistance may avail himself of the services of young people, or such as are specified by the labour overseers as "servants".

Anyone infringing this rule will have to undergo twelve months' forced labour.

Gold and silver must not be coined, but may be worked up for domestic utensils (dishes, cups, etc.) only. "For where money bears all the sway, there is no regard of that Golden Rule, *Do as you would be done by*: Justice is bought and sold: nay, injustice is sometimes bought and sold for money; and it is the cause of all Wars and oppressions."

The sole exception permitted is exchange transactions with other nations that insist on money payments. "Always provided, That what goods our ships carry out, they shall be the *Commonwealth's goods*, and all their Trading with other Nations shall be upon the *common Stock*, to enrich the Storehouses".

These are the main principles of Winstanley's Utopia, which is well worth being rescued from the total oblivion to which it has hitherto been consigned. I have been unable to find any reference to it in any study of the English Revolution, or in any history of democracy or socialism, and the results of my search for further particulars concerning the person and history of its author have been very meagre.[1]

[1] Mr. Beren's book on the Digger Movement appeared after my book was first published.

I

A few hints as to his former life are given by himself in his pamphlet, *A Watchword to the City of London, the Army, etc.* He seems to have been a tradesman in London, of which he was a Freeman. (By birth he was a Lancashire man, as is shown by the preface to his semi-rationalistic book *The Mysterie of God*.) When the struggle against Charles I commenced, he contributed liberally to the support of the Parliamentary Army, but was then driven from his calling and deprived of his property, by fraudulent representatives of the "thievish art of buying and selling, in conjunction with the oppressive imposts for the war", and compelled to accept the help of friends who provided him with the means of settling in the country, where he was eventually ruined by war taxes and the billeting of soldiers. Yet through all these years he was always prepared to work for the good of the nation, but discovered that many who spoke fair words on behalf of the same cause proved to be opponents in the end. At length, one day whilst at work "his heart was filled with beautiful thoughts, and things were revealed to him, of which he had never before read or heard, and which many to whom he related them could not believe". One of these ideas was that the earth should be made a common treasury of all men without distinction of person.

Winstanley then relates the story of the Diggers' venture, and the treatment they met with, adding: "And I see the poore must first be picked out, and honoured in this work, for they begin to receive the word of righteousness, but the rich generally are enemies to true freedome."[1]

The presumption is that *all* writings in which the names of Everard and Winstanley appear were written by Winstanley himself. As a matter of fact, nearly all the historians who mention the Diggers have been led by the somewhat peculiar arrangement of the names on the Diggers' pamphlets to assume that the reverse was the case. But this hypothesis is negatived by the fact that not a single pamphlet has Everard for its sole author, while quite a series of writings is composed by Winstanley alone.

[1] P. 15.

As far as I have been able to ascertain, Robert Coster is the only other pamphleteer among the Diggers. Of his associate Everard, Winstanley speaks in a pamphlet published in December 1649 in these terms: "Chamberlain the Reading man, called after the flesh William Everard." The pamphlet *Truth lifting up its Head* is a defence against the accusation of propagating atheism, and it begins with an explanation why Winstanley uses "the word Reason instead of the word God".

As the leading spirit of a small sect and the champion of an inchoate class, Winstanley has failed to attract much attention from historians. In the eyes of his contemporaries, even the most advanced among them, he and his associates were crack-brained fools; thus, for instance, John Lilburne in his pamphlet entitled *The Legal Fundamental Liberties* repudiates responsibility for the "erroneous views of the poor Diggers of George's Hill". This was written, however, while he was in prison, and previous to the appearance of the other pamphlet referred to, while, strangely enough, in the publication in question Lilburne breaks a lance on behalf of John of Leyden, who was at that time decried even more than now. But even the self-chosen title "the *true* Levellers" indicates that definite differences of principle separated the latter from Lilburne and his associates. The Levellers represented those interests which were common to the artisan and the advanced citizen, while the *"True Levellers"* exclusively represented the labouring interest.

And in this respect we may say without exaggeration as to Winstanley that, although not "armed with the whole of the science of his century", he was as a socialist ahead of his age.

He represents the most advanced ideas of his time; in his Utopia we find coalesced all the popular aspirations engendered and fertilized by the Revolution. It would be more than absurd to criticize, from our modern standpoint, his positive proposals, or to stress their imperfections and inexpediency. They are to be explained in the light of the economic structure of society as he found it. We would fain admire the acumen and sound judgment exhibited by this simple man of the people, and his insight into the connection existing between the social conditions of his time and the causes of the evils which he assails.

It is now practically certain that Winstanley was the author, or part author, of *The Light Shining in Buckinghamshire*, and that his *Law of Freedom* is the exposition, promised in its second part, of the ways and means by which the return to the "time before the fall" is to be achieved. But what became of him? I have been unable to find anything definite, but the title and contents of a publication dating from 1658, the latest to be found from his pen, in the British Museum, suggests that after the failure of his communistic agitation he finally drifted into the same movement as Lilburne did after the collapse of his radical democratic party, viz., into the religious-radical sect of the Quakers, organized since 1652— the date should be noted. This last publication by Winstanley is entitled: *The Saint's Paradise: or the Fathers Teaching the only Satisfaction to Waiting Souls*, with the motto, "The inward Testimony is the soul's strength".

It is a reproduction of a sermon or religious address given by Winstanley in London, and is couched in the rationalistic spirit of the Quakers,[1] and the listeners and teachers are addressed, according to the custom of the Quakers, as "Friends". If we remember, moreover, that Everard and Winstanley when brought before Fairfax refused to take off their hats, because he was "but their fellow-creature", the supposition that we may look upon them and their adherents as the elements from which the Quaker movement was originally recruited becomes a certainty.

[1] But without their mysticism. Thus Winstanley contends against the belief in the Devil, which was still very strongly held by most Quakers.

CHAPTER XI

THE LEVELLERS' REVOLT IN THE ARMY. LILBURNE'S
LAST YEARS AND DEATH

THE "purged" or "Rump" Parliament had meanwhile adopted
drastic measures to end the dispute with Charles I. On December 23, 1648, it appointed a Commission, which was to con-
sult as to the proceedings to be adopted against the King. On
January 1, 1649, the Commission recommended that the
King should be impeached for high treason towards the
nation in having treacherously waged war against it, and
accordingly Parliament decided to appoint a Tribunal of
State to judge him. When the majority of the few Lords still
in attendance at the House refused to sanction this resolution, a further resolution was passed by the House of Commons
on January 4th, declaring that *"the people are, under God, the
original of all just power"*, and that therefore the representatives
elected by the people, viz., the Commons, constituted the
supreme power in England, whose resolutions had the force
of law, even without the consent of King and Lords. On
January 6th the resolution of impeachment was again proposed, and Parliament, on its own authority, appointed 135
persons to constitute a Special Court—"High Court of
Justice"—for the King's trial. Besides Cromwell and other
"grandees" of the Army, Robert Lilburne was also among the
members of this tribunal, and even John Lilburne (as he
himself stated in a pamphlet soon after, without being con-
tradicted) was offered a seat on the tribunal, for which, of
course, none but Republicans were wanted. But John's strict
sense of legality prevented him from taking any part in an
act, which in fact was but an act of the sword clothed in a
legal form. "Honest John" did not object to placing the King
on trial, but he challenged the right of the existing Parliament
to pose as the representatives of the people. Moreover, he
was not prepared to allow the King a special tribunal, but

desired to have him tried by a regular court of law. However, his democratic objections did not prevail any more than his legal arguments. Charles was sentenced to death on January 27, 1649, as being guilty of high treason, and was executed on January 30th. On February 1st the Parliament sanctioned Pride's "purge" by the formal exclusion of the members expelled by Pride; on February 6th a resolution was passed abolishing the House of Lords as "useless and dangerous",[1] and on February 7th it was resolved that government by a king or any individual be abolished as "unnecessary, burdensome, and dangerous". On February 15th a Council of State, consisting of forty-one persons, was appointed, which of course included among its members Cromwell, Fairfax, and other "grandees" of the Army, and also Henry Marten.

On May 19th, by resolution of Parliament, England was declared a "Free Commonwealth".

During the month of January Lilburne had once more been in the North, in order to attend to his private affairs. He was thoroughly disillusioned and wanted to renounce public life altogether. Too proud to accept a well-paid Government post which was offered to him, as his influence in Radical circles was considerable, on his return to London (of which city he was a Freeman) he set up in business as a soap-maker in Southwark. He declared that he would not fatten at the expense of working people who were suffering want. However, he did not long resist the solicitations of his political friends, who were unwilling to abandon the struggle against the dominion of the Army chiefs. As early as February 26th he reappeared on the scene, heading a deputation of London citizens, who presented themselves at the Bar of the House of Commons in support of a petition against certain measures planned by the Council of State for the suppression of "disturbers of peace" in the Army.

[1] Witty Henry Marten moved as an amendment that the word "dangerous" be expunged, or that "not" be inserted before it. As a matter of fact, the Lords, disorganized as they were, played at that time a most pitiful rôle.

These measures were prompted by the discontent that was rife in several regiments quartered near London, due to the growing disparity between the actions of the chiefs and the "agreement" of Newmarket Heath. Much had been done for the rights of Parliament, but nothing for the rights of the people, who showed their dissatisfaction by wearing sea-green ribbons, the badge of the "Levellers". In order to quell this rebellious spirit the new Council of War decided to issue a proclamation prohibiting soldiers from addressing any petitions to Parliament or anyone else except their officers, or corresponding with any civilian on political matters. The Council further resolved to apply to Parliament for permission to have anyone who attempted to incite the Army to "mutiny" *sentenced by court martial to be hanged*. Lilburne's petition was directed against these measures, and attached to it was a memorial, which he published a few days later as a pamphlet, under the title *England's New Chains Discovered*. In this pamphlet he reveals the various modifications which the Army chiefs had introduced into the "Agreement of the People" as originally drafted, and severely criticizes the newly created institution of a "State Council", which he declares to be a mere creature of the Council of War of the Army. He advocates that such State Council should be replaced by responsible commissions, the members of which should be frequently changed, and which should be controlled by Parliament holding permanent session until relieved by a newly elected House of Commons. He further demands complete freedom of the Press as an unconditional right of the people and as a safeguard against conspiracies and tyrannical aspirations of any kind.

But even from the ranks of the Army itself protests were not wanting. On March 1st there appeared a "Letter to General Fairfax and his Council of Officers", signed by eight soldiers in General Fairfax's army, being a protest which boldly enumerates all the complaints of the Army against its leaders,

charging Cromwell with striving after the royal dignity, calling
Parliament a mere reflector of the Council of War, and the
latter a tool of Cromwell, Ireton, and Harrison, and inveighing
in strong terms against the establishment of a "Rule by the
Sword". They declared: "We are English soldiers engaged for
the freedom of England and not outlandish mercenaries to
butcher the people for pay, to serve the pernicious ends of
ambition and will in any person under Heaven", and they
demanded compliance with the terms of the "Agreement" of
Newmarket Heath.

The letter concludes with a hearty recognition of Lilburne's
petition, which the signatories endorse "freely and gladly",
declaring themselves ready to stand or fall by the demands contained therein.

On March 3rd they were brought before a court martial.
In view of the gravity of their situation three of them were
induced to yield, and were consequently pardoned. The re-
maining five, on the other hand, exhibited the utmost firmness. The court martial was most anxious to know who had
drawn up the document, as they "had not the wit of the writing
thereof". But, in separate examination, they, one after the
other, assumed full responsibility for the letter, and the sentence
pronounced on them was that, although "on account of their
grave offence they had really deserved death", they were to be
led past the heads of their detachments seated backwards on
a wooden horse, and to be expelled from the Army after
having their swords broken over their heads, which punishment
was executed upon them on March 6th in Westminster. Their
names are Robert Ward, Thomas Watson, Simon Graunt,
George Jellies, and William Sawyer.[1]

---

[1] One of the three pardoned men, Richard Rumbold, was prominently
concerned, under Charles II, in the famous Rye House Plot (1683) against
the restored King. Warned in time, he escaped to Holland, but in 1685 he
took part in the insurrection of Argyle and his Scots Highlanders against
James II, when he was taken prisoner. Being badly wounded, and lest he
should die a natural death, he was tried with all speed and executed the

But these measures did not avail to stamp out the movement. On the contrary, this result of the court martial simply persuaded the Levellers that more energetic action was required.

A contemporary, the *Mercurius Pragmaticus*, which was then decidedly royalistic,[1] writes in its issue of March 20, 1649, with spiteful glee, that "the gallant Leveller, seeing his addresses laid aside and the agreement of the people violated, and not made good as he expected", . . . "thereupon with his confederate Harry Martyn[2] hath agreed to send away some pokey saints (of their own propagation) into many Counties of England (as Hertfordshire, Berkshire, Hampshire, etc.), who have in several Market Towns not only proclaimed John's addresses, but also posted them desiring the people to stand to those addressed which tend to their freedom, and oppose any power which will enforce them to pay excises and other unnecessary Rates and unreasonable Taxes, imposed on them by an illegal, arbitrary and unjust power of their fellow-commons".[3]

On March 21st a new Levellers' pamphlet appeared, describing the unjust proceedings taken against the five soldiers, and reiterating its charges against the Army chiefs.

It bears the arresting title, "The Hunting of the Foxes

following day (June 27, 1685) with revolting cruelty. But to the last he exhibited the greatest firmness and strength of conviction. During the trial he uttered those words, which subsequently were often cited, that "he did not believe that God had created the greater half of mankind with saddles on their backs and a bridle in their mouth, and some few booted and spurred to ride on the rest".

[1] Subsequently the highly gifted but unprincipled editor, Marchmont Needham, accepted bribes from Cromwell, at whose service he placed his very caustic pen.

[2] Martyn or Marten had little to do with this agitation, although, as stated, he assisted to draw up the "Agreement" of the Levellers and may have been mentioned in this connection. On the contrary, he defended the continued sitting of the Rump Parliament by saying that the young Moses, i.e. the newly created Republic, ought not to be deprived at once of his natural nursing-mother. Moreover, as already stated, he was himself a member of the Council of State.

[3] *Mercurius Pragmaticus*, No. 46, from Tuesday, March 13th, to Tuesday, March 20, 1649.

from Newmarket and Triploe Heath to Whitehall by five small Beagles, late of the Armie, *or* The Grandee Deceivers unmasked. Printed in a corner of freedome right opposite the Council of Warre, Anno Domini 1649". The "Foxes", of course, are Cromwell, Ireton, and the other "grandees," and "Hunting" them means the exposure of their subterfuges from June 1647, when, in the places mentioned, they persuaded the troops to take joint action against Parliament, up to the time when they established themselves in Westminster. A still more scathing denunciation of Cromwell and his staff was read by Lilburne, on Sunday, March 25th, to an enormous crowd assembled in front of his house. Signed by Lilburne, Overton, Prince, and Walwyn, it demanded in vigorous terms the election of a new Parliament, and was entitled, *The Second Part of England's New Chains Discovered.*[1] Its effect must have been disconcerting, for no sooner had it appeared in print than it led to the arrest of Lilburne and his three co-signatories, simultaneously with a public notice to the effect that all who were guilty of distributing this pamphlet, which incited to mutiny and was calculated to make the sending of reinforcements to Ireland impossible, would be considered enemies óf the Commonwealth, and treated as such. A petition addressed to Parliament in favour of those arrested, which is said to have borne as many as eighty thousand signatures, was ignored; a deputation of citizens who spoke on their behalf was dismissed by the Speaker with a sharp rebuke for their "calumnious and seditious proposals", and a deputation of women who presented themselves repeatedly were in the end sent away with the reply that the matter was of more far-reaching importance than they could understand. They were to go home and attend to their housework—"wash their dishes".

[1] Lilburne's remarks, reproduced on page 66, regarding the suspicious game which Cromwell and the "grandees" had played in the autumn of 1647 with Charles I, are taken from this document.

The matter was indeed of far-reaching importance. The Presbyterians and the partisans of the Cavaliers in the Established Church, who by impressive pamphlets on the *Martyrdom* of Charles I, and a forged Diary of his (the famous *Eikon Basilike*, which had a larger sale than any other book before or for long afterwards), had turned many worthy citizens against the "bloodthirsty tigers of the commonwealth", were again raising their heads; Charles' son was proclaimed King in Ireland and Scotland, and troops were raised in his support, while on the Continent Charles himself and the Cavalier refugees and exiles were plotting at nearly every Court against the young republic. How, under these circumstances, could an agitation which threatened to disrupt the Army—the source and mainstay of power of the representatives of the commonwealth—appear to them other than as a blow aimed at the heart of the commonwealth, which would have to be suppressed by sheer force, if needs be? To impress this position upon Lilburne was, according to his own statement, the object of a conversation between him and Hugh Peters, the Republican Field Chaplain, then a zealous partisan of Cromwell, during a visit he paid to Lilburne in the Tower. Peters is said to have answered Lilburne's appeals to the law with the remark that there was no other law than the sword. Evidently Peters intended (and not without Cromwell's knowledge) to make a last attempt at gaining Lilburne over, but Lilburne's distrust could not be overcome.[1] The consequence was that matters remained as they were left on the day after the arrest of the four Levellers, when Cromwell in the Council of State, striking the table with his fist, addressing the chairman, Bradshaw, Milton's brother-in-law, exclaimed: "I tell you, sir, there is no other way to deal with these men but to break them in pieces", which, however, was not quite an easy

[1] Lilburne's account of this conversation, as given in the *Legal Fundamental Liberties, etc.*, is undoubtedly vitiated by his personal prejudices and his fanatical "sticking to legality".

matter. Instead of decreasing, discontent was spreading more and more in the Army and among the people. As we have noted, there was a great dearth in the country, commerce and trade were paralysed, yet the taxes were rising; and while Parliament was granting extraordinary salaries to the "grandees" of the Army and the Council of State, the soldiers' pay was constantly in arrears. In order to replenish the exhausted Treasury, an expedient had already been adopted which was subsequently employed on an immense scale during the French Revolution. The Government had started to make payments in paper notes, which on account of the low level of the national credit soon fell to one-fourth of their nominal value, and even lower. In short, the discontent was not only due to spiritual causes—if we may thus describe the religious or political forms assumed by the class conflict—but also to causes of an economic and material nature.

How was it possible, with a discontented Army, to stamp out discontent in the Army? A loan had been subscribed for fighting the rebellion in Ireland, and a number of regiments commanded by Cromwell had been ordered to quell the Irish insurrection. But just as previously Parliament had intimated to the King that it intended to settle accounts with him before assisting him against the foreign enemy, so the soldiers of the more radical regiments now objected to proceeding to Ireland while Parliament still postponed a settlement of their claims. In order to break down their resistance, the authorities began to move them to other stations. This brought the conflict to a head.

On the night of April 25th a large number of dragoons of Colonel Whalley's regiment appeared in front of the "Bull", Bishopsgate, London, where the colour-sergeant was billeted, and compelled him to give the standard up to them. They were due to leave London next day, but declared they would not go until their demands were granted. This was open mutiny, and if allowed to spread farther, the worst might be expected.

But Fairfax and Cromwell did not allow matters to go farther. No sooner had they heard of the affair next morning, through the commanding officer of the regiment, than they appeared on the spot with other officers, accompanied by a number of reliable soldiers, and by dint of persuasion, combined with intimidation, succeeded in inducing the mutinous soldiers to submit. Fifteen of those who had remained firm were arrested as ringleaders, to be tried by court martial; the remainder were marched off to the new quarters allotted to them. Five of the fifteen were sentenced to death next morning, but of these four were, at Cromwell's request, pardoned, while one only, Robert Lockyer, upon whom the fatal lot had fallen, was shot on April 27th. He was a "brave and pious" soldier, who, although but twenty-three years of age, had served from the very beginning of the struggle against the King and enjoyed great popularity with all his comrades. He went to his death admonishing his friends to remain faithful to the cause of liberty and the weal of the people. "I pray you, let not this death of mine be a discouragement, but rather an encouragement, for never man died more comfortably than I do", were his last words. His funeral, which took place on April 29th, was made the occasion of a great political demonstration by the extreme elements among the population. Thousands of craftsmen and labourers, with their wives and daughters, followed the coffin—decked with rosemary, one bundle dipped in the blood of the "Martyr of the Army", as Lockyer was universally called. They wore sea-green and black ribbons as the token of their opinions. Outside the city they were joined by many more mourners, who did not care to show themselves openly within its precincts. Whitlocke[1] writes that "many looked upon this funeral as an affront to the Parliament and the Army. Others called these people 'Levellers', but they took no notice of anyone's sayings".

Lilburne and Overton, who in the Tower heard of all that

[1] *Memoirs*, p. 385.

happened in London, were unwilling to let this affair pass by in silence. No sooner had they heard of the sentence passed on the five soldiers than they at once, on the same day, drew up a letter to General Fairfax, "in which it is by law fully proved that it is *both* treason and murder for any General or Council of War to execute any soldier in time of peace by martial law". This letter, dated "from our causeless, unjust and tyrannical captivity in the Tower of London", was simultaneously published in print. Its arguments are conclusive, setting forth that Clause 4 of the "Petition of Right" expressly provided that martial law should no longer be applied with regard to soldiers, besides which, in the (Newmarket Heath) Agreement of June 1647, signed by soldiers and officers, the Army had been recognized as an independent organization of free citizens of England. The writers boldly declared that they valued liberty and the rights of the nation above their own lives, and hence felt bound to raise their voices in the face of the bloody sentence passed on Lockyer and his fellow-prisoners. The effect of this letter is shown by the demonstration just described as well as by the events immediately following.

Ten days after Lockyer's funeral, on May 9, 1649, Cromwell held a review in Hyde Park. An ominously large number of soldiers wore defiantly the sea-green ribbon on their hats. Cromwell knew what this sign meant, and earnestly besought them not to endanger the cause of the commonwealth. He promised that all they desired should be done; their pay should be discharged more punctually than heretofore, while Parliament had already decided to dissolve and prepare for the election of a new Parliament. But discipline must be maintained in the Army; for the present they could not dispense with martial law, and whoever objected to this had better quit the Army. Those who were willing to fight with him and their well-tried comrades against the enemies of England must take the green ribbons from their hats. The soldiers yielded to the influence of this harangue, but the general discontent remained unappeased. Nevertheless, a momentary advantage had been gained by spreading indecision among the soldiers quartered in London, for troubles were now growing apace in the regiments stationed in the provinces. News came from Banbury that Captain Thompson, with two hundred horsemen from Colonel Whalley's regiment—presumably a portion of the dragoons transferred from their London quarters on April 25th—had raised the standard of rebellion. In a manifesto entitled "England's Flag," Thompson, who had been prominent as one of the "Levellers" at Ware, strongly supported the revised "Agreement", published in the form of a proclamation by Lilburne and his associates on May 1st, demanded satisfaction for the murders of Arnold and Lockyer, and threatened that if any harm came to Lilburne and his fellow-prisoners, he would avenge it seventy times seven. A Hotspur, but, as will presently appear, no mere braggart. However, the only effect of this threat was that Lilburne, Overton, and others, who hitherto had enjoyed some freedom within the Tower, were kept in solitary confinement.

The 10th of May brought still worse news to London. In Salisbury (Wilts) almost the whole regiment of Colonel Scroope had declared in favour of the "Agreement" of the Levellers, and had placed themselves under the command of Ensign Thompson, brother of the above-mentioned Captain Thompson. The greater part of Ireton's regiment, stationed in the neighbourhood of Salisbury, as well as Harrison's and Skippon's regiments, also revolted. All these elements were about to join forces and to resist any attempt at sending them to Ireland before the promised reforms were carried out at home, intending to enforce these reforms if necessary. Nearly all of them were old and tried soldiers: Scroope's horsemen, for instance, were some of the first levy—men who, as they declared in a manifesto couched in very dignified language, had sold their farms or given up their businesses in order to fight against the tyranny of the King and bishops, and would not allow any new tyranny to arise.[1]

This revolt could not be ignored. Hence Cromwell and Fairfax started at once with all the reliable troops they could muster, altogether about four thousand men, and proceeded by forced marches to Salisbury. On arrival at Andover they learnt, on May 12th, that the rebels had joined hands at Old Sarum with four companies of Ireton's regiment, and turned northward, no doubt with the intention of marching into Buckinghamshire, where troops of the same mind as themselves (Harrison's regiment) were stationed, and where they probably meant to join forces with Captain Thompson. Fairfax and Cromwell at once turned northward to intercept them. At Wantage the Levellers had already met Cromwell's emissaries, who failed to deflect them from their purpose. They then marched towards Abingdon, where they were joined by two companies from Harrison's regiment, the others having found their route cut off by Cromwell and Fairfax. Cromwell's emissaries, who had followed the rebels, now numbering twelve hundred, once more negotiated with them, but again to no purpose. On the other hand, they appear to have kept Fairfax and Cromwell posted as to the Levellers' movements. When the rebels turned to the west, in order to join the troops stationed there, and prepared to cross the Thames at Newbridge, they found the bridge held by a whole regiment of cavalry under Colonel Reynolds. Either to avoid unnecessary bloodshed, or because they did not yet feel strong enough to take the offensive, they desisted from forcing a passage. They sought a ford, crossing the river partly swimming, partly wading, and advanced without a halt through Bampton as far as Burford, which they reached at nightfall, as did also Captain Thompson, whose small band had been scattered in an encounter with Colonel Whalley, but who with a few

---

[1] *The Unanimous Declaration of Colonel Scroope's and Com.-General Ireton's Regiments*, Old Sarum, May 1649.

faithful followers had successfully held the pursuers at bay. Tired and wet through, moreover deluded by the promises of Major White, Cromwell's emissary, who declared the Levellers' demands to be most reasonable, and that he himself would stand up for them, besides assuring them of the friendly feelings entertained by the General towards them, the Levellers retired to rest and put their horses out to grass. Brave men, but unpractical in their idealism, Carlyle was perhaps right when he wrote of their march: "What boots it; there is no leader, noisy John is sitting fast within stone walls." But Cromwell *was* a leader. He and Fairfax had covered fifty miles that day on horseback, and scarcely less the preceding day; yet they would not let the night pass without action. After a short rest outside Burford, they fell upon the place about midnight, being conducted, it is reported, by Quarter-master Moore, whom they had gained over, and who had been entrusted by the Levellers with the posting of sentries. The Levellers, suddenly roused from sleep, defended them-selves as best they could, but, fighting without plan or leader, they were overwhelmed by superior numbers, Cromwell having two thousand men with him. Over four hundred sur-rendered after having received an assurance of pardon and due consideration of their wishes; the remainder fled, aban-doning their horses and arms. Two squadrons only collected under Captain Thompson retired in the direction of North-amptonshire.[1]

The next day a court martial was held on the prisoners. Four of them, including Ensign Thompson, were sentenced to death. Young Thompson and two corporals who were

[1] They succeeded there in taking Northampton by surprise and providing themselves with fresh ammunition as well as a piece of artillery, but, they were too few in numbers to prevail against whole regiments. In the first engagement the men surrendered unconditionally, and Captain Thompson fell a few days later in an almost unparalleled single-handed combat against more than a hundred pursuers. He would not surrender alive at any price, and though bleeding from several wounds fought like a lion. It was not until he was struck by the seventh bullet that he fell.

condemned died courageously. Of one of these we are told:

"Without the least acknowledgment of error, or shew of fear, he pulled off his doublet, standing a pretty distance from the wall, and bade the soldiers do their duty; looking them in the face till they gave fire, not shewing the least kind of terror or fearfulness of spirit."

Even Carlyle, who, as a rule, is hostile to these men, cannot refrain from saying:

"To die the Leveller Corporals; strong they, after their sort, for the Liberties of England; resolute to the very death. Misguided Corporals! But History, which has wept for a misguided Charles Stuart, and blubbered, in the most copious helpless manner, near two centuries now, whole floods of brine, enough to salt the Herring fishery, will not refuse these poor Corporals also her tributary sigh."

The fourth of the condemned, Ensign Dean or Denne was very contrite, and was pardoned. The Levellers henceforth looked upon him as a traitor, and upon his condemnation as a preconcerted farce. After the execution, Cromwell in church gave the captive Levellers one of his half-religious, half-political addresses, which, though much derided, seldom missed fire, and in this instance too the result was that the prisoners addressed promised to abandon all intention of seditiously enforcing the carrying out of their ideas. After a short interval they were reinstated in their regiments, and during the following summer were taken to Ireland, where they either fell fighting against the Irish "Papists" or were settled upon the estates abandoned by the latter. In the afternoon of the day of the execution, Fairfax and Cromwell, with their staff, went to Oxford, where, amidst all kinds of festivities, the University conferred degrees upon them. Parliament conveyed to them the thanks of the nation, and the great merchants of the City, who had often enough execrated Cromwell, and held the purse-strings tight in the face of the financial requirements of the Parliamentary Army, on June 7, 1649, celebrated the overthrow of the Levellers by a splendid banquet given at the Grocers' Hall in honour of Cromwell and Fairfax, now hailed as the saviours of Sacred Property. In order to show that they were no niggards, they presented Cromwell and Fairfax with gold dishes and plates, and at the same time granted £400 for distribution among the poor of London.

Most probably, in fact, they had been trembling in their shoes at the danger they had so luckily escaped. The most absurd rumours had been set afloat concerning the dark plots of the Levellers, and many of the denunciations published at the time read as if they were of most recent date. Thus, for instance, a few days before the banquet there appeared the following, "ENGLAND'S DISCOVERER, OR THE LEVELLER'S CREED. Wherein is set forth their great and unparalleled design against the twelve famous companies of the City of London, and all other trades, mysteries, arts, and callings whatsoever.

"Published by special authority to undeceive the people, the like being never heard of in all former ages." London, 1649, June 6th.

"Let these things be noted from those called Levellers.

"1. It is asserted by them, that Reason is God, and that out of this Reason came the whole creation.

"2. The immortality of the soul they flatly deny, and scoff at such people as believe the soul's immortality. . . .

"4. All that we call the history of the Scripture is an idol, hence they say the public preachers have cheated the whole world, by telling us of a single man, called Adam, that killed us by eating a single fruit."

Their communism is of the worst kind: "They will have no man to call anything his, for it is tyranny that a man should have any proper land; particular property is devillish, the mystery of Egyptian bondage, a destroying of the creation, a lifter-up of the proud, covetous flesh, a bringer-in of the curse again, a mortal enemy to the Spirit, and that which hath brought in all misery upon the creature." And their practice is even worse than their theory. "To these therefore are their emissaries specially sent, to raise the servant against the master, the tenant against the landlord, the buyer against the seller, the borrower against the lender, the poor against the rich, and for encouragement every beggar shall be set on horseback . . ." And they should not allow themselves to be misled by their official statements. "But you heard them say they approve not of this Levelling, unless there did proceed an assent from all the people. Here is a cloak so thin that a man may see through it." The poor and the workers, being the majority, could be easily gained over by such promises.

As will be seen from the above, even at that early date, people knew how to mix up truth with falsehood, theoretical speculations with practical demands, party pronouncements with individual utterances and the declarations of dissenting factions, in order to throw discredit upon the whole movement, and thus justify the employment of the harshest measures. Nevertheless, it must be said that well-meaning mediators were not wanting. Thus, for instance, on the day of the executions at Burford there appeared *A Serious Aviso to the Good People of this Nation concerning the sort of men called "Levellers"*. The author of this publication, who calls himself "Philolaus", admits the justice of many grievances of the Levellers, but warns them against extreme steps. "I am verily of opinion", he exclaims, "that fantastick Eutopian Communities, introduced among men, would prove far more loathsome and be more fruitful of bad consequences than any of these of the basest alloy yet known." Why, even Plato himself, though such a great thinker, had gained nothing but adverse criticism with his imaginary model state.[1]

[1] We may mention, as a very interesting publication written in a conciliatory spirit, which, among other things, pleads strongly in favour of economic reforms for the benefit of the poorer classes, and proposes a suitable programme, the pamphlet, *An Apology, etc.*, by Lieut.-Colonel John Jubbes. Among the large number of publications written by military men on behalf

Nor did the Levellers themselves remain silent. Lilburne and his associates, soon after their arrest, had issued a publication entitled "Manifestation from Lieut.-Colonel John Lilburne, Mr. William Walwyn, Mr. Thomas Prince and Mr. Richard Overton (now prisoners in the Tower of London) and others, commonly (though unjustly) styled LEVELLERS Intended for their Full Vindication from the many aspersions cast upon them, to render them odious to the world", etc.,[1] in which they declared that "Equalling of men's estates and taking away the proper right and title" would be "most injurious unless there did precede an universal assent thereunto from all and everyone of the people", adding that an unrepresentative Parliament had no right to enact measures designed to transform private conditions; even the communism of the early Christians had been a purely voluntary one.[2]

In May "divers well-affected apprentices" within the Cripplegate Ward Without issued a "thankfull acknowledgment and congratulation unto the ever to be honoured Lieutenant-Colonel John Lilburne, Mr. William Walwyn", etc., in which they assert the purity of their endeavours; and in June a Levellers' pamphlet turns the tables on their opponents with the challenge: "Will the *Levellers* take men's estates from them? Truly if it be proved that any of their *nests are feathered* with what is the *Republique's*, and not their own, it may then be so."[3] We may explain that while the Levellers were decried as

of the Levellers, we may also name the pamphlets by Colonel William Bray and his Quartermaster John Naylier. Under the title *A Declaration of Lieut.-General Cromwell concerning the Levellers*, Cromwell published a short defence against the charges brought against the chief authorities of the Army by the leaders of the Levellers. An official report on the negotiations between the Army leaders and the rebels was likewise published, under the title: *A Full Narrative of all the Proceedings between His Excellency the Lord Fairfax and the Mutineers.*

[1] London, 1649, April 14th.
[2] No doubt this is the statement referred to in the denunciatory publication referred to above.
[3] The title of this pamphlet is in rhyme: "Seagreen or blue, see which speaks true, *or* reason contending with treason. In discussing the late unhappy difference in the Army, which now men dream is well composed".

"anxious to share", their opponents carried this "sharing" policy into practice. Parliament was sharing out, with a most liberal hand, the confiscated estates among its deserving adherents, and the wealthy men of the City were injuring the exchequer of the commonwealth to the best of their ability by usurious interest. History repeats itself, in this respect, with remarkable frequency.

But neither the pamphlets quoted nor any that followed them could regain for the Levellers the position that they had lost.

It is true that the number of their adherents among the London populace was by no means insignificant, and that they still had friends in the Army, but they could no longer withstand Cromwell's influence; and it was the Army which determined the policy of the country, the masses being unable to challenge its ascendancy to any purpose by their own effort. Moreover, Cromwell could always win over to his policy, by promises and protestations, many who sympathized more with the Levellers than with any other party, and could immediately suppress any threatening symptoms of opposition. In particular, it was his spirited and intelligent foreign policy that gained him many personal adherents. Hence, after the failure of several attempted revolts, the more desperate among his implacable enemies (which now included nearly all the Levellers, who had ceased to regard him in any other light than as the arch-traitor and conspirator, the chief adversary, and, above all others, the tyrant standing in the way of liberty) now proceeded to plot against his life; but these plots were doomed to failure, their only effect being to spoil Cromwell's enjoyment of the brilliant position of Dictator and Lord Protector to which he had attained.[1] We may here pause to

[1] The first persons who incited to attempts at assassination were, by the way, Champions of Order, Throne and Altar. As early as in the issue of March 20 to 27, 1649, of *Mercurius Pragmaticus* we read: "Why don't you fight *Rogues* to't *Rebels*, ye brave Levellers. . . . What you that are *Rebels* of undaunted valour, it is base for you to deale like Billingsgate

tell of the subsequent fate of Lilburne, who died in 1657. The remainder of his life was no less troubled than the earlier part. About the end of July 1649, while Lilburne was still confined in the Tower, his eldest son died, and Parliament, which had ignored his requests to be permitted to see his sick child while yet alive, now sanctioned his liberation on bail. In consequence of a new political pamphlet, entitled *An Impeachment of High Treason against Oliver Cromwell*, he was re-arrested in September. Being almost ruined financially, and convinced of the impossibility of making headway against Cromwell's influence, he yielded to the entreaties of his brother, Colonel Robert Lilburne, and published on October 22nd an open letter dated from prison, addressed to his persecutors, in which he offered to go to the West Indies if they would release him, pay his arrears, and allow those who wished to accompany him.

His petition remained unanswered, but he was due to be tried on October 24th, in the Guildhall, before a special Court, for high treason, committed in the pamphlet referred to (*An Impeachment, etc.*), and an even more violent one, published on September 1st, under the title *An Outcry of the Young Men and Apprentices of London*. His contention that the constitution of the Court was contrary to the fundamental laws of the country was unheeded, and his claim that the jury was legally entitled to judge not only as to matters of fact but also as to the application of the law itself, as the Judges represented only "Norman intruders", whom the jury might here ignore in reaching a verdict, was described by an enraged Judge as "damnable, blasphemous heresy". This view was not shared by the jury, which, after three days'

---

wenches with nothing but words. I tell you your *claims* of *justice* are not worth a T—, unlesse recorded with the *blood* of them that deny your demands; therefore be ye not baffled, bold Levellers; stand up, be constant and prosecute your claims of Justice against that perjured traytor Fairfax to the death . . . turne Executioners of *Justice* yourselves upon both *Tom* and all his *partakers*."

hearing, acquitted Lilburne—who had defended himself as
skilfully as any lawyer could have done—to the great horror
of the Judges and the chagrin of the majority of the Council
of State. The Judges were so astonished at the verdict of the
jury that they had to repeat their question before they would
believe their ears, but the public which crowded the judgment
hall, on the announcement of the verdict, broke out into
cheers so loud and long as, according to the unanimous testimony of contemporary reporters, had never before been heard
in the Guildhall. The cheering and waving of caps continued
for over half an hour, while the Judges sat, turning white and
red in turns, and spread thence to the masses in London and
the suburbs. At night bonfires were lighted, and even during
the following days the event was the occasion of joyful demonstrations. In fact, Lilburne's popularity among the bulk of
the London populace was so great that a commemorative
medal was struck in honour of his acquittal.[1]

The Government were taken by surprise. They had ordered
Lilburne to be sent back to the Tower after his acquittal, in
order to institute a new trial, if possible, but they were urged
on all sides to respect the verdict of the jury and release him.
Among the members of the Council of State, Henry Marten
and Lord Grey of Groby, one of the few peers who sided with
the Independents, particularly championed Lilburne's cause,
and finally carried their point, not the least circumstance in
their favour being that Cromwell with the major part of the
Army was still in Ireland. The Council of State resigned
itself to its defeat and released Lilburne, Overton, Prince, and
Walwyn on November 8th.[2]

[1] The medal bears the significant inscription, "John Lilburne saved by the
power of the Lord and the integrity of his Jury, who are Judges of Law as
well as of facts. October 26, 1649." A reproduction of it, together with a
picture of Lilburne pleading before the Court, is to be found in the book,
The Trial of Lieut.-Colonel John Lilburne, London, 1649.

[2] After this, Prince and Walwyn no longer figure in the movement. There
exists a sermon, "God Save the King", preached 1660 in honour of the
return of Charles II by a "William Walwyn", but it is doubtful whether

At the end of the following month, December 1649, Lilburne was elected member of the Common Council of the City, but Parliament nullified the election because Lilburne had declined to declare unconditionally in favour of the existing constitution, and because he was incapacitated by his imprisonment from holding this office. On the other hand, in the summer of 1650, Parliament at last assigned to him land to the value of the indemnities still due to him.

In 1651 he was drawn, through a relative, into a civil action against Sir Arthur Hazelrig, Member of the Council of State and Governor of Newcastle. With his customary zeal he took up the cause of his relative against the influential "grandee", who, in his opinion, had robbed the former of his rightful property by an abuse of his position. The matter finally came before Parliament, which appointed a commission of inquiry into the case. The decision turned out in favour of Hazelrig, and Lilburne, who in a pamphlet criticized this decision as unjust and partial, was condemned by Parliament (!), early in 1652, for "contempt", to a fine of £7,000 and banishment for life. All protests and petitions proved unavailing, and in the spring of 1652 Lilburne found himself for the second time an exile in Holland, this time in company with leaders of the very party he had fled from on the first occasion. Holland at that time afforded a refuge to numbers of fugitive and banished Cavaliers.

the author is identical with the "Leveller" Walwyn. Perhaps it was his son, Overton, who had issued several pamphlets from the Tower in which he denounced the members of his party, half bitterly and half humorously, for their inaction, and was subsequently involved in Sexby's plots against Cromwell's life, of which more in the next chapter. In the aforesaid pamphlets he reproaches their London friends with egging him, Lilburne, and their associates on to action against Cromwell, and says that they now forsook them (*Overton's Defiance of the Act of Pardon*, July 1649), and that it appeared to him that the heroes of the great meeting of September 11, 1648, had been dispersed, simultaneously with the Burford affair, like sparrows scattered by a blowpipe. But he hoped that his blunt words had roused them from their stupor and reminded them once more of the Agreement (*The Baiting of the Great Bull of Bashan*).

There was every temptation for him to join these in a conspiracy against the hated "usurper" Cromwell, and in all probability he received overtures in this direction. But we have no reason to doubt Lilburne's emphatic statement that he refused to co-operate in restoring Charles Stuart except on the basis of the "Agreement of the People". It is true that a report was sent to London to the effect that Lilburne had offered the Duke of Buckingham and other Cavaliers to return to England and achieve Cromwell's overthrow for £10,000, but, as Lilburne proved conclusively, the authors of this report were paid spies of Cromwell, and they are scarcely to be believed in preference to Lilburne himself, whose outstanding characteristic was love of truth, carried to the point of reckless disregard of his personal interests. Nor was Lilburne so simple as to imagine that he could, at the moment when Cromwell, fresh from victories over the Irish and Scotch, was stronger than ever, achieve with such a trifling sum the object which Charles I and the City Merchants, under far more favourable circumstances, had been unable to accomplish with adequate financial resources.

Finally, the above imputations are at variance with the tenor of. Lilburne's letters, addressed by him during his exile to his political friends at home. These letters teem with exhortations to adhere to the democratic principles for which they had striven, and to be tireless in asserting them.

When, in April 1653, Cromwell forcibly dispersed the "Rump" of the Long Parliament, and summoned a Parliament consisting of 139 selected notabilities of the Independent party, and known as the "Little" or "Barebone's" Parliament, Lilburne returned to London, contending that the sentence of banishment pronounced against him by the "Rump" was legally annulled by the mere fact that the latter had ceased to exist. But this was not Cromwell's view. He ordered Lilburne to be arrested at once and tried for "breach of exile", which was punishable as an act of high treason. Again monster petitions poured in on Lilburne's behalf, but they had no effect upon the Council of State any more than had an open letter, published by Lilburne immediately after his return, entitled *The Banished Man's Suit, etc.*

Nor could Parliament, to whom Lilburne appealed on its assembling (early in July 1653), do anything for him beyond referring the matter to the competent jurisdiction, i.e. to a jury, which, as a matter of fact, was more in Lilburne's than in Cromwell's interest. The hearing of the case at the Old Bailey Court of Assizes dragged on for several weeks, because Lilburne pertinaciously insisted, supporting his claim by convincing arguments, that a copy of the writ of indictment should be delivered to him *before* the trial, in order to enable him to take counsel's advice upon it. And indeed, as an eminent lawyer puts it, he accomplished the "great deed never before achieved by any man", of enforcing the delivery of the writ of indictment. On August 20th the case came on for final decision. The sympathy of the populace for Lilburne had risen to such a pitch as to cause Cromwell to keep several regiments ready under arms, in order to employ force, if necessary.[1]

Slips of paper with the inscription:

> And what, shall then honest John Lilburne die!
> Three score thousand will know the reason why,

were circulated in large numbers.

As a matter of fact, the number of Lilburne's partisans was not so great as this,[2] but quite apart from the special measures taken by Cromwell, the pamphlets of the period[3] dealing

---

[1] Thurloe, State Papers, p. 336.

[2] Although a publication dating from 1649 states that the "Agreement" of the Levellers had already received 98,064 signatures, and that new ones were being added daily (*The Remonstrance of Many Thousands of the Free People of England*).

[3] One of them, emanating from Sam. Chidley, a radical Independent, which tries to make excuses for Cromwell's political measures, says: "O Lilburne, Lilburne, hear what he saith who said he would be wise but it

with Lilburne's case reveal the intensity of the agitation at this moment, and the enormous popularity acquired by Lilburne. And after a twelve hours' final hearing, in which Lilburne defended himself with his usual skill, the jury pronounced the verdict of "Not Guilty".[1]

But once more it was a case of "acquitted but not set free". The Council of State retained Lilburne in strict custody, and caused a rigorous examination of the whole proceedings to be made in order to have the verdict set aside if possible. The jurymen were separately examined, one by one, but they remained firm and adhered to their verdict. Hence it was impossible to get at Lilburne by means of the ordinary legal procedure, and therefore "reasons of State" were invoked. In December 1653 the "Little Parliament" was dissolved, a new constitution created, and Cromwell proclaimed "Lord Protector" of the Republic with almost regal powers. In March 1654 Lilburne was conveyed to the Isle of Jersey and incarcerated there, as a prisoner of State, by reason of "seditious" statements uttered by him in the course of his trial. In Jersey, where the law is different from that in England, it was easier than anywhere else to ignore any appeal to "Habeas Corpus". As long as Cromwell could depend on the Governor of the Island, he could feel safe from the dreaded demagogue. Lilburne had thus been rendered innocuous, and Jersey did more in this respect than Cromwell could have hoped. They granted Lilburne an allowance of £2 a week, so that at least he was secured against suffering material distress. He appears, however, to have very keenly felt his intellectual

---

was for him. If thou hadst as much wisdom as courage, as much prudence as confidence, if as much meekness and gentleness as strength of memory, if as much depth of apprehension as ready delivery, thou wouldst be a rare Phœnix, or Bird of Paradise." (*An additional Remonstrance to the valiant and well-deserving Souldiers, etc. With a little friendly touch to Lieut.-Colonel John Lilburne, London, 1653*.) In reply to remonstrances of this kind, Lilburne published a pamphlet, *The Just Defence of John Lilburne against such as charge him with Turbulency of Spirit.*

[1] The trial is reported at length in Cobbett's *State Trials*.

isolation, and no less depressing was the effect produced on him by the news he received from England, announcing the failure, one by one, of all the plots undertaken by his confederates against Cromwell. Gradually a mental change was produced in him, such as, in fact, affected many of his partisans in the country. A reaction from his former restlessness set in, and a calmer outlook invaded his mind. He began to doubt the wisdom of his former tactics, and when failing health supervened on his growing scepticism he renounced a continuance of the struggle after the old manner; his fiery spirit was broken. In the autumn of 1655, the Council of State, who had doubtless heard of his change of mind, transferred him from Jersey to Dover Castle, where, although still kept in confinement, he nevertheless had more intercourse with his countrymen. A few weeks later London newspapers received a report, which was confirmed in Lilburne's letters to his friends, to the effect that he had joined the sect of the Quakers, which was then coming into prominence, and had donned the garb of the *"friends of inward light"*. Thus the most eminent leader of the *political* Levellers was eventually absorbed in the same movement into which the most prominent representative of the *True* Levellers had drifted.

But it was not only his political pilgrimage that he had finished. About the end of July 1657 he obtained permission, on finding sureties, to proceed to Eltham, where he took a house for his wife, so that in case of sickness she might be near her relatives. Cromwell had no sooner heard of this than, on August 19th, he issued a peremptory notice, ordering Lilburne to present himself again in Dover within ten days. Probably he had his suspicions. However, the order was useless —a higher power had laid its hand on the still dreaded man. Only ten days later, on August 29, 1657, "turbulent" John was a *stilled* man in every sense—death had finally removed from the ranks of the fighters the quadragenarian whose bodily strength had been prematurely broken by many persecutions.

Lilburne's body was conveyed to London, where it became the cause of a dispute between his old and his new partisans. The former desired to bury him in the customary manner, with a pall over the bier, the latter (the Quakers), according to their custom, in a plain coffin. In the crowd which had assembled outside the house of mourning, the Quakers were in the majority (which is significant), and they gained their point. When the body was carried from the house, an attempt was made to throw a velvet pall, held in readiness for the purpose, over the coffin, but this was frustrated by the Quakers, who took the coffin on their shoulders and proceeded with it to the cemetery in closed ranks.

CHAPTER XII

HISTORICAL SIGNIFICANCE OF LILBURNE AND THE LEVELLERS

HISTORICAL research during the nineteenth century has removed many of the distortions which hitherto disfigured the image of Cromwell as handed down by his contemporaries. The victor of Dunbar no longer appears to us to-day as the double-tongued schemer, as he was considered by many of his brothers-in-arms, as the "great impostor", who for the mere gratification of his ambition would not scruple to tread underfoot what but yesterday he had passionately upheld. Gardiner's book has dispelled almost the last doubts in this respect, and explained many changes hitherto unaccounted for in Cromwell. The various forces, influences, and circumstances which determined Cromwell's actions are more clearly analysed, and assigned with greater chronological accuracy than ever before. It appears on almost every occasion that Cromwell's "deception" turns out to be justifiable opportunism. But what Cromwell gains as a man and a politician he loses as a revolutionist. Whenever the struggle against effete powers threatened to assume a revolutionary aspect, we see him frequently irresolute and even pusillanimous; in every instance he is impelled to decisive action by outside forces. During the period from 1646 to 1648, in every respect a revolutionary epoch, he is inferior, in perceiving the political measures required and grasping a new situation, to others, more especially to the Levellers. The plebeian-radical elements in the Army and in the civil population became prominent during this time, and determined the course of the Revolution. The Levellers among the people and the Agitators in the Army were the first to recognize the necessity of dealing sternly with the anti-revolutionary forces, as they were also foremost in perceiving that so long as the Revolution accepted the irresponsible position of the King, and treated him as a prisoner of war instead of as a prisoner of the State, the issue of the struggle remained in doubt.

But among the Levellers themselves Lilburne was remarkable for his democratic instinct and political sagacity. He was a political doctrinaire, and as such was necessarily one-sided. Yet this theorist had a keen insight into many things, and in not a few points held his own against statesmen. Thus, for instance, he wrote as early as in 1646, when none of the leading politicians had contemplated an attack upon the House of Lords: "All legislative power in its own nature is merely arbitrary, and to place an arbitrary power in any sort of persons whatsoever for life (considering the corruption and deceitfulness of man's heart, yea, the best of men) was the greatest of slavery; but the claim of the Lords is not only to have an arbitrary power inherent in themselves for life, but also to have it hereditary to their sons, for ever, be they knaves or fools, which is the highest vassalage in the world."[1] It was not until three years later that the "grandees" of the Army and Parliament found that he was right, and abolished the House of Lords. We have also seen how his inveterate suspicion of arbitrary power extended to Parliament itself, and how fiercely he opposed the attempted establishment of the "rule of the sword", although he himself was in constant touch with the democratic elements in the Army. We will give one more quotation. In his pamphlet *An Impeachment of High Treason against Oliver Cromwell* he says: "If we must have a King, I for my part would rather have the Prince[2] than any man in the world because of his large pretence of right, which if he come not in by conquest, by the hands of foreigners —*the bare attempting of which may apparently hazard him the loss of all at once* by gluing together the now divided people *to join as one man against him*—but by the hands of Englishmen by contract upon the principles aforesaid—the

---

[1] Lilburne, *A Whip for the Present House of Lords.*
[2] Subsequently Charles II.

principles of the 'Agreement of the People'—which is easy
to be done, the people will easily see that presently thereupon
they will enjoy this transcendent benefit, he being at peace
with foreign nations, and having no regal pretended competitor,
viz., the immediate disbanding of all armies, garrisons, and
fleets, saving the old cinqueports . . . whereas for the present
army to set up the pretended Saint Oliver or any other as their
elected King, there will be nothing thereby from the beginning
of the chapter to the end thereof but wars and the cutting of
throats year after year; yea and the absolute keeping up of a
perpetual and everlasting army under which the people are
absolute and perfect slaves."[1]

"It is impossible", Gardiner adds, "to treat the man who
could write those words as a mere vulgar broiler." If Lilburne
deceived himself in believing that the prince could sincerely
subscribe to his "Agreement of the People", he was right in
predicting that the military dictatorship would not end the
contest, and most apposite in describing the dangers of this
dictatorship. As a politician he showed himself to be far
ahead of the "Fifth Monarchy" men, who held fast to the
external sign of the republic.

Here are a few more opinions on Lilburne:

"Lilburne knew fear so little that he was ready at all times
to fight against any odds."[2]

"Lilburne was naturally of an undaunted courage and an
acute understanding. He defied all consequences, nor was
terror in any instance able to alter his resolution and perse-
verance. Lilburne was a man of generous birth and ardent
disposition; in addition to which his habits were of no common
order."[3]

And Mr. C. H. Firth, in the *Dictionary of National Biography*,
writes at the conclusion of an exhaustive article on Lilburne:

[1] *Vide* Gardiner, *History of the Commonwealth*, vol. i. p. 178.
[2] A. Bisset, *Omitted Chapters of the History of England*, vol. i. p. 145.
[3] W. Godwin, *History of the Commonwealth*.

"Lilburne's political importance is easy to explain. In a revolution, where others argued about the respective rights of King and Parliament, he spoke of the rights of the people. His dauntless courage and his powers of speech made him the idol of the mob. With Coke's *Institutes* in his hand he was willing to tackle any Tribunal. He was ready to assail any abuse at cost to himself, but his passionate egotism made him a dangerous champion, and he continually sacrificed public causes to personal resentment. It would be unjust to deny that he had a real sympathy with sufferers from oppression or misfortune; even when he was himself an exile he could interest himself in the distresses of English prisoners of war, and exert the remainder of his influence to get them relieved. In his controversies he was credulous, careless about the truth of his charges, and insatiably vindictive. He attacked in turn all constituted authorities—Lords, Commons, Council of State, and Council of Officers—and quarrelled in succession with every ally." A life of Lilburne published in 1657 supplies this epitaph:

> Is John departed and is Lilburne gone!
> Farewell to Lilburne, and farewell to John;
> But lay John here, lay Lilburne here about,
> For if they ever meet they will fall out.[1]

This does not do full justice to Lilburne. In reply to the charge of quarrelsomeness he could fairly appeal in his Vindication (1653) to the fact that all his lawsuits and conflicts turned on important questions of right and of the commonweal. He was, in fact, the ideal "champion of right", and as he was hot-tempered into the bargain, he could hardly avoid falling from one conflict into another. He had the makings of a first-class lawyer. But just as, despite his military abilities, he was the implacable foe of military domination, so, notwithstanding his legal knowledge, he was the sworn enemy of the legal profession.

[1] From *The Self-afflicted Lively Described*, London, 1657.

The times were troubled, and whoever championed, as Lilburne did, the cause of the common people "could not but attack, one by one, all the constituted authorities". His hostile attitude towards the "constituted authorities" in no wise differs from that of popular tribunes in other revolutions. We may call him a demagogue in the same sense in which Marat, Desmoulins, and O'Connell were demagogues, and in this category he is second to none. He was a brilliant speaker, wielded the sword and the pen with equal courage and skill, and while some of his comrades in the struggle may have surpassed him in learning (though he was by no means ignorant) and others in consistent radicalism, none among them combined so many brilliant qualities of a popular agitator as this man whom even Hume calls "the most turbulent but the most upright and courageous of human kind". He united the inflexible sense of justice of an ideologist, the resolution of a war-tried revolutionary, and the keen judgment of a practical politician. For all this he was sometimes unjust to Cromwell. He represented another class and different principles from Cromwell's, and he would have been deficient in loyalty had he judged the actions of those in power by any other standard than the principles of the class he championed. A party zealot engaged in continuous strife must be forgiven if he falls short of the impartiality of the historian. Nor have wise politics ever been a strong point with democratic parties. Cromwell himself was devoted body and soul to the cause of the propertied classes, and as such was deficient in his handling of the very question in regard to which Lilburne showed up to advantage. Cromwell beheld in the class division of human society, into aristocracy, bourgeoisie and workers, and the contemporary respective legal positions of these classes, the inviolable "natural" order of things.

"A nobleman, a gentleman, a yeoman, 'the distinction of these': that is a good interest of the Nation, and a great one! The 'natural' Magistracy of the Nation was it not almost trampled under foot, under despite and contempt, by men of Levelling principles? I beseech you, For the orders of men and ranks of men, did not that Levelling principle tend to the reducing of all to an equality? Did it 'consciously' think to do so; or did it 'only unconsciously' practise towards that for property and interest? At all events what was the purport of it but to make the Tenant as liberal a fortune as the Landlord? Which, I think, if obtained would not have lasted long! The men of that principle, after they had served their own turns, w^d then have cried-up property and interest fast enough! This instance is instead of many. And that the thing did 'and might well' extend far, is manifest; because it was a pleasing voice to all Poor men, and truly not unwelcome to all Bad men."[1]

Thus said Cromwell in his speech of September 4, 1654, when opening the first Parliament of the Protectorate. In his speech on the dissolution of this Parliament on January 22, 1655, pointing once more to the danger threatening from the "Levellers", Cromwell said: "It is some satisfaction if a Commonwealth must perish, that it perish by men and not by the hands of persons differing little from beasts! That if it must needs suffer, it sh^d rather suffer from rich men than from poor men, who, as Solomon says, 'when they oppress leave nothing behind them, but are a sweeping rain'."[2]

These words of "Self in the highest", as Lilburne nicknamed Cromwell years before his *coup d'état*, characterize Cromwell's bourgeois opinions, and also indicate that even in 1655 the "Leveller" movement still continued to smoulder under the ashes. This was not surprising, as the causes of discontent, instead of diminishing, were constantly multiplying. Unfortunately, it is very difficult to obtain an impartial account of the strength and extent of the movement. There is

---

[1] Carlyle, *Cromwell's Letters*, Speech II.
[2] Speech IV.

no doubt that it found supporters in the North of England, as emissaries carried the doctrines of the Levellers into the remotest counties. It is, however, very difficult to estimate the degree of cohesion that existed among the supporters of the movement. None of the Leveller publications throws any light on this question, the movement produced no historian, and the accounts of its opponents are extremely inaccurate and contradictory. The expression "Leveller" itself was no strict party term. It signified an equalitarian in the sense of a revolutionary, and was therefore indifferently applied to commotions which had very little, if any, connection with political struggles, but which were of an exclusively local character, produced by discontent with local occurrences, whereas Lilburne and his colleagues repeatedly repudiated the description of Leveller precisely on account of its crude equalitarian connotation. They were democrats, but ought not to be regarded as brutal revolutionaries. It is therefore almost impossible to distinguish mere revolts, to which levelling tendencies were imputed, from movements connected with the party of the democratic "Agreement of the People". The attitude towards the "Agreement of the People" is the attribute of the political Levellers' movement.

For a comparatively short time, viz., from the middle of the year 1648 to the autumn of the year 1649, information about the movement is forthcoming from a journal, which was described as the organ of the Levellers, and which within certain limits may be so regarded, as it reproduces most of the proclamations and pamphlets of the Levellers published during that time, and so far as it exhibits any tendency at all, represents that of the Levellers. Strange to say, this paper, though the organ of the most extreme political party of the period, bears the singular title of the *Moderate*. But this name was neither meant in an ironical sense nor was it chosen in a hypocritical spirit. It indicates the calm and impartial style in which the paper was written. Far from smacking of *sans-culottism*, as the elder Disraeli asserts in his *Curiosities of Literature*,[1] we have nowhere met with a single phrase that could be remotely compared to the vulgar and obscene passages commonly found in the contemporary Royalist press, the *Man in the Moon*, *Mercurius Elencticus*, etc.

The *Moderate* was one of the first papers to publish explanatory *leading articles*, or at least the embryo of such. Several of its numbers open with disquisitions on political and even economical problems, and I venture to reproduce these articles so that the reader may judge whether we are justified in describing the *Moderate* as the pioneer of the Labour Press of our days. The issue of September 4 to 11, 1649 (No. 61), commences as follows:

"Wars are not only ever clothed with the most specious of all pretences, viz., Reformation of Religion, The Laws of the Land, Liberty of the Subject, etc., though the effects thereof have proved most destructive to them, and ruinous to every Nation; making the Sword (and not the people) the original of all Authorities, for many hundred years together; taking away each man's Birth-right, and settling upon a few, a cursed propriety (the ground of all Civil Offences between party and party) and the greatest cause of most Sins against the Heavenly Deity. Thus Tyranny and Oppression running through the Veins of many of our Predecessors, and being too long maintained by the Sword, upon a Royal Foundation, at last became so customary, as to the vulgar it seemed so natural (the onely reason why the people at this time are so ignorant of their equal Birth-right, their onely Freedom). At last Divine Providence crowned the slavish people's attempt with good success against this potent Enemy, which made them Free (as they

[1] Disraeli ridicules the sub-title of the *Moderate*, viz., "impartially communicating martial affairs to the kingdom of England", saying that probably the men of the Republic had evidently not yet had time to obliterate the monarchical title from their colloquial style. But, in point of fact, the *Moderate* came out in the summer of 1648, when England was still a kingdom, as an opposition paper to the *Moderate Intelligencer*, which bore the same sub-title.

fancied) from their former Oppressions, Burdens and Slaveries, and happy in what they could imagine, the greatest good, both for their Soul and Body. But Pride, Covetousness, and Self-Interest (taking the advantage of so unvaluable a benefit). And many being tempted to Swim in this Golden Ocean, the Burthens and Oppressions of the people, are thereby not onely continued, but increased, and no end thereof to be imagined. At this the people (who cannot now be deluded, will be eased, and not onely stiled, but really be the original of all Lawful Authority) begin to rage, and cry out for a lawful Representative, and such other wholesome Laws as will make them truly happy. These not granted, and some old Sparks being blown up with the Gales of new Dissentions, the fire breaks out, the wind rises, and if the fewel be dry and some speedy remedy be not taken for prevention, the damage thereby may be great to some, but the benefit conceived greater to all others.''

This line of argument sounds very modern. The world moves but slowly, and it gives a feeling of humility to realize how old political wisdom is.

Mr. Isaac Disraeli is annoyed because the *Moderate*, in its issue of July 31st to August 7, 1649, when some robbers were executed for cattle-stealing, blames the institution of property for the death of these people, arguing that if no private property existed, there would have been no need for them to steal for their living. The article states: "We find some of these Fellons to be very civil men, and say, That if they could have had any reasonable subsistence by friends, or otherwise, they should never have taken such necessitous courses, for support of their Wives and Families. From whence many honest people do endevor to argue, that there is nothing but propriety that is the loss of all men's lives in this condition, they being necessitated to offend the Law for a livelihood, and being; and not onely so, but they argue it with much confidence, that pro-priety is the original cause of any sin between party and party, as to civil transactions. And that since the Tyrant is taken off, and that Government altered in nomine, so ought it really to redound to the good of the people in specie; which though they cannot expect it in few yeers, by reason of the multiplicity of the Gentry in Authority, command, etc., who drive on all designes for support of the old Government, and consequently their own interest and the people's slavery; yet they doubt not, but in time, the people will herein discern their own blindness, and folly."

From the reports of the *Moderate*, as well as from other contemporary newspapers, it appears that the Leveller movement was not confined to London and its immediate neighbourhood and the Army, but also had followers in the country. Very interesting in this respect is a correspondence from Derby, in the issue for the last week of August 1649, particularly because we find mentioned in it a class of workers who are nowhere else mentioned in connection with this movement, viz., the *miners*, who had appealed to Parliament for redress in connection with a dispute with the Earl of Rutland, and the correspondence states that they were determined, if Parliament did not do them justice, to have recourse to "Natural Law". Their number, including friends and sympathizers, was said to be twelve thousand, and they threatened, in default of a hearing, to form a resolute army. "The party of the Levellers in Town", the article continues "promises them assistance in the prosecution of their just demands." But a few days later, a letter from the "Freeholders and Mine-owners, etc.", of the Derbyshire mining district, published in a Cromwellian paper, states that the miners numbered at most four thousand, and that the Levellers did not have a dozen followers in Derby.

Moreover, the miners were accused of having repeatedly sided with the King, while the far more numerous freehold-farmers and mine-owners supported Parliament. This provoked a reply, in No. 61 of the *Moderate*, which asserted that

the above-mentioned letter was a fabrication of the Earl of
Rutland and his agents; that the farmers and small owners
had nothing to do with it. As to siding with the King, it had
been stated in the original petition of the miners that the
Earl of Rutland, then Mr. Manners, had repeatedly driven
miners from their work, with the aid of Cavaliers, and when
they complained, had sought to throw suspicion on them by
false charges.

No. 63 is the last issue of the *Moderate*. On September 20,
1649, Parliament enacted a press law, which re-established the
system of licences, and prescribed severe penalties for the publication of abusive and libellous paragraphs. This undermined
the position of the paper. On the other hand, negotiations
had just been resumed between the Levellers and representatives of the Army and Parliament, with a view to reaching
a compromise, so that it is by no means unlikely that the
Moderate ceased to appear because the need for a special
organ of the Levellers no longer existed. As a matter of fact,
the *Moderate* reported on September 1st (and its report is
confirmed by the *Perfect Weekly Account*, a paper which was
more sympathetic with the Parliamentary party) that four
representatives each, of Parliament, the Army, and "those
called Levellers", had held prearranged conferences in order
to arrive at a mutual understanding, and if possible a settlement of all differences. "Time will soon show what will be
the outcome of all this." No compromise was effected, but
it seems that, after Lilburne's acquittal in October, a kind of
truce followed, as during the subsequent years the Levellers
adopted an expectant attitude.

The *Moderate* contains a variety of other interesting notices
and reports, which do not bear directly upon our subject.
It consisted of a sheet of eight pages, small quarto size, the chief
contents being the news of the day. It lasted for over a year,
from July 1648 to the end of September 1649. No complete
series of its numbers is extant; they are found, singly and

scattered, among the collections of pamphlets of the so-called King's or Thomason Library in the British Museum.

The whole newspaper is steeped in the sectarian characteristics of the Leveller movement. With all their sympathies for the poorest classes in society, the Levellers do not constitute a class movement. They are the extreme left of the middle-class republican, or, more correctly, middle-class democratic party formation of the period. Like all extreme parties, they tend here and there to overstep the boundary at which they stand, but they remain finally in the middle-class camp. With the class divisions existing in England, as we have studied them, such was bound to have been the case. The class development of the industrial workers had not yet reached a point favourable to the formulation of demands which would have outbid those of the middle-class parties, and among the country population, the peasantry was so preponderant that even Democracy could not advance beyond an agrarian programme suitable for small peasant proprietors. At the end of the seventeenth century—1688—Gregory King estimated the number of peasant freeholders at 160,000, and of peasant tenants at 150,000, in addition to 4,500 families of the nobility and 12,000 families of the gentry, together with 364,000 agricultural labourers and servants and 400,000 cottar tenants and poor persons. In view of these class divisions among the country population, a formidable agrarian movement was out of the question, especially as there was still much common land in England available for squatters. Not until the restoration of the monarchy, and especially after the second revolution, were conditions created which, under favourable political conditions, might have produced a revolutionary agrarian movement.

The eighteenth century, with its many commercial wars and the enormous extension of English colonial possessions, both of which absorbed a considerable portion of the vigorous members of the population, was, on the whole,

sterile ground for the political as well as the social reform
movement.

Engrossed in making money, the middle classes tolerated
the anomaly of a king governing in their name, in conjunction
with a renascent aristocracy, recruited by the sons of kings'
mistresses. They tolerated an electoral system which excluded
from the franchise a large section of wealthy citizens belonging
to their own class. Isolated voices which protested against
such anomalies were silenced by the intrigues of the two aristocratic parties and the sensations of foreign wars, while the
industrial working class, which was increasing rapidly, engaged
in sporadic revolts which bore no trace of their own political
aspirations. Not until the end of the Napoleonic wars was
there a political reform movement, which resulted, after 1832,
in extending the franchise to the lower middle classes, separa-
ting the plebeian and proletarian elements and forming the
great Chartist Party, which in the nineteenth century took
up the cause at the point which the Levellers had reached in
the middle of the seventeenth century. The Chartists are
throughout the heirs of the Levellers. Their People's Charter,
although demanding adult suffrage in response to the higher
level of economic development, is in no other respect more
advanced than the "Agreement of the People" of the Levellers,
which Carlyle ridiculed as a premature "Bentham-Sieyès-
constitution", but which its author, John Lilburne, was more
justified in describing as the legal foundation of popular
freedom. And just as the Chartists issued from the Levellers,
so the great English Utopist of the nineteenth century, Robert
Owen, is in direct line from the "True Levellers". He himself
was wont to appeal to John Bellers as his predecessor, but
we shall see that Bellers himself stood on the shoulders of
Gerrard Winstanley and a Socialist who, seven years after
Winstanley, made a considerable advance from Utopian
communism to the modern idea of co-operation.

CHAPTER XIII

CONSPIRACIES AND RELIGIOUS OFFSHOOTS OF THE POPULAR DEMOCRATIC MOVEMENT

ON April 20, 1653, Cromwell had dissolved the Rump Parliament, whereupon the Council of the Army, which he dominated, summoned a Parliament, or more accurately a convention of important representatives of the republican party, which was known as the "Little" or "Barebone's" Parliament. Composed mainly of persons who united in themselves the puritanical sanctimoniousness and political Radicalism which is peculiar to the Anglo-Saxon world, it showed much zeal for progressive reforms, but in its first blush of enthusiasm it took up so many things at once, and aroused the opposition of so many interests, that Cromwell deemed it advisable to give effect to a resolution passed by the moderate minority of the assembly when the majority was off its guard, and to dismiss the assembly. The Council of the Army then devised and proclaimed an "Instrument of Government", by virtue of which Cromwell was appointed Lord Protector with almost regal powers, save that he was merely to exercise a short veto of postponement upon Parliament.

Although larger constituencies were prescribed for Parliament, some steps were taken to ensure a greater measure of equality in representation, and provision was made for Ireland and Scotland to be represented according to population, so that the Parliament constituted upon this basis embodied a representative principle which did not receive full recognition until after the Reform Act of 1832. In the present case the franchise for both electors and elected was coupled with an oath to make no change in the government of the country, as vested in Parliament and a single person, which meant a recognition of the Republic and of the Cromwellian Protectorate. Parliament had scarcely met, however, before the majority of its members indicated that they were not prepared to accept the new constitution forthwith. The convinced Republicans on the one hand and the Presbyterians on the other went so far as to call in question the principle of the Protectorate itself. The result was that Cromwell, at the head of his officers, rebuked Parliament, and made continued participation in its debates dependent upon signing a declaration, according to which the signatories pledged themselves not to introduce or support any measures which contravened the conditions upon which they had been elected. The convinced Republicans refused to attach their signatures and left Parliament, which, despite this purging, did not last five months.

It may be left undecided whether the Republicans were particularly wise at a time when the Republic was so weak in the country itself, and was exposed to continuous intrigues from abroad, to address themselves immediately to an alteration of the emergency constitution, which the "Instrument of Government" must be regarded as being. This conduct is explained by the fact that the Protectorate was at first a thinly veiled military regime. They resisted on principle being governed by the sword, although the sword rested in the hand of an able man, who adopted a broad-minded attitude in the religious questions which caused so much friction. Thus they saw in Cromwell only the usurper or the protractor of a detestable tyranny, whilst the latter ridiculed those who in a situation of emergency would approve no step necessary to consolidate the Republic until it had been sanctioned, after the delays incidental to parliamentary procedure, by law.

Such were the antagonisms, which aroused all the more feeling when Cromwell apprehended a number of rebellious Republicans and interned them in fortified places. If a certain amount of ferocity was imported into these acts, they were still the measures of a military dictatorship, against which, after the suppression of the rebellions in the Army, no weapon was available save assassination. From 1654 onwards attempt followed attempt upon the life of the Lord Protector, nearly all of which were undertaken by erstwhile Levellers or advanced sectaries closely allied with them, and instigated or even financed by the Royalists. Such in particular were the plots of Sexby and Sindercomb.

Sexby was Governor of the Isle of Portland, with the rank of captain; then he served under Cromwell as Colonel of Cavalry in Scotland, repeatedly distinguishing himself; but in 1651 he was cashiered by court martial for stopping the pay of some of his soldiers, which he maintained he had done, not in his own interest, but for the public advantage. He had in fact attempted to force the seven or eight men to enter a new regiment which he was forming. Despite his transgression, he was then employed by the State Council of the Republic upon a particularly confidential mission.

It was the time when France, in the interest of the Stuarts, sought to injure the young Republic in every way, among other things, financing pirates, who captured English trading-vessels. At this juncture Sexby received from the secret committee of the State Council, consisting of Cromwell, Scott, and Whitelocke, instructions to proceed to France, and report upon conditions in that country and the sentiments of the people, in order that dangers might be avoided and an interest created. With four companions, Sexby repaired to France, and remained there twenty-one months. He entered into relations, among others, with the Condés and the party of the Fronde, and one of the traces of his activity is a sketch of a Republican constitution for France, found among the papers of Mazarin and of Prince Louis Condé. This document, drafted "in the name of Prince Condé and Conti and of the town of Bordeaux", bears the title "L'Accord du Peuple", and on closer examination turns out to be a simple translation of the Levellers' "Agreement of the People". It was to be employed as a manifesto of the Republicans of Bordeaux and of the remainder of Guienne. Condé's secret agent, Lenet, wrote on the draft:

"Mémoires données à son altesse de Conti par les sieurs Saxebri et Arrondel que je n'approuve pas." Saxebri was manifestly Sexby, and Arrondel was one of his companions. This opinion is shared by Mr. S. R. Gardiner, who called my attention to Sexby's mission to France after the first edition of this book had appeared.

Edward Sexby, whom we met in a former chapter as an agitator in the Army and confidant of Lilburne, was undoubtedly a man of great abilities and extraordinary energy. He was a soldier who had risen from the ranks, and advanced step by step to the position of a colonel. It was largely due to him that the Newmarket Heath meeting in the spring of 1647 was held, when the Army pledged itself to uphold democracy.

In the consultations between Cromwell's staff and the agitators in the autumn of the same year, at Putney, Sexby was the doughty champion of the more advanced section. When the franchise was discussed, he pointed to the thousands of soldiers who, poor as himself, had ventured their lives for their "birthright and privileges as Englishmen". Why were they to be told that unless they had a fixed estate they had no birthright? He, for one, would surrender his right to no man.[1]

His criticism of the political strategy of the heads of the Army is drastic:

"We sought to satisfy all men, and itt was well; but in going [about] to doe it we have dissatisfied all men. Wee have laboured to please a Kinge, and I thinke, except we goe about to cutt all our throats, we shall nott please him; and wee have gone to support an house wh. will prove rotten studds, I

---

[1] Gardiner, *History of the Great Civil War*, vol. iii., 2nd ed., p. 389. Cromwell's reply to this speech is most significant. It was in his eyes an unbecoming language, "because it did savour so much of will". Why could not the meeting avoid abstract considerations, and content itself with discussing the question how far the existing franchise could safely be enlarged? Might not, for instance, copyholders be admitted to vote as well as freeholders? (The whole of the debates are fully reproduced in the *Clarke Papers*, vol. i. pp. 226 ff.)

meane the Parliament which consists of a Company of rotten members."

Cromwell and Ireton still favoured a policy of mediation, but before long they recognized that Sexby had accurately forecasted the situation.

In the summer of 1648 it was Sexby who brought Cromwell a letter from Lilburne making pacific overtures,[1] and during the first years of the Commonwealth he remained in the service of the State.

At the end of 1653 we find Sexby again in England, in time to witness the dispersal of the Little Parliament, the driving of the most sincere Republicans out of the first Protectorate Parliament, the internment of Lilburne and other advanced Republicans, and after the dissolution of the first Protectorate Parliament, the complete establishment of military tyranny through the agency of the twelve "major-generals", who ruled with an iron rod over the districts assigned to them. It is not therefore surprising that Sexby, and other equally sincere zealots, persuaded themselves that it was justifiable to make common cause against Cromwell, even with Royalists, Spaniards, and others, and to accept their financial support. As to co-operation with the Spaniards, the "lawful heir to the throne" had set them the example, and early in 1654 a proclamation had been issued, promising an annuity of £500, the rank of a colonel, and other honours to anyone "whosoever will, by sword, pistol or poison", kill the "base mechanic fellow, by name Oliver Cromwell".

But however seductive this offer might prove to "men of spirit in straitened circumstances" (Carlyle), no one managed to earn the promised reward, as Cromwell never rode out without a strong bodyguard, and took other steps to ensure

---

[1] Clarendon, the contemporary historian of the Revolution, reports that Cromwell had repeatedly shared his quarters for the night, "a familiarity which he frequently bestowed on people whom he used for important missions and with whom he could not otherwise converse so freely as during those hours" (*History of the Rebellion*, vol. xv. p. 133).

the safety of his person. The disgruntled Levellers now took up the matter, and they did not mind risking their lives. As the money raised by Sexby did not suffice to finance a rising on a large scale, the only course left open was to make an attempt on Cromwell's life, and some of Sexby's confederates were bold enough to mix with Cromwell's bodyguards, so as to get at him when he was riding in Hyde Park. But they did not succeed, and one of them, Miles Sindercomb, proposed to try a different plan. Sexby gave him £1,600 for this purpose, and went abroad to procure further funds.

Many historians imply that Sexby was a common bravo, whose only object was to make money; but apart from the fact that Sexby's antecedents and his intimate relations with other Levellers and Radical politicians of the period, which continued to the end, cast doubts on this assumption, it is totally refuted by the correspondence during the years 1655–57 between Charles Stuart and his principal agent, Hyde, on the one hand, and the Royalist party leaders, Colonel Talbot, Colonel Silas Titus, Sir Marmaduke Longdale, and Lord Ormond, as well as the Jesuit Father Talbot, on the other. In this correspondence Sexby is frequently mentioned, but invariably only as a highly gifted man, of firm character, whose fierce hatred against Cromwell might be utilized, but with whom they would have to treat very carefully on account of his political convictions. We subjoin a few passages only from this correspondence, which throws much light on the political occurrences and intrigues of the time.[1] Relations with Sexby, Overton, and other "Levellers" having already been established in the spring of 1655 through Count Fuensaldania, Sir M. Langdale, who was the first to inform Charles Stuart of these negotiations, wrote on September 9, 1655, that in an interview held at Brussels Overton and Sexby had declined to suggest that their party should form an alliance with the King. He (Langdale) would warn the King against

---

[1] Extracts from it are given in *Calendars of Clarendon State Papers*.

these people, they should be made use of, but not trusted. Foreigners were the best agents because they had no political interests. On January 7, 1656, Colonel Talbot wrote to Ormond, then staying with the King, that he found Sexby was Cromwell's greatest enemy. But Sexby and his associates detested the King's cause no less than Cromwell's. On March 17th he instructed Ormond how he, or the King himself, was to behave in a projected interview with Sexby. They should emphasize Magna Charta and the powers of a freely elected Parliament. But if it became necessary to countenance extreme ("unreasonable") demands, it should be done—and the advice is most significant—subject to the reservation "as soon as a freely elected Parliament should demand this of his Majesty". Meanwhile Ormond had entered into negotiations with the Leveller Rumbold, and, on June 21st, sought to ascertain from him whether Rumbold's friend, Wildman, was in correspondence "with a certain Sexby", and what Wildman thought of this man. On August 25th Father Talbot wrote to the King that Sexby was "not more favourably disposed towards the King than before", and on October 12th he wrote asking that the King should write a letter which would satisfy Sexby that the King was ready to entertain his political demands, adding that Sexby had "as much moral honesty and sense of honour as could be expected or desired in anyone who is not a Cavalier".

On October 17th Father Talbot reported to Ormond that the King had instructed him to go to Sexby to persuade him to listen to reason, and that he was authorized to make great offers to Sexby personally. But it was not until a month afterwards that the Jesuit was in a position to announce to the King that Sexby was ready to have a private interview with him *on condition that he need not bend his knee to the King*. And this demand was agreed to. About the end of 1656 Sindercomb's attempt was made, from which, however, as Colonel Titus writes to Hyde, Sexby had dissuaded him because too much was left to chance and too many people had to be taken into confidence.

On July 13th Titus reported that Sexby was again in England and much dissatisfied with him because he (Titus) adhered too closely to the King. After Sexby's arrest Titus writes (on November 12th) he hoped that Sexby, who had gone mad in prison, would never recover his reason, and he reiterates this Christian wish on December 13th, after hearing that Sexby's condition was improving.

Whatever might be thought of the wisdom of these negotiations of the Levellers with King Charles II, it will at any rate be admitted that this correspondence puts Sexby's political integrity beyond doubt.

Like Sexby, Miles Sindercomb had entered the Parliamentary Army as a young lad full of enthusiasm, and in 1649 had, as a corporal, joined the Levellers in their rebellion in favour of the "Agreement". He had been taken prisoner at Burford, when he would have undoubtedly shared the fate of the other corporals taken at the same time but for the fact that the night before the execution he succeeded in making good his escape. He went to Scotland, and there joined the Parliamentary Army, or, as it was then called, the Commonwealth Army, and quickly advanced to the rank of a paymaster. In 1654 he took part in the attempt to put Colonel Robert Overton, who was a good Republican, in the place of Monk, the commanding general, whom the Republicans and Levellers in the Army (and as subsequent events showed, not without justice) considered an "unreliable customer". The plot being discovered, Sindercomb was cashiered by Monk, whereupon he returned to London and entered into relations with Sexby and other conspirators. His plan, when Sexby went to the Continent, was to remove Cromwell by means of a kind of infernal machine. For this purpose he took a house at Hammersmith, facing the street which Cromwell must pass on his way from Hampton Court to Whitehall. But his experiments failed;

he gave up this plan and conceived the idea of setting fire to Whitehall, where Cromwell resided in winter, so that during the confusion the "tyrant" might be secured. He had enlisted one hundred persons in support of this plan, and had one hundred horses in readiness for them. He and one of his fellow-conspirators were seen loitering about Whitehall on January 8, 1657, and at half-past twelve at night a basket filled with fireworks "enough to burn through stones", and tied up with a lighted fuse, was discovered by the smell of burning which it emitted. The guard at once reported the matter. All sentries, life-guards, etc., were questioned, and a life-guardsman who knew of the plot (and who possibly may have been a spy) made a full confession. Sindercomb was overpowered, and, notwithstanding a desperate resistance, conveyed to the Tower. On February 9th he was sentenced to death by the High Court for high treason. On the eve of the day fixed for his execution, February 14, 1657, he took poison, which his sister had secretly given him on her farewell visit. The daily report said that "he was of that wretched sect of soul-sleepers who believe that the soul falls asleep at death". He left a declaration to the effect that his soul did not trouble him". We know who the soul-sleepers were. It was a name assumed by the adherents of the materialistic theory of Richard Overton. In a pamphlet published shortly after his death, however, from the pen of a violent opponent of Cromwell, Sindercomb is extolled in fervent terms and placed on a level with the best among the champions of freedom in ancient days, it being said, among other things, that "he has shown as great a mind as any Rome could boast of".

The pamphlet in question is the famous one entitled *Killing no Murder*. On its appearance it made an unprecedented stir, and the demand for it was so great that no copy could be had for less than 5s. As the title suggests, it commends attempts at assassination, the subject of course being Cromwell. It is written in an extraordinarily effective style, and its chief result was utterly to spoil Cromwell's enjoyment of his power and dignities. The all-powerful Protector took elaborate precautions whenever he drove or rode out. The pamphlet was written in exceedingly caustic and clever style, but its authorship was never ascertained, though William Allen was named as the author on the title page. After the Restoration, Colonel Titus, who had gone over to the Royalists, passed himself off as the author, but the statement of this "Flunkey" (Carlyle), promoted to Chamberlain, is not very trustworthy, as it was made for the sole purpose of procuring material advantages for himself. Previous to this Sexby, whose mouth had meanwhile been closed for ever, had already owned to the authorship, and the language of the pamphlet, which, notwithstanding all its violence and acerbity, is dignified, would, in conjunction with the fervent tribute paid in it to the memory of Sindercomb, rather suggest that the author was one who held the same opinion as the latter. The only circumstance which might cast any doubt on Sexby's statement is that it was made in the Tower and under circumstances which did not altogether preclude the possibility that it was forced from him by violence.

Soon after Sindercomb's death Sexby had secretly returned to London, probably to reorganize the disbanded conspirators. It was during this time that *Killing no Murder* appeared, and in July Sexby again tried to take ship to the Netherlands. Notwithstanding his disguise and the full beard he had grown, he was recognized by the Government officials, arrested, and imprisoned in the Tower. According to the statement of the Lieutenant of the Tower, Sir John Barkstead, and other witnesses, he is said to have confessed that he had received money from the agents and allies of Charles Stuart to promote attempts on Cromwell, that he was the instigator of Sindercomb's attempt and the author of the pamphlet *Killing no Murder*.[1] He is said to have lost his reason soon after, and his death ensued in January 1658.

[1] See Cobbett, *State Trials*, vol. v. pp. 844, 845, and 852 ff.

Unless, therefore, as was asserted at the time, and as his speedy end seems to indicate, Sexby's confessions were wrung from him by torture, his statements would at any rate be much more trustworthy than those of the wretched Titus. But after all, it is not impossible that the name given on the title page of the pamphlet was not, as has hitherto been assumed, or suggested, a pseudonym, but the actual name of the author. As a matter of fact there existed a William Allen, who was a staunch Republican, and who (and this is of the greatest importance in this respect) had close relations with Sexby. It was in April 1647—and it is strange that no one should hitherto have referred to this fact—that three "agitators", viz., William Allen, Edward Sexby, and Thomas Sheppard, on behalf of their comrades, presented to the Generals Cromwell, Fairfax, and Skippon a declaration which at that time was by no means unwelcome to them, and which most openly expressed the distrust of the Army towards Parliament. Skippon mentioned this letter in Parliament, which thereupon ordered an examination of the three delegates. The matter finally ended in the great demonstrations of Newmarket and Triploe Heath, followed soon after by the occupation of London by the Army and the purging of the eleven Presbyterian members of Parliament who were hostile to the Army. In short, William Allen was, together with Sexby, one of the first "agitators", hence it is not impossible that he was still alive in 1657, and that he then directed his pen against Cromwell.[1]

[1] Thus, for instance, a letter dated July 28, 1655, from the Jesuit Father Talbot to the King states that Sexby, who had been in Brussels, had received letters from friends in England, giving him absolute authority to act. "He is certain, among others, of Lord Grey of Groby, Wildman, Allen, and several Anabaptists." It is possible that the Allen here mentioned may be the General Adjutant Allen who was an Anabaptist and no doubt sided against Cromwell. But the "agitator" Allen too had no doubt advanced meanwhile to a higher military rank, and his contemporary Edm. Ludlow actually identifies him in his memoirs with General Adjutant Allen, which he would scarcely have thought of doing otherwise. Carlyle disputes this identity, but Mr. Firth has brought forward strong evidence in favour of it. (See *Clarke Papers*, vol. i. p. 432.)

But if, on the other hand, William Allen was dead or had disappeared, the choice of his name would all the more point to his old comrade Sexby as the author.[1]

Killing no Murder appeared at about the same time when Parliament invited Cromwell to alter the constitution and accept the royal dignity (the so-called "Humble Petition and Advice"). After some consideration Cromwell declined the Crown. However favourably the Army was then disposed towards him, it had nevertheless raised its voice against this. But before Cromwell had come to any decision, civilian elements and members of the Army who had returned to civilian life attempted a Republican insurrection in London. Supporters of the "Fifth Monarchy"—we should say nowadays the Republican doctrinaires—agreed with others similarly disposed to meet on April 9th in Mile End, armed themselves, and provided with arms and ammunition for others, and to call on the people to stand up for the hoped-for "Kingdom of God". They relied on the sympathy which these endeavours met with among the populace, in the Army, and with many retired or dismissed officers.

But they had not reckoned with the vigilance of Cromwell and his spies. When the leaders of the conspiracy, on the morning of the appointed day, arrived at the meeting-place,

---

[1] A comparison of the *Letter of the Agitators* with the pamphlet quoted here places the identity of the authors of both almost beyond any doubt. A feature distinguishing this pamphlet from others of the period is not so much the circumstance that it generally justifies attempts on Cromwell's life, but the crushing and trenchant style of argument, to the effect that Cromwell had forfeited his life because he had actually outdone, item by item, every offence laid to the charge of Charles I. I have not met with a single pamphlet of this period which is written so sarcastically, so tersely, and with such acid pungency of argument. And the same arguments, the same trenchant style, are also met with in the letter of the "agitators," in the denunciation it contains of the Parliament ruled by the Presbyterians. Dealing with the proposal to change the quarters of the Army, it states that it was "but a mere cloak for some who have lately tasted of sovereignty, and being lifted beyond their ordinary sphere of servants, seek to become masters and degenerate into tyrants." (Compare Gardiner's *Civil War*, vol. iii. chapter 48.)

Cromwell's horsemen were already on the spot. They arrested some twenty persons and seized the proclamation and pamphlets brought by them, as well as a flag bearing the emblem of a sleeping lion, the "lion of the tribe of Judah", with a motto, "Who shall rouse him up?" During the following days several more persons suspected of secretly promoting or favouring the conspiracy were arrested, and "the fifth monarchy was safe behind bars and bolts". But no trial ensued; most of those arrested were lodged for some time in the Tower and others were confined in safe places.[1]

Venner's first attempt was followed, after the dissolution of the third Parliament of the Protectorate (February 1658), by an attempted Royalist rising, in May 1658, a Presbyterian divine, Doctor Hewit, being· the ringleader, but in this case also Cromwell's men put out the fire at once. An "anarchist" movement by Levellers, Anabaptists, "fifth monarchy" men, etc., against the newly established constitution, was likewise nipped in the bud. But on August 30th of the same year Cromwell succumbed to a violent intermittent

[1] The chief leader of this conspiracy was Th. Venner, a wine-cooper. On January 6, 1661, after the Restoration, and when the restored monarchy had avenged itself on the "regicides" with exquisite cruelty, Venner, with a handful of equally daring followers, whom he had incited by his speeches, attempted a new rising for the "Kingdom of Christ". They were at most some sixty men, but they threw the whole city into a turmoil. Before the superior numbers of the citizen guards and soldiers they fled into a wood situated in the north of London, between Highgate and Hampstead, but returned to London on January 9th, this time numbering thirty-one men only, who were in a completely frenzied state of mind, quite convinced that neither steel nor bullets could touch the soldiers of Christ, and that His Kingdom was close at hand. They "have routed all the train bands that they met with, put the King's life-guards to the run, killed about twenty men, broke through the city gates twice; and all this in the daytime, when all the city was in arms." Thus Pepys, in his Diary (January 10, 1661). Pepys adds, after having stated their number: "We did believe them to be at least 500. A thing that never was heard of, that so few men should dare and do so much mischief." They were finally surrounded on all sides, but broke through into a house, which they defended for some time against thousands. After half of them had fallen, the remainder were taken by force (none of them surrendering voluntarily), only to die on the gallows, Venner being among the number. Venner and a certain Pritchard were drawn and quartered and their meeting-house was pulled down.

fever, continued struggles and emotions having prematurely undermined his health.

The events that followed show how little his death could further the cause for which the Levellers had struggled. Other persons, other groups of the propertied classes, were struggling for dominion, but no movement could be expected from the people.[1]

After the Restoration, the abuses which the Levellers had combated flourished again. Crown lands were squandered, the oppression and expropriation of the farmers by the land-lords increased. The landed nobility discarded the last of their feudal obligations, and instead granted to the King a "Civil List", the burden of which was thrown on the impotent masses in the form of indirect taxes, excise duties, etc. The Whig Revolution of 1688—the replacement of the Stuarts by the House of Orange—so far from benefiting the rural popula-tion, only served to change matters for the worse. The remainder of the Crown lands were squandered and spoliations of common land were legalized in the famous "Enclosure Acts". "About 1750 the yeomanry" (the independent peasantry) "had almost disappeared, and so had, in the last decade of the eighteenth century, the last trace of the common land of the agricultural labourer".[2]

Nor did the Restoration improve the situation of the town workers. The reader will remember what Thorold Rogers says on this subject, as quoted in my second chapter. Artisans and workers remained for a long time without any political rights, and although they sometimes improved their economic

1 What influence Lilburne's name possessed even years after his death is shown, among other things, by a pamphlet published at that time of "anarchy" entitled: "Lilburne's ghost, with a whip in one hand to scourge tyrants out of authority, and balme in the other, to heal the sores of our (as yet) corrupt state, or some of the late dying principles of freedom revived and unveiled, for the lovers of Freedome and Liberty, Peace and Righteous-ness to behold. By one who desires no longer to live than to serve his country." London, 1659. The publication champions the principles of the "agreement".

Marx, *Capital*, vol. i. p. 746.

condition, it was done not through but rather in the teeth of legislation. These classes did not again, either in the seventeenth or in the first half of the eighteenth century, offer notable resistance to the now absolute political dominion of the property owners. Their political champions had been wiped out with the suppression of the Levellers, the spirit of opposition no longer ventured to manifest itself except in occasional riots or in the form of religious sects, and even those sects which outlived the Restoration underwent a change. They tended to lose their revolutionary character and to become respectable.

The moderate Independents—the "gentlemen"—were politically absorbed in the Whig movement, which in 1688 received powerful financial support from the wealthier ones among them. Towards the end of the seventeenth century they represented such a financial power that neither Charles II nor his brother ventured to attack their churches, and were glad to borrow money from them. Some of the "Independents" were founders of the Bank of England. Under the protection of these influential persons, a few Independent congregations managed to subsist, keeping alive radical traditions, and even to this day the Congregationalists, which is a collective name for the Independents, supply their contingent to the advanced political movement.

Some of the more intractable among the Independents at the revolutionary era amalgamated with scattered remnants of the Anabaptist movement to form Baptist communities. It is not easy at the present day to determine exactly the connection between the English Baptist movement and the offshoots of the original Anabaptist movement. Moreover, this would serve no purpose, as from the outset there were various factions among the Anabaptists, moderate and radical, bourgeois and communistic, for all of whom the name of Anabaptist was long used indiscriminately. At the period with which we are dealing the sectarian movement was in a constant state of agitation, one sect recruiting itself from the other, the signification of their names thus being constantly liable to changes. In the case of the "Fifth Monarchy" men important differences have also to be recognized. The Baptists themselves comprise various subdivisions, but all of them, as well as the Methodist (Wesleyan) sect founded about the middle of the eighteenth century, draw their chief support from the ranks of the working classes.

But the English Baptists of modern times do not derive from communistic Anabaptists. Whatever was left of the latter after the Revolution had accomplished its work and the Restoration was impending, we must seek not among the surviving Baptist or Anabaptist communities, but among the early Quakers. This sect, which was a product of the second phase of the Revolution, the period of disillusionment, tended to assimilate the most advanced religious and social elements of the Revolution. We have seen that Lilburne and Winstanley, after the failure of their efforts, joined the Quaker movement. It is fair to assume that, without abandoning their aims, they doubted the methods that had previously been adopted. They discovered, as so often happens in similar cases, that as political agitation had failed to arouse the masses, what was requisite was the creation of a new morality. And at the outset Quaker morality was no doubt strongly tinged with communism. Nor were the first Quakers mere harmless religious visionaries or dreamers of dreams. When Lilburne joined them, they counted propagandists who, although renouncing violent methods, still aimed at reform, and the first person who occupies a prominent position in socialist history after the Restoration is the Quaker John Bellers. For these reasons a subsequent chapter will be devoted to the Quakers.

CHAPTER XIV

POLITICAL PHILOSOPHY OF THE SEVENTEENTH CENTURY. HOBBES AND HARRINGTON

THE literature of the great English Revolution is mainly a fugitive literature, that is to say, it arose from the necessities of the moment. This applies even to works which, like Milton's *The Tenure of Kings and Magistrates*,[1] treated their subject from more general points of view. A revolutionary literature may be said to have preceded the English Revolution in the realm of religion alone, and although religious questions were inseparable from politics, the works dealing with religion did not trench on the secular domain or question the existing social order. Men's minds were not busy with theoretical speculations on the essence or the problems of the State, when the breach came between King and Parliament, and this constitutes one of the main differences between the English and the French Revolution. The latter was preceded by a body of critical literature which sapped the foundations of State and Society, while the former did not produce a special literature on political philosophy until after its close. It is true that we can detect the influence of the writings of Italian political philosophers, especially Machiavelli, of Buchanan, the Scotsman, and Grotius, the Dutchman, on the better-read among the party leaders, but, for the most part, wherever an appeal to ancient English law—real or supposed—did not suffice, the Bible was laid under contribution to sustain the revolutionary argument.

As literature lagged behind events, it is not surprising that the first important work to deal with the theory of government should be hostile to the Revolution. The partisans of the Revolution were far too busy meditating on practical measures to have any time to spare for theories concerning society and the State. Those of them who seized the pen did so in order

---

[1] Milton wrote this book in 1649 in defence of the trial of Charles I.

to justify or criticize, as the case might be, certain measures and proposals. The first author to produce a profound work on the essence and foundations of the State was Thomas Hobbes, the famous philosopher of State absolutism. This work is the *Leviathan*, which appeared in 1651 in the English language. It was preceded in 1642 by an essay, *De Cive*, the fundamental ideas of which are reproduced in the *Leviathan*. We will therefore confine ourselves to a discussion of the social theory developed in the latter work, which exercised great influence on the sociological literature of the eighteenth century, and even in the nineteenth century influenced many socialists.

"Leviathan", being an allusion to the mythical gigantic fish spoken of in the Book of Job, is intended by Hobbes to typify the State, or the power of the State,[1] by which the "war of all against all" which would otherwise reign is reduced to a regular system, thus guaranteeing to man the secure enjoyment of the fruits of his labour or property.

"Leviathan" is the sovereign autocrat of the Commonwealth, and although Hobbes decidedly favours an absolute monarchy as the most suitable form of government, he nevertheless declares the theory to be equally applicable, whether the absolute sovereignty of an individual or that of an assembly is in question. But he is thoroughly opposed to a division of powers. The sovereignty is to rest with a certain person or body. He is, above all, anxious for *order*—in fact we might call him the philosopher of "order at any price". With him all is subordinate to the sovereignty of the State, so much so that after the Restoration he, who himself was a thorough Churchman, was accused by the bishops of the State Church of being a "blasphemer". It was not that he denied God— in spite of his materialism he stoutly maintained the existence

[1] The full title of the work is *Leviathan, or the Matter, Form and Power of a Commonwealth, Ecclesiastical and Civil.*

of God [1]—but because (which in the eyes of the bishops, indeed, was much worse) he denied that the Church had any rights against the State.[2]

And in the same way, the most consistent exponent of State absolutism, temporarily even offended his royal pupil Charles Stuart, afterwards Charles II, because he did not derive the absolute power of kings direct from God, but founded it on purely utilitarian grounds. In his opinion, it is from God in so far only as it results from the nature of things which God has created, and is the most advantageous alternative to a self-abandoned state in which "one man is a wolf to the other" (*homo homini lupus*).

In Hobbes' opinion the absolute power of the State is originally based either on submission to a conqueror or on contract. In both cases the power results from fear: from fear of the conqueror or from fear of the covetousness of others, from which the sovereign is deemed to afford protection. And in both cases the power, once conferred or acknowledged, is irrevocable; it is then vested perpetually in the sovereign, who may abandon it by voluntary surrender, but cannot be dispossessed of it. It is only when he proves incapable of affording legal protection and defending the country that the duty of submission lapses. The individual is indebted to the sovereign for any right legally exercised by himself, but there is no right against the sovereign. The so-called natural law governs relations outside the political right, but does not contravene it. Property exists solely by virtue of the political right. In the natural state all have an equal right to everything, and cunning

[1] Thus, for instance, he declared that to describe God as the world or as the "soul of the world" was to speak of Him unworthily and to deny His existence. If God were the world, He could not be the cause of the world. Nor would it do to describe the world as eternal. "That which is eternal has no cause", and so this doctrine would mean "to deny there is a God".

[2] In Pepys' Diary we read under date September 3, 1668: "To my booksellers for Hobbs' *Leviathan*, which is now mightily called for; and what was heretofore sold for 8/ I now give 24/ at the second-hand, and it is sold for 30s/, it being a book the Bishops will not let be printed again."

or force, practised by one or many, determines the extent of individual possessions. *"The inequality that now is has been introduced by the laws civil."* "The distribution of the materials of this nourishment (land, stock, rights of trading, etc.) is the constitution of 'mine' and 'thine' and 'his', that is to say, in one word propriety; and belonged in all kinds of common-wealth to the sovereign power. . . . From whence we may collect, that the propriety which a subject hath in his lands, consisteth in a right to exclude all other subjects from the use of them; *and not to exclude their sovereign, be it an assembly or a monarch."*[1]

From these and other passages concerning property from the *Leviathan* it is not difficult to draw socialistic inferences, although nothing was further from the author's intentions than any socialistic application of his arguments. His ideas moved in an entirely different direction. Not by any means, however, in the region of pure speculation. On the contrary, these deductions, although formulated in an abstract manner, are intended to convey a very practical meaning bearing on the political struggles of his time. This is very obvious in the twenty-ninth chapter of his book, which treats of the causes of dissolution of a commonwealth. In discussing the various grievances of the supporters of royal power,[2] Hobbes also describes as a great evil—as a "disease" of the political system—the difficulty of raising money for the necessary uses of the State, and more especially at the approach of a war. "This difficulty", he continues, "ariseth from the opinion that every subject hath a propriety in his lands

[1] Loc. cit., p. 116.
[2] Thus, among other things, the grievance as to "the immoderate greatness of a town, when it is able to furnish out of its own circuit the number and expense of a great army"—which, as we have seen, London had done in 1642. Further, the grievance as to "the liberty of disputing against absolute power, by pretenders of political prudence; which though bred in the most part in the lees of the people, yet animated by false doctrines, are perpetually meddling with the fundamental laws, to the molestation of the common-wealth" (p. 152).

and goods, exclusive of the sovereign's right to the use of the same."[1]

This is the secret cause of the tears shed by good Mr. Hobbes over the theory of the sacredness of private property. He describes the excessive accumulation of money in the hands of a few, through revenue-farming and monopolies, as a disease of the State, and compares it to pleurisy in man; but it is only the simile that is remarkable, otherwise *money* is regarded as the "blood" of the social body, and no objection is raised to accumulation of property generally. He does not demur to extensive landownership.

However, questions of pure expediency cannot be raised into theoretical axioms with impunity, and thus "Master Hobbs" (Hobbes is but a Latinized form of the name) has not escaped the fate of being described after his death as a socialist and Utopist. In fact, it is only necessary to substitute "absolute sovereignty of the people" for absolute sovereign or absolute assembly, and the passages we have quoted become texts in a revolutionist's handbook. But Hobbes, notwithstanding his materialism, is a Utopist even in his character as the philosopher of monarchical absolutism, because he derives this from "rights" which are problematical. It is true that in one passage (p. 88) he says the Sovereign might delegate many of his rights to others, and yet remain suzerain, provided only that he retains control of the armed power, the raising of money and the right to decide what doctrines may be propagated; but he gives no indication as to how and under what circumstances this would be possible. On the contrary, he proceeds to impute the origin of the civil war to the propagation of the "opinion" that these powers were divided between the King, the Lords, and the House of Commons. Without the propagation of this *opinion* "the people had never been divided".

Among the replies which *Leviathan* evoked from the contemporaries of Hobbes, undoubtedly the most important, as

[1] Loc. cit., p. 151.

well as the only one that concerns us here, is *Oceana*, by James Harrington. Harrington cannot be called a socialist, any more than Hobbes, but he too, by his literary activity, exercised great and we may add legitimate influence on the evolution of socialistic ideas. In fact, we shall show that Harrington, with his good bourgeois sentiments, has more claim to a place in the history of socialism than many builders of socialistic "States of the future".

But first of all a few facts about the man himself. James Harrington, born in 1611, was descended from a very well-to-do and respected family in Rutlandshire, which was related by marriage to many members of the higher aristocracy. In his youth he was exceedingly studious, and his seriousness is said to have extorted more respect from his parents than he vouchsafed to them. When grown to manhood, however, he developed a bright, cheerful temperament and a very ready wit. After having studied at Oxford University for several years, he travelled, in order to enlarge his knowledge by direct observation, in turn through Holland, Denmark, parts of Germany, France, and Italy, being particularly impressed with the Republic of Venice and its constitution. Returning to England, he devoted himself, as his father had meanwhile died, to the education of his brothers and sisters and stepbrothers and sisters, and for the rest busied himself with his studies and the management of his estates. While at The Hague he had made the acquaintance of Charles I's sister, Elizabeth, wife of the fugitive "winter King" of Bohemia, and in England he became a frequent attendant at Court, although he made no efforts to secure any position there. These personal relations may have contributed to his taking no particularly prominent part in the struggles between King and Parliament, however much he sided with the Parliamentary party, as he openly acknowledged. When Charles I, after his arrest by resolution of Parliament, was confined in Holdenby in 1647, Harrington and Thomas Herbert were permitted to keep him company. Also in the Isle of Wight Charles had Harrington, among others, for a companion. Charles is said to have taken particular pleasure in conversing with him, except when the conversation turned on monarchy or republic, because Harrington did not disguise his sympathy for the latter. When finally Charles was brought to Windsor, Harrington was separated from him and arrested, because he refused to bind himself by an oath to disclose and frustrate any attempts at escape on the part of the King. But Ireton, whose influence was considerable, soon procured his liberation, and Harrington frequently visited Charles at St. James', and finally accompanied him to the place of execution.

After the King's execution Harrington retired for a time to his studies. The violent death of the King, whom he esteemed as a man, seems to have touched him very keenly, but it could not induce him to side against the Commonwealth. On the contrary, he employed himself during his seclusion by writing a work, designed to point a way out of the social confusion. This work is *Oceana*. Before printing it he showed it to several of his acquaintances, one of these being Major Wildman, to whom we have previously referred, and read a few passages of it to them. When at last he sent it to be printed, *Oceana*, concerning which all kinds of awful things had been reported to the Government by their informants, was confiscated at the printer's and brought to Whitehall. In spite of all efforts, Harrington could not get it back, until at last he succeeded in inducing the all-powerful dictator, thanks to the advocacy of Cromwell's favourite daughter, Lady Bridget Claypole, to himself order the return of the work. Subsequently, when *Oceana* appeared with a dedication addressed to Cromwell, the latter is reported to have said that he perceived the author would much like to lure him from his position of power, but he would not abandon, for the sake of a few sheets of paper, what he had obtained by the sword. No one could be more opposed than he was to the government of a *single person*, but he was compelled to assume the office of a High-Constable to avert social anarchy.

Oceana appeared in 1656, and at once produced various replies, nearly all of them coming from theologians. Harrington lost no time in answering his opponents, and his polemical writings, though somewhat diffuse, reveal him as an erudite and witty controversialist. The most important of these replies is *The Prerogative of Popular Government*, directed in the first part against the "considerations upon *Oceana*," by Matthew Wren (son of the Bishop of Ely), and in the second part, against certain theologians, concerning the electoral systems of antiquity and in the early Church communities. A reply composed by Wren, published in 1659, and entitled *For Monarchy*, was answered by Harrington in a small satirical pamphlet, *The Politicaster*. Brief and full of irony is likewise his reply to the publication *The Holy Commonwealth*, which the devout Puritan, Richard Baxter, produced in opposition to the "heathen" system of politics outlined in *Oceana*.[1]

At the request of some friends he issued in 1659 a compact but comprehensive essay on the principles developed in *Oceana*, entitled the *Art of Law-giving*, and after this a publication, written in paragraphs, entitled *Systems of Politics*, which represents a still more concise rendering of *Oceana*. Among other writings by Harrington, we may mention particularly a collection of political aphorisms, a dialogue which develops

[1] Harrington was indeed, for his age, a "heathen". In Oxford he was numbered among the pupils of Chillingworth, that most broad-minded theologian, and subsequently he advocated the most absolute toleration in religious matters. W. H. Lecky, in his *History of Rationalism*, names Harrington, Milton, and Jeremy Taylor as the most eminent authors who, at that period, championed the cause of toleration, the two last named more from the religious and the former from the political point of view. "Of the three", he writes, "it must be acknowledged that the politician took by far the most comprehensive view. He perceived very clearly that political liberty cannot subsist where there is not absolute religious liberty, and that religious liberty does not consist simply of toleration, but implies a total abolition of religious disqualifications. In these respects he alone among his contemporaries anticipated the doctrines of the nineteenth century" (chapter iv).

the principles of *Oceana* in an argumentative form, and a treatise, *Seven Examples of Political Constitutions from Old and Modern History.*

In 1659 Harrington founded a Club for the discussion of his proposals, which Club, on account of the principle of alternate elections—"by rota"—which plays a great rôle in Harrington's ideal State, was called "The Rota". Among its members were the most advanced democrats of the day, as well as many men of literary importance. Besides John Wildman, Maximilian Petty, the Leveller, and William Petty, who subsequently became so famous, it counted among its members the Republican Henry Neville, author of *Plato redivivus*, Major Venner, the "Fifth Monarchy" man, and Cyriac Skinner, Milton's well-known pupil.[1]

To the restored monarchy Harrington was a "suspected" man, and about the end of December 1661, he who had accompanied Charles I, as a friend, up to the very scaffold, was suddenly arrested without ostensible cause, and kept in close confinement in the Tower. After considerable exertions by his sisters, an examination took place, which disclosed that information had been laid against Harrington, accusing him of taking part in secret meetings of representatives of all sections of the Commonwealth party, amongst others Wildman and Barebone, where the forcible re-establishment of the Republic had been discussed and a complete plan for the execution of this proposal had been concocted. But nothing further came of this examination; all his petitions for a regular trial to enable him to prove his innocence were unavailing, and when,

---

[1] Milton himself was no friend of the rotation principle. He considered it unpractical and dubious for the times. In the second edition of his *The Ready and Easy Way to Establish a Free Commonwealth* he wrote: "This 'wheel' might prove a 'wheel' of principles." Men who were indispensable at the moment might perhaps be replaced by incapable men. Milton's work provoked a satire from the Royalist party entitled *The Censure of the Rota upon Mr. Milton's Book, etc., etc.,* being a fictitious report on a meeting of the Rota Club where Milton's book is supposed to be discussed. It is reproduced in the *Harleian Miscellany.*

at last, his sisters applied for a writ of Habeas Corpus, he was secretly removed in great haste, after more than a half-year's close confinement without trial, and lodged in the bleak, rocky island of St. Nicholas. It was not until after he had contracted scurvy there that he was allowed, on heavy bail (£5,000), to sojourn within the forts of Plymouth. There he fell into the hands of a quack, who brought him to the very brink of death with monstrous doses of guaiacum, hellebore, and the like. Luckily, at the eleventh hour, his sisters obtained from the King an order for his discharge, and after using the waters at various spas Harrington returned to London, where he lived till 1677, but without ever completely recovering his health. While he was in Plymouth it was said that his illness had affected his reason, and in London also, although in conversations he expressed himself quite coherently, he was generally considered to be somewhat deranged on account of his remarks on the nature of his disease and physical law in general. He may have suffered from hallucinations, but, on the other hand, it is quite likely that those around him simply did not understand him, and took his figurative language literally. The commencement of an essay on the *Mechanics of Nature* was found among his posthumous papers. Although it contains some rather fantastical speculations upon the nature of his illness, which were inevitable in the then defective state of physical knowledge, it is so harmoniously arranged and finished as to suggest anything but madness. On the contrary, the first part contains many propositions which indicate a very keen intellect. Subjoined are a few specimens:

"Nature is the Fiat, the Breath, and in the whole Sphere of her activity the very Word of God. She is a spirit, that same Spirit of God which in the beginning mov'd upon the Waters, his plastic Virtue, the 'Dynamis' or 'diaplastikē', the 'energeia zōtikē'. She is the Providence of God in his Government of the things of this world, even that Providence, of which it is said, that without it a Sparrow cannot fall to the ground. . . . She is infallible . . . yet she is limited, and can do nothing above her matter; therefore no Miracles are to be expected of her. . . . Nature is not only a spirit, but is furnish'd, or rather furnishes herself, with innumerable ministerial Spirits, by wh. she operates on her whole matter, as the Universe; or on the separat parts, as man's body. These ministerial Spirits are certain Ætherial Particles invisibly mix'd with elementary Matter; they work ordinarily unseen or unfelt, and may be call'd Animal spirits. . . . Animal spirits, whether in the Universe, or in man's Body, are good or evil spirits, according to the matter wherein and whereof they are generated. What is a good spirit to one creature, is evil to another, as the food of som Beasts is poison to man. . . . Nothing in Nature is annihilated or lost, and therefore whatever is transpir'd, is receiv'd and put to som use by the spirits of the Universe."

So far it must be admitted that, apart from the term "spirit", Harrington had arrived as near the materialistic mode of thinking as it was possible in those times. And even the most mysterious and fantastical sentence in this essay is framed on thoroughly materialistic lines of thought, as in fact Harrington says expressly in his introduction that, leaving aside all books and theories, he would picture Nature as "how she first came into my senses, and by the senses into my understanding". This sentence runs as follows: "Animal spirits are ordinarily emitted, streaking themselves into various figures, answerable to little arms or hands, by wh. they work out the matter by Transpiration, no otherwise than they unlock'd it, and wrought it up in the body by attenuation, that is, by manufacture: for these operations are perfectly mechanical, and downright handy work as any in our shops and workhouses."

Just as Harrington in this instance compares the "animal spirits" to arms and hands, so he appears to have occasionally used, in conversation with those around him, still more striking analogies, without always expressing himself so clearly as to make his hearers feel the force of the simile. Hence the reports that he had declared flies and bees that were buzzing about to be emissions of his brain, that he had professed to be visited by devils and angels, etc. Nothing in the essay would indicate such hallucinations; on the only occasion when terms like "angelic" and "devilish" occur, they are derived from the very effects of the "animal spirits" defined above or explained by them. In short, Harrington's madness cannot be deduced from this essay.

Thus much as to the author of *Oceana*. We will now proceed to the work itself and its subsequent amplifications.

As the title indicates, *Oceana* is a political fiction, the description, not of an actual State, but of a State as it should be. In this respect it therefore ranks among the "Utopias". And yet its sole Utopian element consists in Harrington's belief that, provided the existence of a State was not menaced by external force, its perpetual maintenance in a state of equilibrium would simply depend upon the proper constitution and arrangement of its parts. Apart from this, Harrington is remarkable for his historical mode of treatment, which represents a notable anticipation of the materialistic conception of history elaborated by Marx and Engels.

The State of "Oceana" is England—England as Harrington and his contemporaries knew it. Far from disguising this, Harrington is at pains to impress the fact upon the reader's mind. "Oceana" was intended for immediate realization. All names in it are formed from the Greek or Latin so as to characterize, as distinctly as possible, the persons or places which they represent. Thus the name for England herself is "Oceana". London is called by Harrington "Emporium"; Westminster (on account of the Abbey) "Hiera"; Westminster Hall "Pantheon"; King John is "Adoxus" (the inglorious); Henry VII "Panurgus" (the crafty one); Elizabeth "Parthenia" (the maiden); James I "Morpheus"; Bacon "Verulamius";

Hobbes "Leviathan"; Oliver Cromwell "Olpheus Megaletor" (the victorious and generous), etc.

The book is divided into four sections. The first deals with the various *governments or political systems*; the second with the *most suitable mode of establishing a republic*; the third with the *model of a republic established on correct principles*, that is to say, he pictures "Oceana" (England) as such a republic; and the fourth, by way of a supplement, describes some of the probable *effects of the conversion of England into a Republic after the pattern of "Oceana"*.

The Republic is conceived mainly as a republic of property owners. Among its institutions, the "Rota" and "Ballot" are really the most immaterial ones, although Harrington is fond of expatiating on them. He had seen them in operation in Venice, and the Venetian constitution, as being thoroughly adapted to the circumstances of that Republic, appeared to him next to perfect. But being well aware of the difference existing between the material basis of the Venetian Republic and that of the British insular realm,[1] he ought to have reflected that in the case of England other means were available, to provide against an oligarchy, besides the voting by ballot and the "rota" prescriptions of the Adriatic Republic. However, he appears to have been dominated by the idea of proposing only such expedients as had been employed elsewhere, and for which precedents existed, and perhaps it is not his fault that far more discussion was provoked by his "rota" proposal than, for instance, by his "agrarian law". This "Agrarian", as he calls it, was intended to form the main safeguard against

---

[1] Thus he says in the very introduction, after pointing to Venice as an example of how favourable an insular position is for a republic: "And yet that, thro' the streitness of the place, and defect of proper Arms, can be no more than a Commonwealth for Preservation: whereas this, reduced to the like Government, is a Commonwealth for increase, and upon the mightiest foundation that any has bin laid from the beginning of the World to this day. The Sea gives law to the growth of Venice, but the growth of Oceana gives law to the sea." Here we have, by the by, the forerunner of "Rule Britannia".

a relapse into monarchic or feudal conditions. It prohibited the holding of land producing more than £2,000 annually, and set limits on the principle of bequest in order to enforce this stipulation. Harrington calculated on the basis of the total income from land in England at that time that the number of landowners could not fall below five thousand, when his agrarian law was in operation, and this would preclude an aristocratic feudal rule and a monarchy supported by it. But he doubted whether the land would ever be owned by so few as five thousand persons, and confidently reckoned on a preponderance of small over large landowners in the ratio of at least three to one. This being so, he averred that the democratic character of the constitution would virtually already be determined, as "GOVERNMENT FOLLOWS PROPERTY", or as we should say, the political constitution depends upon the distribution of property.

This is the basic idea pervading the whole of Harrington's work, which he tracks down everywhere in history, and which enables him to advance extremely apposite explanations of historical events. Sometimes he indulges in truly ingenious predictions. In view of the economic structure of England as he knew it, he would naturally locate the centre of gravity in real property. He does not attach much importance to personal property, because it has "wings"—and this was undoubtedly true at a time when the great wholesale merchant was still a "Merchant Adventurer" and manufacture was as yet in its initial stages. Attempts to establish an aristocratic rule based on the mere possession of money had been rare and never successful, and it was only in countries where the population lived chiefly by trading, as in Venice and Holland, that the distribution of personal property might have the same importance as that of real property elsewhere. In the case of England, Harrington deduces the inevitability of a political revolution from the development of landownership under the Tudors. He shows how Henry VII, by abolishing feudal duties, altering the laws governing the transfer of land, and making laws to create an independent peasantry, had diminished the amount of feudal real property and increased the property of the "people", that is to say, of the trading classes, thus fostering the very power which in the long run could not fail to become a menace to the Throne; how Henry VIII, by abolishing monasteries, while the nobility was on the down grade, had given a fresh impetus to this development, had thrown open to the "industry of the people" such rich "booty" that even under Elizabeth the change in the basis of power had led to an almost complete ignoring of the nobility by the advisers of the Queen; and how, finally, nothing was wanting for the complete overthrow of the Royal prerogative but that the people themselves should become aware of the power which resided in them. And then "a prince, as stiff in disputes as the nerve of monarchy was grown slack", received from his clergy that unhappy encouragement which cost him his life.

"For the house of peers, which alone had stood in this gap, now sinking down between the King and the Commons, showed that Crassus was dead and the isthmus broken. But a monarchy, divested of its nobility, has no refuge under heaven but an army. *Wherefore the dissolution of this government caused the war, not the war the dissolution of this government.*"[1]

Harrington declared a restoration of the monarchy impossible except by means of a fresh readjustment of the conditions of ownership (the "balance of property", as he calls it). Wise critics, like the elder Disraeli, have derided this, and pointed out triumphantly that but four years after the appearance of *Oceana* a restoration of the monarchy took place after all.[2] But this only shows that they misunderstood Harrington. What he maintained was the impossibility of abolishing the political rule of the middle classes, except by a material alteration in the balance of property, and this contention has been

---

[1] *Oceana*, ed. Routledge, p. 60.   [2] *Amenities of Literature.*

amply confirmed by history. Harrington was fully aware that there are mixed forms of government; he discusses quite a series of historical examples, but in these cases he always attempts to ascertain the class in which the centre of gravity of the government resided, and he determines its character accordingly. The final establishment of the parliamentary monarchy was a triumph for Harrington's theory, not its refutation.[1] The failure of the attempt of the Stuarts to restore absolute monarchy justifies Harrington's polemic against Hobbes.

He writes:

"To erect a monarchy, be it never so new, unless like Leviathan [i.e. Hobbes] you can hang it, as the country-fellow speakes, by geometry (for what else is it to say, that every other man must give up his will to the will of this one man without any other foundation?), it must stand upon old principles—that is, upon a nobility or an army planted on a due balance of dominion."[2]

The last remark is to be understood to mean that the army would consist of another tribe, and that the land on which it is settled would belong to the monarch, for instance after the manner of the Mamelukes in Egypt. Hobbes had ridiculed, among other things, the "Agreement State" as the Republicans conceived it, maintaining that law was based on the power of the sword, without which it would be a mere piece of paper. Harrington replies to this:

"But so he might have thought of this sword, that without a hand it is but cold iron. The hand which holds this sword is the militia of a nation. . . . But an army is a beast that has a great belly, and must be fed; wherefore this will come to what pastures you have, and what pastures you have will

---

[1] He writes in 1659: "In the present case of England, Commonwealth men may fail thro' want of art, but Royalists must fail thro' want of matter; the former may miss thro' impotence, the latter must thro' impossibility" (*Works*, ed. 1737, p. 540).

[2] *Oceana*, p. 61.

come to the balance of property, without which the public sword is but a name or mere spitfrog."[1]

In short, whoever had the means to send this animal with the large belly on the pasture, as the Grand Turk does with his Timariots, might laugh at the "Agreement State" too, but "if the landed property of the (feudal) nobility, stocked with their tenants and retainers, be the pasture of that beast, the ox knows his master's crib; and it is impossible for a king in such a constitution to reign otherwise than by covenant; or if he break it, it is words that come to blows."[2]

Harrington's objection to Hobbes is confined to Hobbes as a politician. To Hobbes the philosopher he pays the highest respect. "It is true, I have opposed the politics of Mr. Hobbs . . . with as much disdain as he oppos'd those of the greatest authors. . . . Nevertheless in most other things I firmly believe that Mr. Hobbs is, and will in future ages be accounted the best Writer, at this day in the world. And for his Treatises of Human Nature, and of Liberty and Necessity, they are the greatest of new Lights, and those wh. I have followed, and shall follow."[3]

After dealing with Hobbes, Harrington proceeds to apply his definition of Will to history. In *The Prerogative, etc.*, he writes: "The Law must proceed from the Will," and Will "is not presum'd to be, much less to act without a mover . . . the mover of the will is interest."[4] It is therefore absurd to say of any form of government or constitution that it is the most natural. "Government" (always to be taken in the widest sense, as constitution), "whether Popular or Monarchical, is equally artificial; wherefore to know which is more natural, we must consider what piece of Art comes nearest to Nature; as for example, whether a Ship or a House be the more natural; and then it will be easy to resolve that a Ship is the more natural at Sea, and a House on Land." . . . "Each govern-

[1] P. 20.
[2] P. 21.
[3] Loc. cit., ed. Toland, p. 257.
[4] Loc. cit., p. 241.

ment is equally artificial in effect or in itself; and equally natural in the cause, or the matter upon which it is founded."[1]

Harrington speaks of Machiavelli with the greatest veneration; with him he is always the "admirable", the "prince of political authors".[2]

Nevertheless, he asserts his own intellectual independence, and repeatedly corrects Machiavelli in the most felicitous manner. Thus, e.g., he writes in *Oceana*: "A people (says Machiavel) that is corrupt, is not capable of a commonwealth. But in showing what a corrupt people is, he has either involv'd himself or me; nor can I otherwise come out of the Labyrinth, than by saying, the Balance altering a People, as to the foregoing Government, must of necessity be corrupt: *but corruption in this sense signifys no more than that the corruption of one Government (as in natural bodys) is the generation of another.* Wherefore if the Balance alters from Monarchy, the corruption of the people in this case is that wh. makes them capable of a Commonwealth. But whereas I am not ignorant, that the corruption wh. he means is in Manners, this also is from the Balance. For the Balance leading from Monarchical into Popular, abates the Luxury of the Nobility, and, inriching the People, brings the Government from a more private to a

[1] P. 381.
[2] "A man may devote himself to death or destruction to save a Nation, but no Nation will devote itself to death or destruction to save mankind. Machiavel is decry'd for saying, that no consideration is to be had of what is just or injust, of what is merciful or cruel, of what is honorable or ignominious, in case it be to save a State, or to preserve Liberty; wh. as to the manner of expression is crudely spoken. But to imagin that a nation will devote itself to death or destruction, any more upon Faith given or an Ingagement thereto tending, than if there had bin no such Ingagement made or Faith given, were not piety but folly. . . ."
"Corruption in government is to be read and consider'd in Machiavel, as Diseases in a man's Body are to be read and consider'd in Hippocrates. Neither Hippocrates nor Machiavel introduc'd Diseases into man's Body, nor Corruption into Government, wh. were before their times; and seeing they do but discover them, it must be confest that so much as they have don tends not to the increase but the cure of them, wh. is the truth of these two authors" (Harrington, *A System of Politics*, ed. Toland, pp. 509, 514.)

more public Interest; wh. coming nearer as has bin shewn, to Justice and right Reason, the People upon a like alteration is so far from such a corruption of manners, as sh^d. render them incapable of a Commonwealth, that of necessity they must therby contract such a Reformation of manners as will bear no other kind of Government. On the other side, where the Balance changes from Oligarchical or Monarchical, the public Interest, with the Reason and Justice included in the same, becomes more privat; Luxury is introduced in the room of Temperance, and Servitude in that of Freedom. . . . But the Balance of Oceana changing quite contrary to that of Rome, the Manners of the people were not therby corrupted, but on the contrary adapted to a Commonwealth."[1] The discovery of the revolutionary side of corruption is certainly no slight achievement.

We might quote many more passages to show that Harrington came as near to a scientific conception of history as was possible in the seventeenth century. In his frequent references to *property* as the sole basis of political and other institutions, he makes it clear that his conception of property is sufficiently elastic.

He says in his *System of Politics*: "Industry of all things is the most accumulative, and Accumulation of all things hates levelling." The Revenue of the People "being the Revenue of Industry", the risk that the people would submit to forcible Levelling is reduced to a minimum. This is a valid inference from contemporary conditions. And Harrington's statement that the existence of a "gentry", or a class of well-to-do proprietors, is not only not dangerous but even useful to the democracy, provided only that the greater part of landed property remains in the hands of small freeholders, is similarly justified with reference to the time when he wrote. Progress in agriculture was stimulated by the large estates. In *Oceana* Harrington assigns the highest praise to the man who could

[1] *Oceana*, pp. 64–65.

contrive to stop rent-racking by competition, while preventing neglect of rational cultivation of the soil.

In making the political constitution dependent on the balance of property Harrington is not blind to the fact that other factors, for instance the geographical situation of a country, may exercise a distorting influence on the political conditions; just as he deduces from the protected insular position of England the possibility of an undistorted development. We need not quarrel with Harrington because he understood the "people" to comprise the middle classes. The earning classes in Harrington's time differed in the size of their property or income only; there were paupers, but not as yet a class of proletarians condemned to a state of permanent dependence. It is in this sense that *Oceana* classifies the populace.

The people in Harrington's model republic are divided into "freemen" or "citizens" and "servants", but the latter word is limited by the proviso, "while such". "For", he adds by way of explanation, "if they attain to liberty, that is, to live of themselves, they are freemen or citizens." "Servitude", i.e. economic dependence, "is inconsistent with freedom, or participation of government in a commonwealth."[1]

A further division of the people, adopted in "Oceana", pertains to the size of their incomes, the dividing-line being £100. This is intended to be operative in the question of national defence. Persons enjoying incomes over £100 are obliged to serve in the cavalry, while those who earn less than £100 are to serve in the infantry. All men under thirty years of age are to belong to the field army, those over thirty are designated for garrison service. In striking contrast to the Levellers, Harrington will admit no exemptions; conscription must be universal if it is to form a safeguard against the appearance of anti-democratic tendencies in the armed force. For military reasons also he favours general conscription, as it is wasteful to try to conduct a war with a small army.

[1] *Oceana*, p. 78.

The classification according to income, moreover, determines the electoral division. The class whose members have incomes over £100 elects, by direct vote, the Senate, which consists of three hundred members, and which discusses and proposes laws and regulations.

The popular assembly, constituting the "prerogative tribe" (the whole country is territorially divided into fifty "Tribes", these into "Hundreds", and these again into "Parishes", all with self-elected officials), consists of six hundred elected by citizens with less than £100 income, and four hundred and fifty elected by citizens with over £100 incomes, so that the former have the majority. This popular assembly has the final voice in deciding the enactment of laws. Whatever it determines is the "law of the land". If it rejects individual clauses only, these will be referred back to the Senate for reconsideration in order to be presented again, if thought fit, to the popular assembly in a modified form. Printed copies of each Bill are to be submitted to the popular assembly six weeks before they are introduced, but when it meets the popular assembly does not discuss; it merely votes. In proposing that each of the two classes of income shall elect their own special representatives, i.e. "class election", Harrington's object is not to secure a representation to the more prosperous class, but, on the contrary, to ensure that the less prosperous shall have a majority in the popular assembly. In a dialogue *Valerius and Publicola*, written in October 1659, in which he discusses the principles of "Oceana", he shows that hitherto the British Parliament had consisted of members of the upper classes only, *notwithstanding* the partial franchise of the lower classes, and this not merely because of their dependence on the lords. Even apart from this, in a general election men of the well-to-do classes would in the main be elected. A stronger representation of the lower classes must therefore be ensured by a separate election.

For the rest Harrington considered the democracy sufficiently

safeguarded by making the qualification for an elector to the
Senate conditional on an income which should not be beyond
the reach of any industrious and capable member of the
community. He held it to be a useful stimulus to industry that
certain posts of honour should be dependent on a certain
income.

As a matter of course, schools, education in technical arts,
cultivation of sciences, etc., would be amply provided for
and industry fostered in "Oceana", adequate provision being
made for the aged and infirm. As we have already indicated,
religious liberty too was to reign in "Oceana". Again and
again Harrington reiterates that political liberty cannot exist
without religious liberty, and vice versa. This explains why
Churchmen and Presbyterians assailed him so savagely. In
return he frequently makes theologians, and especially the
theological faculty of Oxford, the target of his wit.

Before taking leave of Harrington we will quote just two
more passages, demonstrating his historical foresight. He
predicts the industrial supremacy of England over Holland in
the following words: "In Manufacture and Merchandize the
Hollander has gotten the start of us; but at the long run it
will be found, that a people working upon a foren Commodity
dos but farm the Manufacture, and that it is really intail'd
upon them only, where the growth of it is native: as also that
it is one thing to have the carriage of other men's Goods, and
another for a man to bring his own to the best market. Therefore (Nature having provided incouragement for these Arts
in this nation above all others, where, the people growing, they
of necessity must also increase) it cannot but establish them
upon a far more sure and effectual Foundation than that of the
Hollanders."[1]

[1] *Oceana*, p. 211. Readers of Karl Marx's *Zur Kritik der politischen Oeko-
nomie* (Contribution to the Criticism of Political Economy) will remember a note on page 30, where a similar dictum by Petty is quoted. But Petty
wrote his essays almost a generation later than Harrington, from whom
he has quite obviously borrowed a great deal.

Harrington explains the absolutism which prevailed in seventeenth-century France from the fact that the landlordism of the nobility was opposed by a strong, landowning hierarchy, which still sided with the monarch, while the great mass of the people were too deeply immersed in misery to think of asserting themselves politically. And he goes on to say: "If it is said that in France there is Liberty of Conscience in part, it is also plain that while the Hierarchy is standing this Liberty is falling, and that if ever it comes to pull down the Hierarchy it pulls down that Monarchy also: wherefore the Monarchy or Hierarchy will be beforehand with it, if they see their true interest."[1]

Some twenty years after this was written the "Edict of Nantes" was revoked. But when the people, that is to say the middle classes, had grown stronger, both the hierarchy and absolutism were overthrown.

Harrington has exercised a far greater influence on the revolutionary literature of the eighteenth century than is generally known. Authors have frequently made use of him without acknowledging it. It would be too discursive to pursue this further, but we may mention what David Hume said of *Oceana*: "Even in our time", he writes, "it (*Oceana*) is justly admired as a work of genius and invention." So late as in Sieyès' writings the influence of Harrington's teaching is unmistakable,[2] and similarly in the case of St. Simon and

---

[1] Harrington, ed. Toland, p. 506.
[2] The Consular Constitution introduced by Napoleon Bonaparte on the 18th of Brumaire (November 9, 1799), the so-called "Constitution of the year VIII", has the same division as is found in Harrington's *Oceana*, one legislative body, which is deliberative only, and the other which votes, and it is more than likely that Sieyès, from whom the original draft of this constitution emanated, had borrowed this division from Harrington. In other respects also his draft displays striking points of resemblance to the institutions described in *Oceana*. For instance, as regards Harrington's favourite idea as to elections by rotation, and where it deviates from the original, it does not always improve on it from a democratic standpoint. The power of decision, in Sieyès' draft, is vested in the executive power, and the number of voting legislators is reduced to three hundred, which considerably facilitates their being influenced by the holder, for the time being, of the executive power. But at any rate the powers of the executive are re-

his disciples. In this sense it will certainly be no exaggeration for us to describe him as a precursor, not in his postulates but in his theoretical expositions of modern scientific socialism.

The seventeenth century in England saw the birth of political economy. We have already pointed out that most writers on political economy of the period are more or less pronounced representatives of protection and mercantilism as, for instance, is Hobbes, and it is in the nature of things that as protection was to foster the industrial classes, while these were still the "people", this protectionist literature bears a strongly popular or democratic stamp, and it is easy therefore to discover therein socialistic phrases. We believe, however, that we may safely content ourselves with the examples already given. Further, the question, "How are we to foster industrial progress?" goes always hand in hand with "How are we to provide for our poor?" and they both blend in the question, "How are we to educate our poor to agricultural and industrial activity?" Like P. Chamberlen, quite a series of other authors—economists and philanthropists—propose the establishment of *industrial* and *agricultural Labour Colonies*, which, in all cases, are to form model institutions of their kind. As may be seen from Sir Fr. Eden's *The State of the Poor*, there existed already, at the end of the seventeenth century, quite a literature of proposal son this subject; they remained ineffective because the various parishes had neither the power nor the desire to give themselves up to such experiments, and the State had still less desire or time for it. Instead of this, the State, under the

stricted by all sorts of safeguarding provisions, and both the deliberative and the voting body—the Tribunate and the Legislative—derive their mandate from the electors. Bonaparte caused all this to be struck out; he cared still less than Cromwell to have taken from him by a piece of paper what he had gained by the sword. But, more cunning than Cromwell, he let as much of the draft remain as was necessary to invest the legislative bodies with a semblance of independence from the holder of the sword, and this garbled rendering of "Oceana" was sanctioned by a plebiscite with 3,011,700 against 1,562 votes. According to it, a Senate consisting of sixty persons was to elect the members of the Tribunate and the Legislative from among the proposed candidates, but the Senate was nominated by Napoleon himself.

Restoration, solved the "poor" question by means of the "Laws of Parochial Settlement", under which the poor, apart from other hardships had to bear the brunt of the disputes between the parishes as to who was liable to support them. But the history of the poor law since the Restoration, and of the first movements of the workers in the industries carried on by capitalists, ought to be discussed in connection with the development of the social conditions in England in the eighteenth century; we will therefore content ourselves here with these general suggestions.

CHAPTER XV

PETER CORNELIUS PLOCKBOY

IN 1659 two pamphlets were published in London, the author of which signed himself Peter Cornelius van Zürickzee. They were ascribed for a long time to Hugh Peters, Cromwell's former field-chaplain and secretary,[1] but they originated, as a matter of fact, from a Dutchman named Pieter Corneliss Plockboy, of Zierickzee, which at that time was a very important commercial town in the province of Zeeland. One of these pamphlets was originally intended for Oliver Cromwell, with whom the author stated he had had personal relations; but Cromwell having meanwhile died, the author dedicated it to Richard Cromwell and Parliament. It contains proposals for the establishment of the Republic and internal peace (abolition of tithe and of any State religion, equal rights for all Christian sects, free speech, etc.), and while interesting for the style of its argument, is outside the scope of our discussion.

Not so the second pamphlet. Its somewhat prolix title runs as follows: "A Way propounded to make the poor in these and other nations happy by bringing together a fit, suitable and well qualified people unto one Household government or little Commonwealth. Wherein every one may keep his propriety and be imployed in some work or other, as he shall be fit, without being oppressed. Being the way not only to rid those and other Nations from idle, evil, and disorderly persons, but also from all such that have sought and found out many inventions to live upon the labour of others. Whereunto is also annexed an invitation to this Society or little common-wealth."[2]

[1] Thomason, bookseller and book-collector, to whose diligence, as a collector, we are indebted for the preservation of most of the pamphlets of those times, put on the pamphlet with which we are here concerned: "I believe this pamphlet is written by Hugh Peters, who has a servant named Cornelius Glover." Under Charles I Peters lived much in Holland, and maintained close relations with the sectarians there.

[2] By Peter Cornelius van Zürick-Zee.

The annexed "invitation" is from people who supported the project and had subscribed some hundred pounds towards it. They speak of the author as "our friend Cornelius". At the end of the pamphlet it is intimated that all who are interested in the project may learn the address of the author from the publisher, Giles Calvert, with whom we have already become acquainted. Hence there can be no doubt whatever that the project was designed to be carried out forthwith. It was not a dream of the future, but "practical" socialism, to be realized by the devisers themselves. But the originator and his associates actually appealed to *experience* gained. The contributions asked for were to be administered by trustworthy persons until the association to be founded could properly stand on its own legs. The English supporters of the cause say on this point: "Which we believe may soon be from the credible information of divers persons, relating that many hundreds in Transylvania, Hungaria, and the Valtsgraves Countrey, from a small beginning have attained, not only to a very comfortable life among themselves, but also ability of doing much good to others, not of their Society."

The instances quoted refer to the dispersed remnants of the Moravian Anabaptist communities, whose communism eventually found a footing in England. It is true that the end of the Republic, which came soon after the pamphlet appeared, shattered the hopes of the plan's supporters, but the ideas behind the proposal had taken root in the minds of some Englishmen, and have influenced the evolution of ideas in England.

It was natural enough that England should receive an impetus from Holland, which was then the most advanced country in economic respects in Europe, but the Dutch origin of the proposals imparted to them an air of modernity, which heightens their importance in this investigation. As one might expect, the economic aspect is stressed, while the religious argument occupies a secondary place. The first part of the

pamphlet, which elaborates the actual plan, is purely sociological; it is only in the second part, which is a kind of corollary,
that Christian charity and the moral doctrines inculcated by
Christianity are appealed to.

Plockboy commences as follows: "Having seen the great
inequality and disorder among men in the World, that not
only evil Governours or Rulers, covetous Merchants and
Tradesmen, lazie, idle and negligent Teachers, and others,
have brought all about under slaverie and thraldom: But
also a great number of the common handycraft men, or
labourers (by endeavouring to decline, escape, or cast off
heavy burthen) do fill all things with lyes and deceipt, to
the oppressing of the honest and good people, whose con-
sciences cannot bear such practises, therefore have I (together
with others born for the common welfare) designed to endeavour
to bring four sorts of people, whereof the World chiefly consists
out of several sects into one Familie or Household-govern-
ment, *viz*. Husband-men, Handy-crafts people, Marriners and
Masters of Arts and Sciences, to the end that we may the
better eschue the yoke of the Temporall and Spirituall
Pharaohs, who have long enough domineered over our bodies
and souls, and set up again (as in former times) Righteousnesse,
love and Brotherly Sociablenesse, wh. are scarce anywhere to
be found, for the convincing of those that place all greatnesse
only in domineering, and not in well-doing, contrary to the
pattern and doctrine of the Lord Jesus, who came not to be
served but to serve, and gave his life a ransome for many."[1]

Here follows a diatribe against "those that are called spiritual
persons or Clergymen, who perswade people (that they may
the more willingly drudge for them) to believe that they take
care of their souls (as if they c[d] love the soul wh. they cannot
see, and have no compassion on the body wh. they see)."[2]

This is the introduction to the project, which may best be
described as a socialistic community with limited private

[1] P. 1.   [2] P. 4.

property. Exploitation is abolished within the pale of the
association, but not property, which is to be allowed to con-
tinue in accordance with the tenth commandment. Whatever anyone has contributed to the company in the way of
land, money, or movable goods, shall be put to his credit and
shall be secured to him, but he shall receive *no interest*. In
the event of his death, unless he should bequeath his property
to the Company, his children and relatives shall inherit all
that stands to his credit. Anyone resigning his membership
is bound to give notice to the effect, and whatever stands to
his credit will then be returned to him, if under £100, as
soon as he desires it, if over £100 within one year, "paying
them a quarter of the summe presently (if they desire it) that
so none may be hindered to leave the Society".

If the Company is disturbed or broken up by tyranny, the
cash assets and the real property shall, after satisfying all
creditors, be distributed, in equal shares, *exclusively among
the poor members* who have nothing standing to their credit,
and any *poor relatives* of other members. Young people who
desire to leave the Company (whether to marry non-members
or for other reasons) shall receive on leaving a proportionate
share of the surplus realized since the date of their birth
or joining, or if no surplus should have been made, an amount
to be fixed by the Company.

To begin with, a fund is to be collected by suitable persons,
as "fathers" of the Company. Out of this fund two large houses
are to be bought or erected, one in the City of London, which
is to be large enough to accommodate twenty to thirty families,
and which is to serve as a warehouse containing shops of all
kinds, and a second and larger one in the country, near to a
river, which is to be the centre of production and the common
residence of the association, for agriculturists, mechanics,
teachers, and seamen.

Between this house and the river there is to be sufficient
space to serve as a "key", and if practicable, the house is to

be so situated that it can be isolated from the surrounding parts by a drawbridge.

The house is to be "built after a convenient manner, with public and private places for freedom and conveniency". It is to contain "a chamber and a closet for every man and his wife, with a great Hall, to lay all things ready made in order, a place to dress victuals, another to eat together, a third for the children, also Cellars to keep meat and drink in, a place for the sick, one for the Physicians and Chyurgeans, furniture and medicines, one other for all kind of usefull (as well naturall as Spirituall) Books, Maps and other instruments belonging to liberal Arts and Sciences".

The managers and officials are to be elected by the members to serve for one year, so that no official hierarchy may be established. The manager of the stores is to be changed each six months, and the cash-box is to have three locks, and be placed in the custody of three persons holding one key.

As few rules as possible are to be fixed, and each member is to enjoy the maximum liberty compatible with the common weal. All things are to be free to them that is not contrary to the "Kingdom of God" and Reason.

It is recommended that at first chiefly unmarried persons should be brought into the Society, so "that with laying out little money may presently be on the getting hand".

As regards production itself, six hours a day shall be the rule for all members of the Society, to be worked, at the option of the members, either three hours in the morning and three in the afternoon, or (which many might prefer, especially in hot summer) six hours in the morning; Sundays always excepted in this as in other cases. However, workers whom the Company might employ by contract are to work twelve hours a day until they are "fit and willing to come unto us". The best men are to be selected for foremen, who are also to work six hours.

Each of the members employed in the City warehouse is to

work for a period at the country settlement, in order to increase his technical knowledge and to enjoy other benefits.

All children are to be taught two or three trades. With the prospect of having to work no more than six hours daily, their lot would be enviable compared with that of children in the world outside. In their leisure hours they might study arts and sciences at their free choice. For children still being taught in school, the number of hours of work in trade or agriculture is to be three. All this is to apply equally to rich and poor.

The girls, too, are to learn proper trades as well as domestic work, so that if at any subsequent period they should leave the Company they may find their living in the world.

The author goes on to show that the Society is bound to prosper economically, and to go on increasing in extent, for the following reasons: "The first is that there will not be overasking in price, but all will be sold at the lowest rate; . . . The second is that we, dwelling at a cheaper rate and living less costly, can make all things better at the price."

The author describes all the advantages of co-operative economy, and of combination in agriculture and industry; he shows how one branch of production dovetails into another and how the extension of one will entail that of another; how the multiplicity of the branches of the system would be a guarantee for the stability of the concern. He paints an alluring picture of its gradual expansion, and shows how even shipbuilding is to be carried on. Boats for deep-sea fishing as well as vessels for the exportation of manufactured goods to the Continent would be built in their own dockyards.

In the actual domestic arrangements, joint management would be advantageous in every respect. In the first place through lightening the work. "Everyone shall be able quietly to do his work . . . 25 women in our Society, when all things are done orderly, shall have no more business to trouble their

heads with, than one woman in her own private family."[1]
"Besides the quiet and ease . . . it will also be very profitable
to dwell together." If a hundred families live together twenty-
five women can do the work which otherwise a hundred would
have to do; the other seventy-five could do *productive* work,
which many of them would prefer. And even in other respects
economy could be effected. Instead of a hundred fires, perhaps
four or five "great fires" only would be required: one in the
kitchen, one "where the children are", etc. Moreover, as far
as their own consumption might not be covered by the pro-
ductions of their own industry, they could purchase more
cheaply by buying wholesale. In this way a co-operative
system and the combination of agriculture and industry
would be remunerative in every respect. "Whereas the
Traders in the World do oppress their workmen, with
heavy labour and small wages, instead thereof with us, *the
gain of the tradesmen will redound to the benefit and refresh-
ment of the workmen*." Tradespeople in the world are always
in suspense "betwixt hope and fear", while in the Society
everyone "is quietly to mind his own business".

The Society need not fear any competition. Even if other
dealers, in order to entice customers from the association, were
to refrain from charging exorbitant prices (which is to be
desired in every respect), the advantages of working on a large
scale would enable the association to produce cheaper than
they. They ought, however, to be careful to avoid repelling
customers by doctrinary fads. If, for instance, a purchaser
desired to have articles of clothing trimmed ornamentally, they
ought not to offend him by pointing out that finery is sinful.
Plockboy adds humorously that it is certainly a great pity
that Adam ate of the tree of knowledge, but we should never
be able to cure men of their love of finery except by example
and education. The refusal to make finery would also be
impolitic for this reason, that if the young people brought up

[1] P. 10.

in the association should subsequently have to seek work, they would have much less chance of finding it if they did not know how to make finery.

The members themselves, however, should dress as plainly as possible, but those who have the means of doing so should not be debarred from having their clothes made of a better material, in order that—if for no other reason—the poor might recognize him as a person from whom they might justly expect help.

Some of the further advantages offered by the association would be, that young people need not get married prematurely, as was but too frequently done, simply in order to avoid slavish dependence on the parents—they might choose their partners for their life with deliberation and with full liberty, as they need not marry members; the teachers in the association would not be under the necessity of teaching, for the sake of their livelihood, things which they did not believe themselves, as there would be no coercion of conscience, all sects being afforded equal rights; and no one need entertain any fear of sickness or as to his support in old age, or as to the welfare of his children after his death.

In the same way as the association was to trade with the outside world, and open its schools to outsiders for payment, their physicians and surgeons too were to afford medical aid to outsiders, to the rich for remuneration, to the poor gratis; and while some were visiting patients, other medical men would be at home at certain hours in order to give advice to visiting patients.

Rich people who desired to enjoy the advantages of life in company might live with the association as boarders for the cost of their maintenance. If, for the sake of good example, they were willing to join in doing some work, they might, in return, receive gratuitous lodging and clothing. In every sixth and every twelfth month of the year accounts were to be balanced and a part of the surplus realized distributed, in order to enable members to give to the poor, make presents to friends, and the like.

The association was also to build a large meeting hall, with seats arranged in ascending tiers, each seat to be fitted with a desk for reading or writing. In this hall lectures, discussions, etc., would be held, in which non-members also might take part, and all might freely express their opinions. Meals would be eaten joyously with an absence of ceremony. The waiting at table would be attended to by the young people alternately, in order that none might give himself up to false pride.

In conclusion, seventy-two trades are mentioned to which the society would be of advantage. The author then continues: "Our Society being settled in order (as a nursery) about London, to imploy the poor, we may have a second about Bristole, and another in Ireland, where we can have a great deal of land for little money; and plenty of wood for building of Houses, Ships, and many other things."

In the second section, which contains the religious and moral arguments in favour of the project, the following passage is particularly characteristic: "This Society or fellowship hath not alwaies been so rare, and so thin sowen, but was very rife in the primitive times, till the enemies of the first innocencie did insinuate themselves thereunto, whereby the life wh. men were bound to live, as in obedience to the laws of Christ, began to be accounted such as a man may chose whether he w^d imbrace or no, and take up a meritorious and super-erogatory life, comprising such a sanctimony or holyness, as was more than necessary to Salvation . . . wh. opinion gave a beginning to many orders of lazie and wanton beasts (I mean monks and the like) and of many thousand fables and cheats."[1]

This was written in 1659. Three years later Plockboy, who had meantime returned to Holland, reappeared with a new project for an economic association, to be established

[1] P. 31.

in the Dutch colony of New Amsterdam in America. It is related that Plockboy, with twenty-four companions, received a loan of £1,500 from the Amsterdam municipal authorities on their joint security, and thereupon issued the invitation. The enterprise did not prosper, as the colony of New Amsterdam was soon afterwards captured by the English and renamed New York, after the Duke of York, who subsequently ascended the throne as James II.

Plockboy was a clear-headed person, and his economic insight was considerable. Apart from the fact that his proposal deliberately aimed at the combination of agriculture and industry, it also contains an attempt to establish what may be called a more intimate organic connection between town and country, so that, although the differences are not removed, the division of labour is placed on a more rational footing, production being reserved to the organized colony, and the exchange of commodities being reserved to the town establishment. Moreover, Plockboy made a definite stand against the ascetic tendencies which prevailed among the great bulk of the communists of the period, and which had so far formed one of the most salient characteristics of communism, with which everybody would have to reckon. There is a certain irony in his remarks to his followers that they were acting against their own interests in declining to make articles of luxury, and that the world could not be altered in this way. But he is not prompted solely by commercial considerations. Among the subjects to be cultivated in the colony, there figures in his scheme, next to the sciences and other "liberal arts", *music*, which many Quakers condemned, while others would only suffer it so far as it applied to singing hymns. In short, it is a contemporary and countryman of Rembrandt and Jan Steen whose temperament we are analysing; his proposals bear no trace of the desire to flee from the world, but, on the contrary, are redolent of a healthy enjoyment of the world. He relies, in nine cases out of ten, upon the economic advantages derived from production organized on a large scale, upon mass operations in production and trading. In the latter respect he anticipates the departmental store of modern times. What is the town establishment of the association with its many shops but the germ of modern establishments, such as Selfridge's or the Magazins du Louvre?

This brings us to another aspect of the scheme. What it sheds in the way of Utopian thought it makes up for in commercialism. It produces to make a profit, and notwithstanding all its regulations for the benefit of the poor, it is more distinctly a trading, or even a joint-stock company, than any other communistic scheme of the period. The other schemes were designed for religious ends and in antagonism to the world. If they nevertheless became commercialized, this was contrary to the original intention, and in the nature of an historical accident. In Plockboy's scheme the opposition to the "world" had not quite disappeared, but it was greatly toned down. It was, in fact, not religious at all, and has little reference to the mode of life of the members. Plockboy's quarrel with the surrounding world is mainly of an economic nature. He desired to free the members of this commonwealth from economic exploitation, from people "who live on other men's labour". The colony would leave everyone free to seek happiness in his own way—in heaven, and, apart from questions relating to production, to the best of his ability, also on earth. He expressly laid it down that liberty should prevail wherever necessity did not ordain otherwise. Another remarkable feature is the provision which facilitates withdrawal for those who wished to part from the Company. The Company is intended to make things better than they are in the world, but the members are not to be deprived of the advantages of the world.

Given such an outlook, concessions to the commercial spirit of the period were inevitable. Nevertheless, we do not detect in Plockboy's proposal any retrogression as compared with his communistic predecessors and contemporaries. In fact, just the reverse. We have seen that all the communistic enterprises of the time ended by becoming commercialized, and at best they were isolated communities which managed better and accomplished more than the outside world, but they competed with it and frequently proved themselves very able competitors.

All this information was available to Plockboy, who must have been aware of the practices of some of these communities. It was no small achievement, even for a native of the most highly developed commercial country of the age, to have learned all the lessons that could be imparted thereby, and to have based his schemes on the logic of undeniable facts. Socialism has to take account of a commercialized state of society, and Plockboy is the first whose guiding principle is to anticipate developments rather than lag behind. But his ideas could not be realized except by means of a co-operative association organized on a large scale. Plockboy may well rank among the pioneers of the modern idea of co-operation.

CHAPTER XVI

THE QUAKERS IN THE SEVENTEENTH CENTURY

1. THE RISE AND PRINCIPLES OF QUAKERISM

Johannes Becoldus redivivus; or, the English Quakers the German Enthusiasts Revived, is the title of a publication which appeared in 1659 in Boston.[1] It was naturally hostile to the Quakers. At a time when the worst calumnies concerning the vanquished of Münster found ready credence, the worst that could be said about any movement was that it was a revival of the Münster movement. However, the comparison was not altogether unwarranted. What was then suggested merely to prejudice men's minds against the new sect is now generally admitted as far as regards the spiritual descent of Quakerism from or its spiritual connection with the Continental Anabaptist movement.[2]

---

[1] It is an extract, published for party purposes, from a French work (by Guy du Brez) on the Anabaptists of Münster, "translated into English for the benefit of his countrymen by J. S." (Joshua Scotton).

[2] See, for instance, the excellent work already cited of H. Weingarten, *Die Revolutionskirchen Englands*, where both the spiritual relation of the Quakers to the German Anabaptists and the original revolutionary character of Quakerism are treated with keen perception. Most of the English essays on the history of Quakerism neglect the latter point, while the writings of the Quakers themselves and their friends studiously endeavour to efface all that might serve to throw doubts on the purely religious-ethical character of the original movement, or else they treat any such symptoms as mere vagaries of single individuals. But even they point out the relation existing between the Quakers' ideas and those of the Anabaptists, or, going still farther back, of the Waldenses and their predecessors. Thus, among others, Robert Barclay in *The Inner Life of the Religious Societies of the Commonwealth* (London, 1876); William Tallack in *George Fox, the Friends and the Early Baptists* (London, 1868); further, W. Beck in *The Friends, Who They Are and What They Have Done* (London, 1893). Tallack, in fact, does not hesitate to write: "And no friend need be ashamed of tracing his spiritual ancestry to Baptists and Anabaptists . . . .Even those Münster men were rebels against the cruelty of German tyrants, whose oppressions over the souls and bodies of the commonalty . . . were often, without exaggeration, diabolical. They failed and were rebels. Had they conquered men would have styled them heroes and patriots. Their rebellion was ferocious because their oppressors had been far more ferocious" (Tallack, pp. 84, 85).

P

In fact, the Quaker movement at the outset was really a revival of the original tendencies of the Anabaptist movement, of which the representatives of the new movement were unconscious, clothed in a new garb suited to the altered circumstances. The Lollard movement in England in the fourteenth and fifteenth centuries had been a primitive reaction against the rapacity and ostentation of Rome and of the Roman clergy, rather than a profound spiritual movement; while Puritanism, which was a genuine spiritual manifestation in the sixteenth and even in the first half of the seventeenth century, had through its conflict with monarchic absolutism become increasingly formal and shallow from a religious point of view, especially in the degree that it had been espoused by the proprietary classes. This was clearly apparent from the moment when Puritanism .triumphed over Charles I. The Presbyterians, on the one hand, repelled many people by their want of toleration and their pedantic insistence on formal church discipline, while, on the other hand, the Independent Ministers, after 1649, and after the rigorous measures adopted against the Royalist priests, had fallen into ill-repute on account of their sycophancy towards the new rulers. The Independents and Baptists now set up as recognized, regular "churches", and began to dogmatize, and in some cases to excommunicate. The Baptists had meanwhile split up into two sects, viz., the "General Baptists", who allowed a certain freedom to the human will, and the "Particular Baptists", who held fast to the Calvinistic doctrine of predestination. Both sections insisted on baptism by immersion. But many people who had been stirred by the religious conflicts failed to find satisfaction in any sect. All dogmas had been shaken, one faction in the Church decried the other, and these disputes were carried on in the streets and open places, the public joining in, as in the case of modern political meetings. The result was that scepticism spread among the people, many of whom turned their backs on religion altogether. Judging

from the reports of Quaker missionaries, there were in England
at that time a considerable number of people who denied the
truth of the Biblical story of the creation, and declared that
"all comes by nature".[1] But such sceptics were lost in the
great bulk of the nation. Others attached themselves to obscure sects, brooding on the mysteries of creation (the so-
called "seekers"), or waiting for a sign from heaven which
was to solve their doubts (the so-called "waiters").

One of these "seekers" was George Fox, son of a Leicester-
shire silk-weaver. Born in 1624, and bred during the period
of Puritan persecutions, he developed at a very early age a
strong religious bent. He was apprenticed by his father, who
was in comfortable circumstances, to a shoemaker, who was
also a sheep-breeder; but he abandoned his apprenticeship
at the age of nineteen, and driven by a restless, roving spirit,
he went from place to place, from county to county, preaching
and arguing. None of the existing Churches satisfied him;
they were all too worldly to his mind, they did not correspond
with primitive Christianity, and obeyed the letter rather than
the spirit. Through debating, reading, and the influence of
his environment, he eventually reached a state of mind which
was a compound of rationalism and mysticism, of democracy
and political abstention. Strange as it may appear at first
sight, it will nevertheless become intelligible in the light of
contemporary events as set forth in the preceding chapters.
The civil war had claimed untold sacrifices, without any
satisfactory result; political struggles had succeeded each
other without bringing a solution of social difficulties any
nearer; men who had been hailed as deliverers, when once
raised to power, assumed the mien of oppressors, and thus
the conclusion seemed inescapable that the chief evil lay
in *man* himself, in the *weakness* of human nature, which

---

[1] A letter, reprinted in the *Harleian Miscellany*, from a Frenchman who
came to London in 1659, expresses the greatest horror at the great spread of
atheism in the capital of the insular realm.

the existing Churches had proved powerless to overcome. Enthusiastic natures were likely to incline to this view, and thus we see George Fox, who up to the proclamation of the Commonwealth had been like the "voice of one crying in the wilderness", after 1650 making converts in increasing numbers. They flocked to him from all parts, a large contingent coming from the former soldiers of Cromwell's Army, who, owing to their discontent with the course of events, had either obtained a discharge or been dismissed from the Army. This element was, at first, so strongly represented in the communities established by Fox that in many of them a different spirit from his own prevailed. The Ironsides concurred with Fox in rejecting the formal element in Church matters, having been trained to this in Cromwell's Army, where, after the withdrawal in 1644 of the official ministers of religion, anyone would preach whom the spirit moved.[1] After this we can understand the following passage from John Evelyn's Diary: "On Sunday afternoon I frequently staid at home to catechize and instruct my family, those exercises universally ceasing in the

[1] "Thus, during the war, a peaceful village church was often startled by the violent entrance of a band of these military reformers, who ordered the priest to close his prayer-book and come down from the reading-desk, with terrible threats if he disobeyed. If he complied, their errand was done. . . . One other occasion, after discharging the preacher from the pulpit, a gifted brother would assume his place, and hold forth to the astonished auditories such wondrous revelations as had never entered their hearts to imagine. . . . Occasionally, also, the doctrines of these teachers were illustrated by practical examples which were not always convenient to the taught. To show that the birds of the air were given as a common property to the dominion of the saints, they sometimes demolished a harmless dovecot. To enforce the duty of even modern Christians to abstain from eating 'things strangled', they would, in a march, reject the fowls which had been got ready for their dinner in the houses upon which they were quartered, because their hosts had killed the poultry in the usual fashion by twisting their necks; and would themselves go to the barn-yard and prepare materials for an orthodox meal by chopping off the heads and pouring out the blood of all the hens, geese, and turkeys that remained. To burn the Bible itself, also, before the eyes of a horror-struck assembly was sometimes the daring act of the wildest of these sectarians, to show that their inward light was superior to all written revelation" (Macfarlane and Thomson, *The Comprehensive History of England*, vol. vi. p. 749).

parish churches, so as people had no principles, and grew very ignorant of even the common points of Christianity; all devotion being now placed in hearing sermons and discourses of speculative and notional things." But their objection to war and politics was not the same as Fox's. His objection was based on principle, after the manner of the Mennonites, from whom on the whole Fox differed little in doctrine.[1] while their objection was largely one of expediency. They stood aloof from war and party contentions, but did not abandon the hope of eventually realizing their social ideals by political methods.

It was not until after the Restoration that Fox's doctrine of abstention from politics was generally adopted by the Quakers. During the Commonwealth this was so little the case, that when representatives of the Army (in April 1659) presented a petition to Parliament in favour of a resumption of the "good old cause" of liberty and of the republic, Quakers supported it by a memorial which added a few further demands to those of the petition. During the first years of the Commonwealth Fox was generally overshadowed by the republican Quakers who headed the religious-revolutionary opposition to Cromwell. They "marched through the streets of London, denouncing with uplifted voice Cromwell's Government, and predicting its downfall". Publicly they were better known than Fox. The best-known person among the Quakers, against whom the pamphlet referred to at the commencement of this chapter is directed, was James Naylor, an ex-quartermaster of the Army.

But before dealing further with this man, and the incident which made him notorious, and which throws much light on the first period of Quakerism, it will be expedient to discuss the ideas chiefly propagated by the Quakers.

The Quakers believe in God and are Christians, adhering as

[1] "There is no feature of Fox's character more striking than his absolute separation from all the political aims and objects of the men of his time" (Barclay, loc. cit., p. 193). "Keep out of the powers of the earth" Fox repeatedly exhorted his followers.

strictly as possible to primitive Christianity; but what they mainly rely upon is not the traditional "word of God", the Bible, but the living word, the inward light. Consequently they call themselves the *"professors"*, or else the *"Children of Light"*. The name of Quakers was first given to them by opponents in derision, and then came into general vogue.[1] This cult of the inward light, down to the very name "Children of Light", forms a connecting-link between the Quakers and many German Anabaptists, as also the German Mystics, and it is a suggestive fact that the first English edition of writings of the German theosophic mystic, Jacob Böhme, was issued in 1649 by the bookseller who issued the Quaker publications of the period, viz., Giles Calvert of London, who, as we know, was also the publisher and in some cases even co-signatory of the pamphlets of the "Levellers".[2]

According to Quaker doctrine, this "inner illumination" can only come as a result of *concentration* of the thoughts on God, for which purpose neither a learned sermon nor a liturgy is necessary. On the contrary, a professional learned priest-hood, appointed and *paid* by the State, is an evil; everyone shall preach, or rather he shall say what he has to say, whom the inner voice prompts to do so, and *whenever* it prompts him to, whether he be a man of education or not. Fox and the first

[1] This name, according to some, is derived from the fact that Fox in his itinerant preaching called upon his hearers to hear the word of the Lord with "quaking", while others derived it from the fact that the professors of the new doctrine in their prayer meetings frequently fell into religious ecstasies, with trembling and convulsions. According to an anecdote, a judge whom Fox addressed with the above-mentioned words replied: "Then you are Quakers?" and the name is supposed to be derived from this episode. Fox first appeared in the character of an agitator in 1649. In the church at Nottingham he interrupted the preacher, who admonished the congrega-tion to test all doctrine by the Bible, with the words, "Oh no, it is not the Scripture by which opinions and religions should be tested, but the Holy Ghost, for it was the Spirit that led people to truth and revealed it to them."

[2] Böhme or Behmen (1575–1624) was, like Fox, a shoemaker by trade, and undoubtedly was under the influence of the sect of Schwenkfeldians, whose doctrine resembles that of the Quakers. Many of his followers had fled to Holland and England during the Thirty Years War.

Quakers inveighed with real fanaticism against a priesthood paid out of public funds. Repeated instances occurred when Quakers entered churches and shouted at the preacher in the pulpit: "Come down, thou false prophet, thou impostor, thou blind leader of the blind, *thou hireling*!" We read in Fox's diary that the priests "trade", that they "sell" their Gospel, that the bells of their "steeple-houses" (the Quakers will not allow the name of "church" for any building) resemble *market-bells*, which call the people together in order that the priest may "spread out his *wares for sale*"; and "the enormous sums which are obtained by this *traffic*, what other traffic in the world can be compared to it?"[1] But even without using such invectives, the Quakers frequently interrupted preachers, or took the Word after the regular service was finished and preached to the assembled multitude their own doctrine. But they did not always get a quiet hearing; sometimes the whole community, and in the majority of other cases the bulk of the inhabitants, showed themselves hostile to the passionate apostles and vented their indignation on them by ill-treatment of the most brutal kind. Again and again we read that the Quaker apostles were beaten, stoned, kicked, and often the apostles of the new doctrine, after such an attempt to win the people, would be lying unconscious on the ground, bruised and bleeding, for hours, until some charitable soul took pity on them. The sequel was in most cases an inquiry before a Justice of the Peace, ending with the Quakers being sentenced to fines, imprisonment, and whipping. All other sects taken together did not at that time supply half as many inmates to the prisons as the "Professors of Light".[2]

[1] *Journal of Fox*, edition of 1891, vol. i. p. 117.

[2] A memorial addressed to Parliament in 1657 showed that between 1651 and 1656 no less than 1,900 Quakers were sent to prison, and twenty-one *died in prison*. This was the time when John Lilburne joined the Quakers; certainly a sign that this step did not constitute a humble submission to the authorities.

Between 1661 and 1697 no less than 13,562 Quakers were imprisoned, 338 died, either in prison or from the effects of ill-treatment, 198 were transported (Barclay, *The Inner Light*, etc., p. 475).

The rejection of the letter led the Quakers, among other things, to reject the strictly literal conception of the *Sabbath rest*, which was observed by the other Puritans, whom they often reproved on account of their "Judaizing tendencies". As regards asceticism in their mode of life, they outstripped all other sects; they strictly prohibited all boisterous amusements and every luxury, and the peculiar and severely plain dress retained by them for a long time is well known. They interpreted the Sermon on the Mount literally. They would suffer the severest penalties rather than take an oath. They likewise rejected the Church sacraments of *Baptism, Communion,* and *Holy Matrimony.* Their cult, in some of its forms, was extremely rationalistic; they assembled in plain meeting-houses, where they gave themselves up to religious meditation.[1] Following the precepts of the Sermon on the Mount, they repudiated *war* and *forcible resistance,* and however impracticable their ideas may sound, it cannot be denied that when endeavouring to carry them out the early Quakers frequently displayed heroic strength of character. Men who had helped to fight Cromwell's battles bore quietly the worst brutalities from excited ruffians, and risked death rather than defend themselves. A training of character was further supplied by their rule to address everyone as "thou", and not to doff their hats to anyone; the first because they considered it tantamount to a lie to address an individual as if he represented a plural number, and the second because equal respect was due to *all men*, whether poor or rich, high or low, and that it was therefore an unworthy act to bow to any man.[2] The judges and other authorities, of course, took a different view from that of the Quakers, and in most cases cast them into prison

[1] But during the time of the first enthusiasm it seldom happened that no one *was* "moved by the Spirit" to speak. Subsequently members who obviously had a "call", that is, who had proved efficient apostles, were specially appointed and paid for proclaiming the true doctrine. But anything like a hierarchy or any monopoly of preaching was strictly avoided.
[2] The reader will remember, in this connection, the behaviour of Winstanley and Everard in April 1649, i.e. before Fox's public appearance.

for "contempt of court", and frequently had them whipped into the bargain. And prison, where the bulk of the inmates were vagrants covered with vermin and criminals, generally proved to the Quakers veritable hells on earth.[1] Nevertheless, they stuck to this rule with iron tenacity; it was not relaxed under the pressure of persecutions, but only after the Quakers had succeeded in gaining for themselves political toleration and social acknowledgment. "And albeit no Reason can be given why we should be Persecuted upon this account, especially by *Christians*, who profess to follow the Rule of Scripture, whose Dialect this is; yet it would perhaps seem incredible, if I should relate how much we have suffered for this thing, and how these Proud Ones have *fumed*, *fretted*, and *gnashed* their *Teeth*, frequently *beating* and *striking* us, when we have spoken to them in the *Singular Number*: Whereby we are the more confirmed in our Judgment, as seeing that this *Testimony of Truth*, which God hath given us to bear in all things, doth so vex the Serpentine Nature in the *Children of Darkness*." Thus wrote the most prominent exponent of Quakerism, Robert Barclay senior, in his principal work, published in 1675, *An Apology for the True Christian Divinity, as the Same is Held Forth, and Preached, by the People, called in Scorn, Quakers* (4th Edition, pp. 528, 529).

[1] In the everyday private intercourse also the persistent use of "thou," and the refusal to doff the hat to anyone, for a long time brought the Quakers continually into much and serious trouble. Apart from Fox, we may find significant instances of this in the autobiography of Thomas Ellwood, his contemporary, which, in many respects, affords us much insight into the social life and the internal condition of Quakerism of the period. "The countless autobiographies and pamphlets of the early Quakers, from the time of Barebone's Parliament to the Restoration, contain a super-abundant quantity of unused materials for the social history of England, the history of the common man and the common people" ("Early Quaker Politics," by the Rev. Thos. Hancock, in *Weekly Times and Echo* of February 1896). Mr. Hancock rightly says that as a religious movement early Quakerism was both *ultra*-Puritan and *anti*-Puritan. "They (the Quakers) said the last word of Puritanism; they were its Extreme Left." But by their proclamation of the Light of Christ within every man, simply because he *was man*, the Quakers "gave a theological basis and impulse to the principle of social equality, freedom and brotherhood".

A further source of persecution was the Quakers' persistent refusal to pay tithes. Among all the more important sects they upheld most consistently the principle that religion was a private matter. And certainly greater moral courage was required for a member of a moderately numerous sect, mainly composed of members of the poorer classes, of the "vulgar" (Hume), to refuse to pay taxes, than for John Hampden, when supported by more than half the nation, to refuse to pay ship-money.

The constitution of the Quaker communities was thoroughly democratic; it was modelled, in its cardinal features, upon that of the early Christian communities, and presents all the essential characteristics to be found in the communities of the more consistent among the Anabaptists, viz., regular meetings for exercising discipline and moral censorship, settling disputes, and regulating financial affairs. From these local meetings the organization (which grew but gradually) extends to the quarterly district meetings and the annual general meetings of the whole community.

The writings of Fox and of the better-known advocates of early Quakerism reveal no distinct social or economic tendencies; they are of a purely religious and ethical character. Whether and to what extent communistic tendencies were propagated among the early Quakers, or certain sections of them, by *clandestine teaching*, is difficult to ascertain.[1] The

[1] On the other hand, as Mr. Hancock states, there exist a number of the earliest Quaker pamphlets which "show a distinctly socialistic tone of thinking", and numerous proofs are extant that Quakers declaimed in their meetings against private property—in England as well as elsewhere. For at a very early period they sent out apostles of the new doctrine to the Continent and America. How these fared in Holland, for instance, we find recorded, among others, in Otto Pringsheim's *Beiträge zur wirthschaftlichen Entwicklungsgeschichte der Vereinigten Niederlande im 17 u. 18 Jahrhundert*, Leipzig, 1890, pp. 65 ff. Pringsheim relates that in 1657 some Quakers caused great excitement in Zeeland and Rotterdam by preaching that *all goods ought to be held in common*. He quotes a bourgeois paper, the *Hollandse Mercurius*, of 1657, where the communistic preaching of the Quakers is ascribed to the fact that they were themselves mostly "loafers and paupers". There is nothing new under the sun. In Hamburg, where the

only thing certain is that at a very early date they established among themselves an organized *system of charitable relief*, and that the more prosperous among their members exhibited in this respect a noteworthy spirit of sacrifice. Significantly enough, a beginning was made with the *relief of the victims of coercion and persecution*, but soon this was followed by arrangements for the relief of *poor and sick* members of the community.[1] Anything beyond this was utterly impracticable during the period of propaganda; even avowedly communistic sects were obliged, unless special circumstances favoured a fuller community of goods or incomes, to limit the realization of their ideal in practice to the relief of the poor.

On the other hand, it was possible to apply communism to *education*, and we may observe in the case of the Quakers a feature that is peculiar to all the communistic sects of the period, namely, a contempt for academic learning combined with a great interest in education. Barclay the elder, for instance, in the book already quoted, after condemning theatres, dancing, sports, and other diversions as detracting from true Christianity, mentions as permissible amusements the following: to visit friends, to read or hear history, to converse soberly on the events of the present or of the past, to engage in gardening, to make geometrical and mathematical experiments and the like.[2] Fox, in his letters, never tires of impressing upon his friends the importance of educating

Quakers had also sent emissaries, there appeared in 1661 a book entitled *The Quaker Abomination—that is, Detestable, Seditious, Damnable Error of the New Enthusiasts Called Quakers*. At Dantzic the trade guilds demanded the expulsion of the Quakers.

[1] "But an excellent order, even in those early days, was practised among the Friends of that city (London) by which there were certain Friends of either sex appointed to have the oversight of the prisons in every quarter, and to take care of all Friends, the poor especially, that should be committed thither", is what Th. Ellwood wrote in 1662, at the same time describing in what manner this was done. "Friends" is the designation adopted by the Quakers among each other, which subsequently became the official denomination.

[2] *Apology*, 4th edition, pp. 540, 541.

the young. The first years of their propaganda, however, were
not a favourable time for the promotion of this purpose. The
numerous persecutions exhausted all the resources of the
"friends"; their most capable members were alternately in
prison; and many of their followers were inclined to believe
that the "inner light" compensated for all knowledge except
that required for daily pursuits.

It was only gradually that much of what we have been describing took definite shape as the Quaker movement, and
came to be generally recognized as such. Originally, in this as
in similar movements, the negative side, the *protest*—in this
case protest against the establishment of new hierarchies—was
uppermost. It was during this early period of fermentation
and persecution, in some respects marking its very climax, that
the James Naylor episode occurred.

2. JAMES NAYLOR, THE KING OF ISRAEL

James Naylor was the son of a comfortable farmer in Ardsley,
a village near Wakefield. He received a good education, and
in 1642, when aged about twenty-five (and already a family
man), his enthusiasm prompted him to join the Parliamentary
Army. His conduct as a soldier was blameless, and his superiors,
who included Major-General Lambert, subsequently gave
him the best of characters. While in the Army he went over
to the Independents, and gave religious addresses which, like
his subsequent speeches, were full of eloquence, depth, and
power. An officer who heard him preach after the bloody
battle of Dunbar on September 3, 1650, subsequently wrote
that "he had been inspired with greater fear by Naylor's
sermon than he had felt in the battle of Dunbar". Soon after
the battle of Dunbar Naylor obtained his discharge on account
of illness, and returned home in order to attend to his farm.
In 1651 he heard George Fox preach, and quickly embraced
his ideas, which, as we have shown, expressed what thousands

of disappointed enthusiasts were feeling at the time. In the spring of 1652, while following the plough, he suddenly felt within himself the "call" to work, like Fox, as an itinerant preacher, for the propagation of the new doctrine, and he at once started on his journeyings. He met Fox in Lancashire, where an ardent adherent had been gained to their cause at Swarthmore, near Ulverstone, in the person of the wife of Judge Fell, a granddaughter of Ann Askew, the martyr, and her house became the centre of the Quaker organization.[1]

As early as in the late autumn in the same year Naylor was called to account at Orton, Westmoreland, for having preached a "blasphemous" sermon. He had said, among other things, that the body of Christ after the resurrection was to be taken as being "not carnal but spiritual", and refusing to recant, he was kept in prison for nearly six months. Out of a sum of five pounds which Margaret Fell sent for his sustenance, he accepted the twentieth part and refused the rest. Like many other Quakers, he imposed on himself an ascetic mode of life.

A sample of the opinions then held by Naylor, and an illustration of the general *political* disillusionment, is to be found in one of Naylor's pamphlets, dated from 1652, and entitled, "A Lamentacion (By one of England's Prophets) Over the Ruines of this oppressed Nacion, To be deeply layd to heart by Parliament and Army, and all sorts of People, lest they be swept away with the Broom of Destruction, in the Day of the Lord's fierce wrath and Indignation, which is near at hand. Written by the Movings of the Lord in James Naylor." It begins with the words: "Oh England! how is thy expectation failed now after all thy travails! The people to whom Oppression and Unrighteousness hath been a Burden, have long waited for Deliverance, from one year to another, but none comes, from one sort of men to another. . . . For as power hath come into the hands of men, it hath been turned into violence,

[1] After her husband (who had always adopted a benevolent attitude towards the movement) died in 1670, Margaret Fell married George Fox.

and the will of men is brought forth instead of Equity. . . .
He that turns from iniquity is made a prey to the wicked, and
none lays it to heart through the nation, for all hearts are full
of oppression, and all hands are full of violence, their houses
are filled with oppression, their streets and markets abound
with it, their Courts which sh^d afford remedy against it
are wholly made up of iniquity and injustice. . . . Oh!
Foolish People . . . are not these the choicest of thy Worthies,
who are now in power? Hath it not been the top of thy desires
and labors to see it in their hands, and are not they now become
weak as other men, and the Land still in travail but nothing
brought forth but wind?" No reliance could therefore be
placed on men, nor could any hope be set upon an alteration
in the government, but improvement could only follow the
cultivation of the right *spirit*. This attitude of mind may be
observed after all great political reactions. The most striking
modern example of it may be found in the works of Tolstoy,
who may be described as a Russian Quaker of the late nineteenth century.

After finishing his term of imprisonment Naylor at once
resumed his missionary activity, and early in 1655 came to
London, where a fairly strong Quakers' community already
existed. His fervent, stirring speech soon made him their
favourite speaker, and even outside the narrower circle of
Quakerism he attained to a certain degree of fame. He moved
in circles where he met prominent representatives of the
Republicans who were then opposing Cromwell, such as
Bradshaw, Sir Henry Vane, and others, and on the other hand
many of these, and even members of Cromwell's "Court",
visited the Quaker meetings where Naylor spoke. Eventually
a Naylor cult grew up, especially among the female members
of the Quaker community. People would hear no one but
him, and would interrupt the addresses of those who had
hitherto been leaders of the community. Naylor had to be
the chief speaker, the principal representative. He himself

resisted for some time, but in the end this adulation proved too much for him. In the summer of 1656 Naylor set out for Launceston, where Fox was then imprisoned, in order to discuss with him more fully the differences which had arisen in London, and which probably had reference to the attitude to be adopted towards contemporary politics. Several of his admirers insisted on accompanying him, and thus his journey tended to assume a Messianic aspect. The Quaker gospel, with its mystical idea of the inner light, did not preclude this. The inner light, the divine illumination, varied in the strength of its manifestations. Why should not James Naylor with his enthralling eloquence be called to perform a special work? Why should not the Spirit manifest itself in him with the same power as in the Son of Mary? The Quakers were Christians in the sense of the teachings of primitive Christianity, but during the earliest days very heretical views obtained among them concerning the Godhead of the person of Christ.

In the West of England, in the centres of the cloth-industry, the new doctrine had made rapid strides. It was reported, as early as in 1654, that the Quaker meetings in Bristol were always attended by three to four thousand persons. The actual number of members of course was much smaller than this, but nevertheless very considerable in proportion. In a town of a little over thirty thousand inhabitants they had, in 1658, over seven hundred members, most of whom were mechanics. Among the soldiers of the garrison also they had many adherents, and even some of the officers were favourably disposed towards them.

When Naylor, on his journey to Launceston, passed through Bristol, demonstrations naturally took place, and it even came to disturbances, from which, however, nothing followed. Yet in Exeter Naylor was arrested and cast into prison as a disturber of the peace and agitator. But this only increased his authority among his admirers. Women praised him in their letters as the incomparable champion and "only son" of

God, and their husbands improved upon this in their post-
scripts. The husband of Hannah Stranger wrote: "Thy name
shall no longer be James but Jesus", while Thomas Simmonds
called Naylor "Thou Lamb of God". They visited him in
prison, and the women fell down before him and kissed his
feet. A certain Dorcas Ebury loudly proclaimed that she had
been lying dead for two days, and Naylor had called her to
life again. Towards the end of October he was liberated, and
Fox too having meanwhile been set free (he had visited
Naylor in prison, but no understanding had been arrived at), the
return journey was entered upon. First they made for Bristol,
Naylor being on horseback, and his companions either mounted
or on foot. Already at Glastonbury and Wells garments had
been spread on the road and shawls waved, but when they
arrived outside Bristol the procession became an imitation of
Christ's entry into Jerusalem. Naylor was quiet, but his
companions sang hymns, "Hosannah in the highest", "Holy,
Holy, Holy", etc. Unfortunately for them, England was not
Palestine. The rain poured down in torrents, and Naylor's
companions had to wade knee-deep along the quagmire-like
roads. Rain acts as a deterrent to all manifestations, even
"Messianic" ones, and this is probably why, when the procession had entered Bristol, its heroes could be arrested without
any trouble. Even as it was, large crowds had assembled in
spite of the rain. The local authorities appear to have been
reluctant to keep Naylor long in Bristol or to bring him to
trial there. After a first hearing, he with six others were sent
to London on November 10th in order to be finally heard and
judged by the House of Commons as an extraordinary male-
factor. His case occupied for weeks almost the whole time and
attention of the Second Parliament of the Protectorate, which
had only just assembled. The matter was first inquired into
by a Committee of fifty-five members, who, after meeting
four times, reported to Parliament; thereupon, on December 6th, Naylor was tried at the bar of the House, and two

days afterwards was found guilty of "abominable blasphemy", whereupon the House debated for seven days as to whether sentence of death should be passed.[1]

On December 16th the more lenient view prevailed by 96 against 82 votes. But the punishment still proved severe enough—so severe, in fact, that its execution had to be interrupted. On November 18th Naylor was to be exposed in the pillory for two hours, whipped through the streets of London by the hangman, then pilloried again, his tongue was then to be perforated with a hot iron, and the letter B (Blasphemer) branded on his forehead. He was then to be taken to Bristol, conducted through the town seated backwards on a horse, and whipped back through the town. Finally, he was to be sent to the penitentiary, and being prohibited altogether from any use of the pen, and dependent for his sustenance on the proceeds of his own work—of picking oakum—he was to be kept in strict solitary confinement as long as Parliament pleased.

Naylor had not uttered anything during his examination beyond what he and other Quakers had said on previous occasions as to the power of the "inner light", and as regards the homage done to him he declared it was not meant to apply to his mortal being, but to God speaking through him. He suffered the punishments inflicted on him with the stoicism of a fanatic. But his friends did not look on idly. When, after the first whipping, Naylor was so lacerated that the further execution of the sentence had to be postponed, petitions in his favour literally poured in—among the number, some from people of influence such as Colonel Scroope—so that Cromwell himself was prompted to ask Parliament for the grounds of the verdict. This question led to a further day's debate by the House, before the termination of which, however, a further part of the sentence was executed upon Naylor, viz., perfora-

[1] "Interminable debates about James Naylor—excelling in stupor all the Human Speech—even in English Parliaments, this Editor has ever been exposed to. . . . To Posterity they sit there as the James-Naylor-Parliament" (Carlyle, loc. cit., vol. x.).

tion of the tongue and branding. His adherents stood round the scaffold in great numbers, while one of them, Robert Rich, a merchant, stood beside him, and held a placard over Naylor's head, bearing the words: "This is the King of the Jews", which was, of course, torn up by the hangman's assistants. After the completed branding Rich threw himself over Naylor, stroked his hair, kissed his hands, and endeavoured to suck the fire from the burnt wound; others pushed forward in order to kiss his hands or feet—in short, he was still the divine messenger. Moreover, during the mocking ride through Bristol Rich and other Quakers rode in front of Naylor and sang hymns which had reference to Christ.

There is no need to deny the religious character of this ecstatic outbreak—religion, and above all, *this* religion, provided an outlet for the tension caused by the proceedings on the political stage. We are dealing with the period when Cromwell's despotic power was at its zenith. Monarchical risings had been suppressed, and had afforded an occasion for having the country administered by military Deputies, viz., the *Major-Generals*. Shortly after their appointment Naylor's procession to Bristol took place. Was it meant to be the prelude to a revolt, or was it intended as a counter-demonstration? We can scarcely imagine that Naylor and his friends, nearly all of whom were recruited from among the most advanced elements of the political world, were indifferent to passing events, and it is still more difficult to conceive that Parliament should have devoted weeks and months to this affair unless they suspected that some movement hostile to the existing order of things was hidden beneath the religious cloak. In this respect the express prohibition in the sentence of the use of the pen by Naylor during his imprisonment is very significant.[1]

[1] In a speech made by Cromwell in the spring of 1657 on a constitutional reform under discussion, we find a passage which, if not exclusively aimed at the Quaker doctrines as being, both politically *and* religiously, hostile to the State, at any rate includes them in this category. The passage (which is contained in the address described by Carlyle as Speech 13) speaks

Such a prohibition, and so appalling a punishment, would not be pronounced against a man who is considered insane. We may mention that Quakers subsequently endeavoured to explain Naylor's ride to Bristol as being an act of temporary mental derangement, and other authors also speak of him simply as a madman. But Naylor's writings and letters show no trace of mental aberration. Moreover, Ellwood states that Naylor, even after his discharge from solitary confinement (which certainly was not calculated to cure mental aberration), showed himself a debater of the first order. "James Naylor interposing", he writes of a debate which took place in 1659, "handled the subject with so much perspicuity and clear demonstration that his reasoning seemed to be irresistible." Contemporary Quakers treated Naylor's case as one of passing spiritual intoxication, and in fact his madness did not amount to more than this. How many of the followers shared this infatuation we will not stop to examine.

A further circumstance typical of the general situation is that even before Naylor's affair had quite disappeared from the orders of the day this Parliament addressed itself to the second question which dominated the session, that is, the constitutional change which aimed at creating a new Peers' Chamber and conferring the regal dignity on Cromwell. It is true that in the meantime Sindercomb's plot had been discovered. It was only in deference to the Army, in which the republican, or perhaps the anti-monarchical, spirit still predominated, that Cromwell was constrained to decline the

ironically of some hundreds of "friends", who with *their* friends—the "Fifth Monarchy" men—proposed to override all legitimate powers and threatened all civil and religious interests. Cromwell intended to expose both sides of this movement, but got entangled at once, speaking of the religious when he proposed to speak of the temporal aspect, and vice versa. It is just because the two sides of the question cannot be kept apart, because the movements themselves sometimes present one and sometimes the other phase. But in the constitutional reform project the number of those declared to be *ineligible* includes, in addition to atheists, revilers of religion, etc., *all those who deny the divine institution of sacraments and priesthood.*

crown. Otherwise he might have safely accepted it. The great majority of citizens were apathetic, and longed for peace. A firmly established government, which could promise to satisfy this longing, was certain of the approval of these classes. Many of the aristocrats and gentry and municipal corporations, formerly hostile to Cromwell, now went over to his side in ever increasing numbers, as he represented the cause of *order*, while the bulk of peasants and petty citizens were indifferent about the form of government. No one cared any longer to risk his skin for the cause of Charles Stuart, nor would anyone have cared to risk it for the preservation of the republic save a handful of enthusiasts. These were not dangerous in civil life, but in the Army they, and the schemers who relied on their support, could not be ignored.[1]

In the person of Naylor, who was discharged from prison in 1659, and died soon after, in 1660, the extreme political section among the Quakers lost its principal representative. There is evidence that this section did not disappear all at once, but that it continued to exist for a considerable time. It tended more and more to be supplanted by Fox's supporters. While Naylor's resistance was broken in prison, the spirit of rebellion among the "friends" outside was likewise crushed. From 1656 to 1658 no less than three thousand Quakers were imprisoned for longer or shorter periods—let us pause a moment to consider what this meant to so young a movement. It was bound to divert all its energy in one distinct direction, and in view of the apparent futility of all political endeavours, this could only be the ethic-religious direction. In 1659 the political tendency flared up for the last time in the petition already referred to "for the good old cause of the Commonwealth",

[1] Hence the great disappointment of Sexby, the Leveller, when Cromwell declined the crown. Colonel Titus wrote to Ed. Hyde, on May 23, 1657, that Sexby was quite altered and melancholy thereat. (Cf. *Calendar of Clarendon State Papers*, vol. iii.) Sexby knew that the only power which might possibly have been capable of supplying the elements required for Cromwell's removal was the Army.

but after the Restoration the Quakers became so non-political as to be the only non-Catholic sect which approved of the toleration manifesto issued by James II in favour of the Catholics.

But they still had to suffer many persecutions under Charles II. The insurrection of the adherents of the "Fifth Monarchy" in January 1661 (Venner and his associates) once more caused all extreme sectarians to be suspected of political intrigues. All subjects were ordered to take an oath of loyalty, and as Quakers refused to take any oath, they also declined to take this, and thereby incurred one punishment after the other.

Notwithstanding all this, they continued to increase. At the time of the Great Plague (1665) their number, in London alone, must have amounted to at least ten thousand, and although, being chiefly recruited from the lower classes, they would probably have had the very highest death-rate, besides having at all times a large percentage of emigrants to record, their number went on steadily increasing up to about the year 1680. But from the moment when they enjoyed full official recognition as a religious community, their numbers began to decline, at first slowly, but later on at an ever increasing rate. At the present moment, at least in Europe, they may be said to be dying out. Among all the more important religious communities of the epoch of the Revolution, none has so bravely borne persecutions as the Quakers. While Baptists and Independents temporized, the Quakers practised passive resistance in such a manner as to have, we may well say, tired and worn out their persecutors. But to none of those Churches of the Revolution has the toleration obtained, and the equality of rights subsequently gained, proved so fatal as to the Quakers.

3. The Economic and Social Aspects of Quakerism

We have already mentioned that the Quakers proceeded at a very early date to organize a system for the relief of the persecuted among them. But as their communities became more compact, this form of relief tended to be supplemented by the relief of poor and incapacitated members. We need scarcely add that this institution became a source of great anxiety and much unpleasantness to the community, but no doubt many will be surprised, at first, to hear that it was just on this account that the number of their poorer members decreased most. Nevertheless, on closer examination this seems feasible enough.

Even during the period of persecutions people were tempted to enrol as "friends" simply in order to obtain relief fraudulently, that is to say, to live at the expense of the enthusiasm and devotion of others. But these were isolated instances which could be easily controlled. But as persecution slackened and it became less dangerous to be a Quaker, there was greater temptation to obtain, as a Friend, assistance, which was far more liberal than the public poor relief. In this way the Quaker communities were at a very early date confronted with an actual problem of the poor, and it is interesting to read in Barclay the younger what was done in order to cope with the difficulties encountered in this respect. The problem was not solved with the raising and distribution of relief funds, but involved settling principles of distribution, exercising some control as to the merits of the recipient, and providing a check against lazy and false brethren. What had been gladly offered, under the pressure of persecutions, as an act of charity, now that the pressure had ceased, was in many cases simply felt as an imposed duty, or else a less lenient view was taken of the matter because it was seen that the relief frequently demoralized rather than afforded actual help. In addition to this, questions of jurisdiction arose, as to whether a community should immediately be liable to relieve a newly arrived member, or whether this duty should not devolve upon the community to which he had hitherto belonged. As early as in 1693 we find mentioned, in the report of the national annual meeting, how many poor "friends" had migrated from the country to London and became there a burden to the community. In 1710 a complete poor

law system was created for the members of the association of
"friends". Regulations were made as to domicile for purposes
of relief, and new arrivals were scrutinized with somewhat
more critical eyes. Meanwhile, however, the society itself
became more respectable. Its austere manners and sobriety,
the still close cohesion of its members, explained why the
Quakers developed into very successful men of business. This
was observed to be a characteristic feature of the Lollards.
Asceticism is a commercial virtue, and was particularly so before the rise of the wholesale industry, in social conditions,
where new fortunes were in fact very frequently made by saving.

In a polemical pamphlet published about the end of the
seventeenth century against Quakerism, entitled *The Snake
in the Grass*, we read: "For tho' the Quakers, at first left
their houses and Families, to run about and Preach: and
cry'd down Riches when they had none; yet since that time,
they have Grip'd Mammon, as hard as any of their neighbours, and now call Riches a Gift and Blessing from God."[1]

The same thing is enunciated in other words in a letter
published in 1699 from the pen of William Edmundson, the
Quaker. "And as our number increased it happened that such
a spirit came in amongst us as was amongst the Jews when
they came out of Egypt, and this began to look back into the
world, and traded with the credit which was not of its own
purchasing, and striving to be great in the riches and possessions
of this world." Luxury had developed, people had built
themselves fine houses, were wearing fine clothes, had begun
to enjoy luscious and abundant meals, and were most "un-

[1] *The Snake in the Grass*, 2nd Edition, 1697, pref., p. 16, by J. Leslie. In
the *Anti-Jacobin* of September 1798 is a vehement onslaught on the Quakers
based on Leslie's book. Both the book and the article are full of misrepre-
sentations, but some of the facts they adduce in order to prove the inconsistencies of Quaker theories and Quaker practices are undeniable, except
that these inconsistencies were the natural result of the contradiction
between the actual conditions of society and the type of society the Quaker
doctrine presupposes, and not of a particular hypocritical turn of mind in the
Quaker.

comely" smoking tobacco.[1] But even in other respects the comparison with the Jews is by no means inapposite, and is a pretty example of how, in the course of history, movements will always develop differently, and often in a diametrically opposite way, to what their originators had planned. Even Barclay the elder still represents Quakerism as being primarily a reaction against the "Judaizing" spirit of the Puritans then in power. But their principles, copied from primitive Christianity, forbade them the cultivation of fine arts, and their early traditions even caused the great bulk of them to be indifferent to sciences. They were precluded from occupying public offices by their objection to taking oaths; they were obliged to forgo all chance of lucrative Government offices, livings, etc., while drinking and sports were strictly prohibited to them; hence it was almost unavoidable that they should direct their whole energy towards money-making pursuits, and notwithstanding their ethical principles[2] become as dangerous commercial rivals as were the Jews. In the seventeenth and eighteenth centuries Quakers played a rôle in agriculture too, some being pioneers of modern agriculture,[3] but after 1760 the refusal to pay tithes was made obligatory among the Friends, and hence there remained for the farmers and yeomen among them no alternative but to emigrate, to move to town and engage in trade, or else to leave the community of Friends. Some did the first and some the latter, and then the agricultural Quaker disappeared in England.

[1] From J. S. Rowntree, *Quakerism, Past and Present: an Inquiry into the Causes of its Decline,* London, 1859.
[2] Thus the Quakers are credited with having been mainly instrumental in bringing about the system of fixed prices in trade. Early in the eighteenth century the Friends in their annual meetings were exhorted to ensure genuineness and fair quality of manufactures and to discountenance adulteration of goods. As at that time they were very strong in Ireland, this injunction is said to have greatly benefited the Irish linen industry. Many subsequent State enactments had been anticipated by the Quakers. Thus as early as in 1705 a resolution of the annual conference of the Friends prohibited them from catching salmon or trout during the spawning season.
[3] Thorold Rogers, loc. cit., p. 85.

On the other hand, the list of famous English Quakers includes many eminent bankers, one of the greatest of whom was Gurney, whose bankruptcy in 1866 made a world-wide stir.

With their increasing commercial success the Quakers acquired another Jewish characteristic, the incapacity or loss of inclination to make proselytes.

These developments were of course only in germ during the period with which we are dealing, but the movement had already begun to lose its proletarian character. More caution was observed in admitting working men, and the working men received into the community, or at least the children of such working men, would generally soon cease to be proletarians.

The children received in the Quakers' schools, or through the school funds of the Quakers, a better education than the average of working men's children, as well as better advancement afterwards, and would then attain to a good "bourgeois" position. Early in the eighteenth century the peasant and wage-earning element still predominated, to such an extent that the Friends made an attempt to establish employment registries. But although working-class members of the Quaker sect might improve their economic situation, and were enabled to bring up their children to a social position superior to their own, Quakerism, by virtue of its asceticism, its political passiveness, and its general quietism, lost its attraction for those working men in whom the commercial spirit had not taken sufficient root. Moreover, as Rowntree points out, the generous relief system of the Quakers prevented the spread of Quakerism among working men, who were reluctant to join, lest they might be suspected of being animated by mercenary motives.[1]

[1] Concerning the Quakers' relief system, Sir Fr. Eden wrote about the end of the eighteenth century: "The particular economy and good organization to be found with the Quakers deserves general imitation" (*The State of the Poor*, vol. i. p. 588). A very sympathetic but not uncritical description of the features of Quakerism is given in the book, *A Portraiture of the Christian Profession and Practice of the Society of Friends*, by Thomas Clarkson,

In short, the proletarian Quaker was overtaken by almost the same fate as the agrarian Quaker. He has not yet quite disappeared, but has become a *rara avis*. According to Rowntree's calculation, the Friends, during the first half of last century, had not a third of the average number of poor and indigent members which, according to the ratio of their total number to the entire population, they should have had. The number of their rich members, on the other hand, would be considerably more than three times in excess of the average.

Why Quakerism was subsequently unable to make any more proselytes among the prosperous classes scarcely requires explanation. It required an enthusiasm, such as Quakerism of itself was no longer able to evoke, in order to induce a member of the bourgeois classes to join a community with such peculiar customs as were maintained by the Quakers as late as the present century. Its religious principles had lost their significance above all to the modern bourgeois. What is the use, to him, of a religion which is neither the established one of the State, nor a creed which has any influence on the masses, which has neither fine churches nor any distinguished or highly gifted preachers, which is not rationalistic enough for the "cultured" spirit of our times nor symbolic enough to fascinate the surfeited mind? In short, Quakerism to-day vegetates simply as a survival from former days. But although Quakerism since the end of the seventeenth century has been steadily decreasing in membership, it still exerted a great influence in the eighteenth and in the early part of the nineteenth century—not as a political, but as a *philanthropic* movement, and the philanthropic movement was certainly useful at a time when industrial capitalism, then in its youthful vigour, was ruthlessly exploiting a working class not yet strong enough to offer an organized resist-

the famous crusader against negro slavery. One chapter (the thirteenth) of the book deals very judiciously with the question how far the Quakers are really to be blamed for their "money-getting spirit".

ance. We find Quakers taking a prominent part in all great reform movements of the eighteenth century. Both in England and America they were the pioneers and the most indefatigable champions of the anti-slavery movement; they were in the forefront of the movements for the reform of the penal code and prison reform. Eminent protagonists of science and education, and subsequently also of political reform, issued from their ranks. We meet with Quakers in the Chartist movement, belonging, conformably to their doctrines, to the "moral force" section, yet labouring assiduously for the cause, and we also find Quakers among the Owenites.

When in 1809 Robert Owen was in danger of having to abandon his scheme for the benefit of the working people of New Lanark because his partners demanded this sacrifice in the interest of their profit, it was (apart from Jeremy Bentham) none but Quakers and sons of Quakers who provided the capital for the continuation of his reforms. One of them, William Allen, caused Owen much trouble, mainly, however, on account of religious differences. Of his other associates from the ranks of the Friends, and more especially of a certain John Walker, who had invested £30,000 in the concern, Owen speaks in his autobiography in terms of highest acknowledgment. And a circumstance which is worth mentioning is the fact that *before* Owen went to New Lanark, two young Quakers with whom he was intimate in Manchester greatly influenced his intellectual development. One of these, who subsequently achieved great fame in the scientific world, was the chemist, John Dalton. It is a peculiar coincidence that Owen's other fellow-student (who was then twenty-one years of age) at Manchester College, described by Owen himself as "his intimate friend",[1] was a Quaker, and bore the name of Winstanley—the same name as that of the most pronounced

[1] See *Life, etc.*, p. 36. Owen tells us there that he had, with Dalton and Winstanley, "much and frequent interesting discussion upon religion, morals, and other similar subjects", and that "occasionally we admitted a friend or two to join our circle, but this was considered a favour".

communist of the Cromwellian era. It is not altogether unlikely that he may have been a descendant of the "True
Leveller" Winstanley, who was, as we know, a Lancashire
man.

But between Gerrard Winstanley and Owen there is, as
we have already mentioned, another Quaker, John Bellers.

CHAPTER XVII

JOHN BELLERS, CHAMPION OF THE POOR AND ADVOCATE OF A LEAGUE OF NATIONS

1. THE COLLEGE OF INDUSTRY

ALL historians who have dealt with the social conditions of England in the seventeenth century agree that the situation of the poorer classes, more especially that of the agricultural labourers, from the end of the Commonwealth in 1660 to the close of the century was invariably bad. The legislation enacted by the restored monarchy, as far as it concerned the economic life of the nation, was throughout class legislation in favour of the great landlords, and the "revolution" of 1688 only changed this in so far as it admitted the commercial classes to a greater share in the government of the country. The landed class ruled as the representatives of their own *and* the commercial interests. As far as the working classes were concerned, this meant a change for the worse in their situation for a long time to come. Any neglect under the Stuart dynasty to promote the interests of the possessing classes was now remedied. The enactments before referred to for the benefit of the landlords, under Charles II, had been supplemented in 1677 by an Act which declared all tenantships to be short-term leases, in default of the production of tenancy agreements to the contrary effect. Such agreements, however, could not be produced in the great majority of cases, partly because no such deeds had ever reached the hands of the farmers, and partly because the tenure was based on relations passed on from father to son since the feudal times. In such cases, and frequently enough in others, small freeholders and farmers were unable to assert their freehold or leasehold rights at law. Thus the way was prepared for a transformation of agrarian conditions, under which small farmers could have managed to subsist, into such as

compelled them either to toil like serfs or else make room
for a capitalist tenant. To make up for this, in addition to
the import duties on corn, export bounties were fixed lest
improved cultivation should bring about a greater reduction
in the price of corn. The situation of small holders and agricultural labourers was further worsened by the enclosure or
monopolizing of forests, marsh lands, and heaths by the landlords. Formerly farmers and agricultural labourers were able
to supply their wants to a great extent by shooting or snaring
game, or to add to their income by the sale of game; this, too,
was gradually prohibited from the time of James I, one of the
reasons given being that poaching promoted idleness, which
meant that it prevented the labourers working for the land-
owner.

The commercial growth and the expanding incomes of
the proprietary classes, of which the economists in the latter
part of the seventeenth century, such as Sir William Petty,
Josiah Child, and others, write with rapture,[1] brought slender
benefits to a very small section of the working classes, while
the situation of the great bulk of them changed for the worse.
For while profits and prices went up enormously, wages were
kept down by judicial assessments. Even if we knew nothing
of this from the documents extant, this one fact would speak
volumes, that the weekly pay of the private soldier, who,
under Cromwell's Commonwealth received 7s. 6d., in 1685
was 4s. 8d. only.[2] The fact that men were willing to enlist
at this rate of pay shows that the general condition of the
workers must have considerably deteriorated. Wages remained
so low that in the country and in domestic industry they had,

---

[1] Child states, among other things, that in 1688 there were more people
represented at the London Exchange with a fortune or income of £10,000
than there were in 1651 with fortunes of £1,000 and over, so that a dowry
of £2,000 in those cases was not thought of so much as sixty years earlier
one of £500 would have been.
[2] Macaulay's *History of England, etc.*, vol. i. chap. 3. Macaulay at the
same time quotes many instances of the low rate of wages in those days.
The weavers' wages in Norwich fell to 6d. a day.

in most cases, to be supplemented by grants from the poor fund. The poor rates assumed colossal proportions, amounting to over one-third of the whole Government budget. Charles Davenant estimates the number of poor and beggars in 1696 at nearly one-fourth of the whole population; it is not surprising that everybody was debating how to remedy this state of things. An entire literature on the problem of the poor and poor relief sprang up.[1]

In all these essays we may trace two fundamentally different views, although they are not always clearly expressed. One view is concerned, in the interest of the comfortable classes, with finding means of getting rid of the "pauper plague", while the other aims at raising the poor for their own sakes, and seeks to discover a better organization of society. Andrew Tarranton may be taken as a typical representative of the first view, while the more humanitarian outlook is best represented by John Bellers the Quaker.[2]

John Bellers was born in 1654 of well-to-do parents. Himself a Quaker, he married a Quakeress, as was almost obligatory by the matrimonial traditions of the Friends, and through this marriage became "Lord of the Manor" of Coln Aldwyns in Gloucestershire. Precluded from a political career by belonging to a sect which, at that time, was still ostracized in this respect, he occupied himself with all kinds of studies and philanthropical undertakings. Among his friends was William Penn, the famous founder of Pennsylvania, as well as John Sloane, the physician and philosopher, whose great institu-

---

[1] A bibliography of this as well as of the literature of the problem in general up to the end of the eighteenth century is given by Sir Fr. Eden, *The State of the Poor*, 1799.

[2] We say best, as Bellers does not stand alone with this opinion. He simply summarized the ideas of an entire generation of philanthropic authors and placed them on a more solid basis. Even William Petty, whom we cannot count among these, writes in favour of the unemployed, "rather burn the work of a thousand people than let this thousand lose, through non-employment, their capability for work". And again: "There need no beggars in countries where there are many acres of unimproved improvable land to every head, as there are in England" (*Essays on Mankind*, vol. i.).

tion laid the foundation for the establishment of the British Museum. Although not of a very strong constitution, and frequently indisposed, he attained the age of seventy-one years. He died in 1725, one of the best men of his time, and as Marx writes concerning him, "a veritable phenomenon in the history of political economy".

The first of the publications before us from the pen of Bellers dates from 1695, one of the seven consecutive years of distress, the notorious "seven lean years", which befell the English working community at the end of the seventeenth century, and which depressed the purchasing power of work-men's wages to an extraordinarily low level. *Proposals for Raising a College of Industry of All Useful Trades and Husbandry* is the title of Bellers' essay, but as a matter of fact, what Bellers has in view is a labour colony or association. He declares in his essay in two places why he has selected the name of College of Industry.[1]

On page 11 he says he would rather call it a College than a Workhouse, because it is a more pleasing name, and, moreover, because all kinds of useful instruction can be imparted there; and in the concluding chapter, when discussing the objections that might be raised against his plan, he says that "Workhouse" savoured too much of the "Bridewell". Nor was the name "community" considered suitable, because everything was not to be in common. College, on the other hand, suggested the idea of a voluntary sojourn. Bellers is fully conscious of the hybrid character of his proposal, and clearly indicates that considerations of a purely practical nature prevented him from going further. With truly Quaker-like ingenuousness, in which, however, his opinions reveal themselves enlivened

---

[1] The full title runs as follows: "Proposals for Raising a Colledge of In-dustry of all usefull Trades and Husbandry with Profit for the Rich, a plentiful living for the Poor and a good education for Youth, which will be advantage to the government by the Increase of the People and their Riches. Motto: Industry brings Plenty.—The Sluggard shall be cloathed with Raggs. He that will not work shall not eat."

with a certain waggish humour which occasionally recurs in his writings, he answers the question as to why the poor, that is to say the working men, are not to have all the profit of the college, by giving the following reason: "Because the Rich have no other way of living but by the Labour of others; as the Landlord by the Labour of his Tenants, and the Merchants and Tradesmen by the Labour of the Mechanicks." However, he advances other reasons, besides this concession to the rich, why the college should yield a profit. In order to set it to work on a sufficiently large scale much money is required, and "a thousand Pound is easier raised where there is Profit, than one hundred Pound only upon Charity". Besides, the more money is put into an undertaking the more guarantee is offered that people will see to its being properly worked so that the interest therein may not be diminished. But the college is not meant to be a benevolent institution, for the additional reason that the working man, when he enters it, shall have a *right* to it. A comfortable life at the college is to be "the rich man's *debt* to the industrious labourer, and *not their Charity* to them". Only the surplus which is left beyond the yieldings required for this purpose is to go to the capital of the association.

Bellers estimates this capital, for a colony of three hundred able-bodied persons, at £15,000, provided that the ground is not leasehold but freehold, the latter being decidedly preferable. (The calculation is £10,000 for the ground, £2,000 for live and other stock, £3,000 for installations, tools, etc., for the industrial workmen.) The minimum contribution shall be £25; every £50 shall entitle to one vote in the Administrative Council, but no one, however much he may invest, shall have more than five votes.

The working population of the college is divided by Bellers, with regard to its Budget, as follows:

Forty-four industrial workmen (mechanics, etc.), including one manager and one deputy-manager.

Eighty-two women and girls, who are to do household work of all kinds (including spinning, etc.), as well as dairy work.

Twenty-four field and other labourers (men and boys), including one manager and his wife.

Altogether, one hundred and fifty persons whose labour supplies all the requirements of the college.

Another ten men will supply, by the produce of their labour, the requirements of fuel, iron, etc., the labour of five more would supply the rent of the buildings, and that of thirty-five more (if required) the rent for the ground. If no rent is to be paid, the produce of the work of these latter would be added to that of the other hundred workers, constituting the surplus shown by the enterprise. But even if the ground was held on lease only, the surplus, assuming the value of the yearly produce per man at £10 per annum, would amount to $100 \times 10 = £1,000$. However, Bellers estimates the average of productive capacity at £15 for each worker.

Bellers states that he has arrived at this estimate of the surplus of production, which corresponds to a rate of surplus value equal to $300 : 135 = 45$ per cent., "from a view of the Nation, where I suppose not above Two Thirds, if one Half of the Nation are useful workers; and yet all have a living". Furthermore, the college offers a number of economic advantages. It would save the cost of shops, the maintenance of middlemen and other useless trades, lawyers' fees, bad debts, etc.; there would be a reduction in the cost of dwellings, heating, cooking, and food to be bought. Many women and children would be productive workers, and loss of time through periodical want of employment could be avoided. In addition to this, the college would reap the benefit of a combination of industry and agriculture. The fields falling to the share of the industrial population would be better cultivated than the allotments of mechanics would otherwise be, because more cattle would be kept at the college, and hence more manure would be available, and altogether a more economical mode of working

would be possible. A further advantage would be afforded
by the fact that at harvest time not only the actual field
labourers, but also mechanics and others might assist, and
altogether the available forces might be distributed as required.

Besides abolishing the middleman and avoiding the loss
entailed by the separation of agriculture and manufacture (a
subject to which Bellers reverts in another place), the elimina-
tion of speculation would be an advantage to the college.
The greater part of the production of the members is destined
for their own consumption, and whatever is not consumed by
them would, as far as possible, be employed for stock and for
the expansion and development of the enterprise. The profit
is to be ascertained annually and credited to the shareholders
according to their investments. It might be drawn out or
added to the "principal" as desired, but no kind of stock-
jobbing to be allowed with the shares because this "will ruin
any good thing". If any member desires to sell his share, the
other shareholders should have the right of appointing a purchaser, who would then enjoy the rights of his predecessor.
In no case would any surplus arise until all the requirements
of the workers at the college had been amply provided for in
every respect. Contrary to what obtains outside in ordinary
life, where "the Tradesmen are endeavouring to get one from
another what they can; so they are all *straining the necessity
of the Mechanick*, not regarding how little he gets, but to get
as much as they can for themselves".

At the college the workers, as long as they were in the prime
of their life, should observe the general hours of work, but
"as they grow in years in the college, they may be allowed to
abate an Hour in a Day of their Work, and when come to
Sixty years old (if Merit prefer them not sooner) they may be
made Overseers; wh. for ease and pleasant life, will equal
what the Hoards of a private purse can give".[1] The rules of

[1] Compare with this and other proposals those of Winstanley in Chapter
VIII.

work should be based on the rules in force for the time being with the best situated "prentices" in London.

Further notable institutions of the college are:

The managers and other officials (overseers) of the college, like the actual workmen, shall be paid in kind, not cash.

The dwelling-house of the college shall consist of four wings: one for the married people; one for single young men and boys; one for single women and girls; and one for sick and invalid members. At meals, which are to be taken together, the young people, boys and girls, are to wait alternately.

The workrooms are also to be divided. The young men at the college shall be apprenticed up to the twenty-fourth, and girls up to the twenty-first year; they may then leave the college if they like, or may marry.

At first great care shall be taken to engage a number of trustworthy workers who are likely to set a good example; the others may at first consist of apprentices. They must begin with young people. "Old people", he says in the Introduction, "are like earthen vessels, not so easily to be new moulded, yet children are more like clay out of the Pit, and easy to take any form they are put into." Hence if the poor should perchance at first "prove brittle", the rich who had found the money for the college should not lose patience. "Seven or fourteen years may bring up young ones that Life will be more natural to."

Great value is to be attached to education, not only as to the "what" but also as to the "how" thereof. It shall combine work with instruction, and endeavour to act more by object-lessons than by theory, more by practice and experience than by rote learning. And what children read for instruction they had better read together. "Children reading and discoursing one to another, gives a deeper impression than reading to themselves, we remembering a man's voice longer than his face." Well-to-do people may become boarders at the college

at certain fixed contributions, and on condition of orderly
conduct. Similarly the college would afford board and education to children of well-to-do people for payment, and to
these, too, the combination of work and instruction would be
of the utmost advantage. "Seeing others work, at spare times
instead of Playing, w^d be learning some trade, work not
being more Labour than Play; and seeing others work, to
imitate them w^d be as much diversion to the children as
Play." The development of bodily strength and skill is as
important for the rich as for the poor, for the learned as for
the mechanic. Work and learning must go hand in hand, for
*"an Idle Learning being little better than the learning of Idle-
ness"*. . . . "Labour it's a primitive institution of God. . . .
Labour being as proper for the body's health as eating is for
its living; for what gains a man saves by Ease, he will find in
Disease. . . . Labour adds Oyl to the Lamp of Life when
thinking Inflames it. . . . Men will grow stronger with working." . . . And the work is to be on a definite plan, not mere
tiring out of the body. "A Childish silly employ leaves their
minds silly."[1]

Of course the college is to have a proper library. Also a
"physick-garden", laboratories for the preparation of medicine,
and the like.

In calculating the working strength of the college, the number of three hundred was only selected for the purpose of more
clearly illustrating the proportion of necessary and surplus
work. The college, however, might be considerably larger; it
might number three thousand members, especially in districts
where staple products are manufactured. Nor need it be confined to the trades enumerated. Even seafaring men might

[1] The above sentences are quoted by Marx in *Capital*, vol. i. He adds that
"as early as at the end of the seventeenth century Bellers conceived with
fullest clearness the necessity of the abolition of the present mode of education and division of labour which generate hypertrophy and atrophy in the
two extremes of society, although in opposite directions", and it is certainly
no exaggeration to say that Bellers' proposals contain the germs of the best
principles of modern pedagogy.

join it and enjoy its advantages, provided that they undertook to endow it with their goods or the value thereof.[1] In short, it should be "an epitome of the world".

"A College thus constituted cannot so easily be undone as single men, whatever changes comes (except the People are destroyed), for if plundered, Twelve months time will recruit again; Like the Grass new mowed, the next year supplies again; Labour bringing a supply as the Ground doth; and when together, they assist one another; but when scattered are useless, if not preying upon one another."

The first edition of the *Proposals* was dedicated by Bellers to his co-religionists, the "Children of Light named in scorn Quakers". "The consideration of your great Industry and diligence in all affairs of this Life, your great charity in relieving your own Poor, and others also, as occasions offer, your great Morality acknowledged by all, and your religious Sincerity known to the Lord; Hath induced me to Dedicate these following Proposals to your serious Consideration, whilst I think you a very regular Body, willing and capable of such an Undertaking. . . . I often having thought of the misery of the Poor of this Nation, and at the same time have reckoned them the Treasure of it, the Labour of the Poor being the mines of the Rich, and beyond all that Spain is Master of; and many thoughts have run through me how then it comes that the Poor sh^d be such a Burthen and so miserable, and from it might be prevented; whilst I think it as much more charity to put the Poor in a way to live by honest Labour, than to maintain them idle, as it w^d be to set a man's broken leg, that he might go himself, rather than always to carry him." The dedication is followed by an introductory disquisition in which the leading economic ideas of Bellers are developed.

It commences as follows: "It's the interest of the rich to

[1] In the second edition of the *Proposals* we read: "As also at the sea coast may be raised several colleges as nurseries to the most effectual and successful fishery."

take care of the poor and their education, by wh. they will
take care of their own heirs."

But Bellers knew that by stressing the need of provision
for future generations he would gain but little sympathy from
the rich for his proposals, and hence he was careful to promise
them an immediate advantage, namely the profits of the
college. He held that a profitable enterprise would attract
money, last longer, and do most good. What sap is to a tree,
profit is to a business; it stimulates its growth and keeps it in
vigour. We see that Bellers was by no means a dreamer. He
recognized with a keen eye the spirit of his time, and in this
respect is even ahead of the thinkers of his period.

He observes that out of consideration for their profits the
rich would find it advisable to provide for the poor.[1]

"For if one had a hundred thousand acres of Land, and
as many pounds in money, and as many cattle without a
Labourer, what w^d the rich man be but a Labourer. And
as the Labourers make men rich, so the more Labourers,
there will be the more rich men (where there is land to employ
and provide for them)." The rich therefore had an interest
in seeing that honest workers married as soon as they had
come to mature age.[2]

"For is it not strange to consider how industrious the world
is, to raise corn and cattle, wh. only serves men, and how
negligent of (or rather careful to hinder) the increase of
men?" "The increase of the Poor is no burthen, but advantage,
because the conveniencies increase with them", he writes a
hundred years before Malthus.

The mercantile system which in the seventeenth century
was represented in England by Thomas Mun, Josiah Child,
Charles Davenant, and others with more or less ability, was
partly a reaction from the preceding monetary system. A cardinal

[1] Poor is always used as meaning all those who depend on their work or on
charity for their living.
[2] P. 2.

principle of this system was the prohibition of exports of gold
and silver, or, more properly speaking, it was the theoretical
expression of a practice perfectly normal in a state of society
which produced mainly for direct consumption, that is, the
feudal system. According to this system, foreign trade consists
almost exclusively in the exchange of surplus home production
for foreign products. Simultaneously with the decay of the
feudal units of production and with the rise of the monetary
system, foreign trade lost the characteristics of primitive
barter and became increasingly differentiated in independent
purchases and sales. Consequently the prohibition of the
exportation of money was felt to be a serious inconvenience, and
the champions of foreign trade combated this prohibition by
arguing that the main point was not the separate transaction
but the final result: who laughs last—that is to say, who makes
a surplus in the end—laughs best. Applying this to the whole
country, the main thing was that its trade with other nations
should in the end show a balance in its own favour (the theory
of the balance of trade), in this case any money exported would
return with interest and compound interest, as the corn, cast out
in seed-time, is returned many times over in the harvest.[1]

It may be contended that this theory was based upon a
greater reverence for money than the monetary system which
it combated. But in arguing against the monetary system, or
the monetary policy, it emphasized the importance of *production*, of *labour*, in obtaining a favourable balance of trade,
and enunciated a system of Protection designed to stimulate
production and develop manufactures. In thus stressing productive *labour* as the source of wealth it prepared, at the same
time, the way for a new school of thought which strove to be
emancipated from money. In 1662 Sir W. Petty ascribed the
value of commodities to the labour embodied in them, and in
the person of Bellers we encounter the first socialist who tried

[1] This simile is used by Th. Mun in his publication, *England's Treasure
by Foreign Trade*.

to put this idea into practice, that is to say, to justify the antagonism to money which he shares with all communists.

"This College-Fellowship will make *Labour*, and *not money*
the *Standard to value all Necessaries by*; and tho' money hath
its Conveniencies, in the common way of living, it being a
pledge among men for want of credit; yet not without its
mischiefs; and call'd by our Saviour *The Mammon of Unrighteousness*; most Cheats and robberies w^d go but slowly
on, if it were not for money: And when People have their whole
dependence of Trading by Money, if that fails or is corrupted,
they are next door to ruine; and *the Poor stand still, because
the Rich have no money to employ them, tho' they have the
same Land and Hands to provide Victuals and Cloaths, as ever
they had*; wh. is the true riches of a nation, and not the money
in it, except we may reckon beads and pin-dust so, because
we have Gold at *Guiney* for them."[1] Money is a "crutch"
which a country, in a sound condition, does not require any
more than a healthy body requires a crutch.

"Whereas often now the Husbandman and Mechanicks
both are ruined, tho' the first have a great crop, and the second
industriously maketh much manufacture; money and not
Labour being made the Standard, the Husbandman paying
the same Rent and Wages, as when his crop yielded double
the Price; it being no better with the mechanicks, where
it's not who wants his commodity, but who can give him
money for it (will keep him) and so often he must take half
the value in money, another c^d give him in Labour that hath
no money."[2]

In conclusion, Bellers traverses a number of objections
which might be raised against his proposal. We quote those of
his answers which throw most light on his trend of thought.

To the objection of the *difficulty* of the undertaking, Bellers
answers that what would be impossible of an individual would
be quite possible for a number working together. And he gives

[1] P. 3.   [2] Pp. 12, 13.

the example quoted by Marx in *Capital*, vol. i.: "As one man cannot, and ten men must strain, to lift a tun weight, yet one hundred men can do it only by the strength of a finger of each of them."

Scarcity or Famine was not to be feared in the college, since there would be no temptation to waste their stores in order to heap up money. "And there hath seldom been any years of Scarcity, but years of Plenty have been first."[1]

But would the more highly paid workmen join the college which only offered them a mere subsistence? To this he replies that the college offers far more than this, since it relieves them of anxiety concerning their children, cases of sickness, etc.[2] Extra pay might moreover be granted for performances beyond a certain average standard. However, not all poor people would be so foolish as the Spanish beggar-woman who would not let her son accept a situation with an Englishman as he would thereby lose the chance of becoming King of Spain. "For tho' some Poor get estates, how many more become miserable?"

Another point raised is whether people would submit to the confinement of the college.

This confinement need not be an absolute one, no more than "absolutely needful for the good government of the college". And he thinks the "Plenty and Conveniencies in the College will sufficiently allay the hardness of the College rules".

Bellers excuses his proposals as to differences in dress with the remark that these would only correspond to actually existing distinctions. Probably he simply meant to make a concession to the more prosperous elements he desired to

[1] P. 20.

[2] "From being poor they will be made rich, by enjoying all things needful in health or sickness, single or married, wife and children; and if Parents die, their children well educated and preserved from misery, and their marrying incourag'd, which is now generally discourag'd." There is no competition or overreaching to be feared at the college, and all these advantages are purchased by "doing only an easie day's work".

attract. Moreover, the prescription of a uniform clothing would have no doubt been worse still.

But however plausible he made his proposals he does not appear to have found, with the "Children of Light", the support he expected, or at least sufficient support. Possibly this was simply due to lack of means, as the pockets of the members were severely taxed.[1] However this may be, the first edition of Bellers' *Proposals* was followed by a second in the following year, which, instead of being dedicated to the Quakers, was inscribed to the Lords and Commons of Parliament and to the thoughtful and those concerned for the public weal. The former are requested to examine the proposals made in the pamphlet and to carry them out for the benefit of the nation. They were urged to grant any concessions necessary for the establishment of these associations. It was not to be inferred from this that he required a monopoly for his societies; if others tried to put into execution any similar or somewhat modified plans, they should by all means be encouraged therein. The "thoughtful", etc., are requested to deposit subscriptions and contributions for the projected enterprise with two inhabitants of the City mentioned by name, one a merchant and the other a lawyer. For the rest this edition differs little from the first. The working capital required is put at a somewhat higher figure than in the former edition, as the £15,000 for ground, livestock, and working materials is supplemented by £3,000 for buildings. Moreover, the amount of the shares is fixed at a higher rate; and the author also discusses a further objection that might be raised, namely, that the college might engender laziness and monkish habits. Finally, the readers and friends are requested, in a special appeal, to forward com-

[1] At the conclusion of a pamphlet by Bellers published in 1697, and which is specially addressed to the Friends, there is an appeal, signed by about forty-five Quakers, to the Friends, in favour of giving such a college a trial. Among the signatories we find William Penn, Robert Barclay, Th. Ellwood, and John Hodgskin. This pamphlet, *An Epistle to Friends Concerning the Education of Children* (in the sense of the "Proposals") is to be found in the library of the London Central Office of the Quakers.

munications as to available sites that might be suited for the college, etc. The second edition, however, does not contain any fundamental alterations in the plan of the enterprise or the arguments in its favour.

The following additional sentences which it contains, as compared with the first edition, deserve special notice: "I believe the present idle hands of the poor of this nation are able to raise provision and manufactures that w^d bring England as much treasure as the mines do Spain, if send them conveniencies abroad; when that can be thought the nation's interest more than breeding up People with it among ourselves, wh. I think w^d be the greatest improvement of the lands of England that can be; *it being the multitude of people that makes land in Europe more valuable than land in America, or in Holland than Ireland."* The college is a "Civil Fellowship rather than a religious one".

A copy of this edition, as Robert Owen tells us in his autobiography, was accidentally found, about 1817, by Francis Place, the well-known Radical, while sorting out some useless books from his library, and he at once brought it to Owen with the words: "I have made a great discovery—of a work advocating your social views a century and a half ago." Owen asked for the pamphlet, and told Place he would have a thousand copies made of it for distribution, and would acknowledge that the author deserved the credit of being the parent of the idea, "although mine had been forced upon me by the practice of observing facts, reflecting upon them, and trying how far they were useful for the every-day business of life".[1]

Owen kept his word, and thus Bellers became at that time more generally known.

2. BELLERS' ESSAYS AND OTHER WRITINGS

We must suppose that the general public did not evince sufficient interest for Bellers' proposals and that new objections

[1] *Life, etc.*, p. 240.

were raised. Anyhow, in 1699 Bellers published a new pamphlet which, to a great extent, turns upon the views set forth in the *Proposals*. This is the publication entitled *Essays about the Poor, Manufactures, Trade, Plantations and Immorality, and of the Excellency and Divinity of Inward Light*.[1]

The essays are remarkable in many respects and worthy of the best passages of the *Proposals*.

In a dedication addressed to the Houses of Parliament, the pamphlet opens with a reference to the weavers' disturbances in London during the preceding Parliamentary session. If the indigent of any single trade could venture to defy, for a time, the whole of Parliament, what might be expected if a hungry multitude entered the houses of some of the possessing class? The legislators should consider this. The possessing classes might be influenced by fines, the healthy by the infliction of bodily pain; but "what can awe the misery of starving?" This is followed by a short discussion of three questions with reference to establishments for the employment of healthy unemployed. The question as to whether the working of these establishments by the State or by private persons is preferable is answered by Bellers in favour of the latter. He says that the State works expensively and administers badly.[2]

The State should only be left to provide for those totally unable to work. The question as to whether it would be better to select certain specified trades for the employment of the unemployed poor, or whether it would be better to place the poor in individual households, is answered by Bellers with the arguments already known to us in favour of joint house-keeping and of co-ordinating the most various branches of production and employment.

[1] On the front of the title page we read verses 1 to 3 of the 41st Psalm, and on the back page some sentences from William III's Speech from the Throne, from a publication by Chief Justice Sir Matthew Hale and from another by Sir Josiah Child—"as powerful a King, as honoured a judge, and as rich a merchant, as England ever had". All of which passages refer to the necessity of sufficient provision for the poor.

[2] This was at Bellers' time undoubtedly the case.

Bellers then deals with the question, *"How the Poor's Wants will be best answered, and the nation's strength and riches increased."*

He says that the poor suffer from four evils, namely: bad education in their youth, want of regular employment, want of constant sale for the products of their work, and want of sufficient sustenance in return for the work performed. All these evils could be remedied by the colleges or colonies proposed by him. They would at the same time increase the value of the land of the nobility and gentry, populate districts which were then thinly populated, and counteract the congestion in other places. Thus they would, for instance, draw away the excess of population from London, which, containing 10 per cent. of the total population of the country, was decidedly too populous. "The nation can maintain but a number of tradesmen and gentry, in proportion to the number of labourers that are in the nation to work for them."

The first essay is to *"shew that 500 Labourers, Regularly Imploy'd, are capable of Earning £3,000 a year more than will keep them"*.

The demonstration, supported by figures, is introduced with the remark that if productive labour had not from the first produced more than it had cost, the human race would have vanished long ago. "By computation, there is not above two-thirds of the People or Families of England that do raise all necessaries for Themselves, and the rest of the people by their labour; and if the one-third, wh. are not Labourers, did not spend more than the two-thirds wh. are Labourers, one-half of the People or Families Labouring c^d supply all the nation." People might object to his budget that according to it every worker was, on an average, to earn 16d. per day, while in reality at the time many, with the greatest exertion, would scarcely earn 6d. or 8d. This, he says, is quite correct, but it was so just because the other 8d. or 10d. went into the pocket of the ground-owner or dealer. "For it [the product] commonly stands the user in double the price the master had." Again, the great difference between the amount paid to the actual producer—the artisan—and the price of the goods was also due to the bad social organization of production. It "is the great Unhappiness of many of our mechanicks, that they make Commodities when nobody wants them". With a better organization of labour, therefore, more wages could be given and less work could be demanded from the individual, and still the working of the colony would remunerate the investors of capital.

The second essay endeavours to "*shew how 500,000 poor are capable to add 43 millions value to the nation*".

As regards the calculation, the proof relies on the surplus work which the poor are capable of performing and which Bellers "capitalizes" at 5 per cent., as well as on the value imparted by their work to land. More interesting than this antiquated calculation are the propositions brought forward by Bellers in support of his ever-repeated thesis that "the Increase of regular labouring people is the Kingdom's greatest treasure, strength and honour".

"Land, cattle, houses, goods and money are but the carcas of riches, they are dead without people; men being the life and soul of them.

"Double our Labouring People and we shall be capable of having double the noblemen and gentlemen that we have; or their estates will be worth double what they are now: But if it were possible to increase our houses and treasure (and not our people) in such excess, that the poorest man in the Kingdom were worth a million of money. There must be as many of those rich men hewers of wood and drawers of water, plowmen and threshers, as we have of such Labourers now in the Kingdom, or else we sh^d be under Midas' Golden Curse, starve for want of bread, tho' we had our hands fill'd with gold.

"To say foreigners w^d supply us for money. Yes, but it is their labouring people must do it; who also being subjects to foreign princes, may take their turn to come and plunder as well as feed us.

"There are no increasing of rich men, but as poor labourers increase with them; *where there is no servants, there can be no masters.*"

Passing on to the question of the organization of labour, Bellers points, among other things, to the increase of the "necessitous poor" through "the uncertainty of fashion", a subject which he, as a Quaker, had particularly at heart. He points out that in winter many industrial labourers were out of work because dealers and master weavers would not invest any money before they knew what would be the next fashion. In the spring, on the other hand, sufficient hands could not be obtained at short notice. Then large numbers of apprentices and chance helpers were set to work, hands were withdrawn from the plough, and future beggars were introduced in the town.

Passing over a rather interesting digression to the effect that "dear bread will make dear manufactures and ruin trade", in which almost the whole Free-Trade gospel is anticipated, we will turn to Bellers' criticism of trade in general, and of foreign trade in particular.

In the *Essay on Tradesmen* he writes: "Merchants and tradesmen are to a nation as Stewards, Bayliffs, and Butlers are to great Families," and are therefore useful as a good government is to a nation. "But as traders are useful in distributing, it's only the Labour of the Poor that increaseth the Riches of a nation, and tho' there cannot be too many Labourers in a nation, if their imployments are in a due proportion; yet there may be too many traders in a country for the number of labourers." Tradesmen might become rich while the nation might be impoverished through "extravagancy". An instance as to the consumption of wine forms the transition to the *Essay on Foreign Trade*. He says that this trade also is useful by introducing into the country, among other things,

articles of art and of consumption which the country itself
does not produce, but this trade also is profitable to a country
inasmuch as "ornamental or delightful" things are brought over
which are not produced in the country. But in this matter a
"voluptuous age may easily fall into excess, with dress and
pleasure, whilst nothing can be strictly said to inrich a nation
but what increaseth its people. . . . But how much of the
silks, oyls, pickles, fruits and wine we receive from Turkey,
Italy, Spain and France . . . are an equivalent and of equal
use to us, wh. the more lasting and needful clothes and provision we send out for them w^d be, may be some question.

"Supposing we send 400 thousand pound a year of *English*
manufacture to them 4 Countries, and by the returns, the
merchants and retailers may get 30 per cent. wh. makes
250 thousand pounds value imported, to be spent in *England*.
Now, Quere, whether this 400 thousand pounds first sent
out, is not rather the nation's expence, than the 120 thousand
pounds the traders get, may be supposed to add to the nation's
stock? And another question is, what of it is prudently spent
with comfort, and how much is extravagantly wasted, to the
ruin of the bodies and estates of the spenders?

"If we send 100 thousand pound of manufactures to Holland
and Germany, we have commonly some useful manufactures
for them; however, if we did employ our own idle poor upon
them things, it's possible they w^d be able to raise most of them
foreign goods we want.

"But then our woollen manufacturers that supply them
countries w^d complain of such new manufacturers; as some
Lancashire men lately petitioned the Parliament, that Flanders
lace sh^d be allowed to come into England that thereby they
might have better vent for their cloth in Flanders. And thus",
Bellers writes, and in doing so he really says the last word on
the eternal dispute of free trade and protection, "whilst our
manufactures are disproportioned to our husbandmen, *we
are, and shall be like limbs out of joint, always complaining*,

lay us wh. way you will. For wh. reason several Laws, made
for incouraging of Trade, doth but raise an intestine war
among our mechanics, because the advantage of one Trade is
often the ruin of another."

And the essay concludes with the query: "If we do not
depopulate our country by pineing many at home for want
of them manufactures, and especially food, wh. we send
abroad, to supply the pride and luxury of others by the
returns?" "120 thousand pounds", adds Bellers, "imported
to be spent at home, for 100 thousand pound sent out, leaves
the publick never the richer at the yeare's end."

There follows next an *Essay on Money*. It expands the ideas
set forth in the introduction to the *Proposals*. "Land, stock
upon it, Buildings, and money are the body of our riches, and
of all these", Bellers says, "money is of least use." . . . "Land
and live stock increase by keeping, buildings and manufactures are useful, whilst kept, but money neither increaseth,
nor is useful, *but when it's parted with*." "So what money is
more than of absolute necessity for a home Trade, is dead
Stock. . . . Money hath two qualities, it is a pledge for what
it is given for, and it's the measure and scales by wh. we
measure and value all other things, it being portable and
durable, and yet it hath altered far more in value to all things
than other things have among themselves, when there was but
the one 20th part of the money in England to what there is
now . . . the same number of days' work of a man w^d pay
for a sheep or cow 300 years ago as will now, and the same
labour will plough an acre of land now as would then."

We must remember that this was written when the methods
of agriculture and manufacture changed but slowly. And even
where Bellers starts from false premises, the idea which he
aims at is nevertheless correct.

The essay on the *Abating of Immoralities* asserts that all economical improvements are useless unless they are combined
with moral elevation. The essay *Against Capital Punishment*, or,

as Bellers entitled it, *Some Reasons Against Putting of Felons to Death*, is a very fine anticipation of the best works of Beccaria and others. He calls the premature death inflicted by the State "a stain to religion", and compares the relation of the criminal to society to that of a scapegrace to his family. "If a man had a child or near relation, that sh^d fall into a capital crime, he w^d use all his interest to preserve his life, howmuch soever he abhorred his fact, in hopes he might live to grow better, especially if he c^d have such a power of confinement upon him, as might prevent his acting such enormities for the future. And this child, and near relation, is every one to the publick." Moreover, it should not be forgotten that man is not wholly responsible. "The idle and profane education of some, and the necessities of others bring habits almost invincible."

Bellers stresses the economic loss caused to society by killing criminals instead of employing them in useful work in penitentiaries, but adds that this is not the cardinal point. He appeals to the petition in the Lord's Prayer, "Forgive us our trespasses", and inveighs against the excessive punishment then in vogue, of the gallows or penal servitude for small thefts. Finally, he demands that the detestable conditions existing in the prisons should be altered, and that the prisons should be freed from exploitation by speculative gaolers.

The booklet, which concludes with the *Essay on the Inward Light*, stamps Bellers as one of the most unprejudiced minds of his time, not on all points free from its errors, but almost in all points far in advance of the majority of even his more enlightened contemporaries.

The same may be said touching the next publication of Bellers, the contents of which are sufficiently indicated by its title, which we therefore reproduce in full: "*Some Reasons for an European State proposed to the Powers of Europe*, by an *universal guarantee* and *an Annual Congress, Senate, Dyet* or *Parliament*, To settle any Disputes about the Bounds and Rights of Princes and States hereafter. With an abstract of a scheme formed by King Henry the Fourth of France, upon the same subject. And also A Proposal for a *General Council or Convocation of all the different Religious Perswasions* in *Christendom* (not to Dispute what they Differ about but) to Settle the General Principles they Agree in: By wh. it will appear, that they may be good subjects and neighbours, tho' of different Apprehensions of the way to Heaven. In order to prevent Broils and War at home, when Foreign Wars are ended." London, 1710.

In this, as in his other proposals, Bellers is notably in advance of his predecessors, although he is careful to make allowance for existing circumstances. This pamphlet is by no means an abstract essay, but is closely related to contemporary occurrences, from which he endeavours to show the expediency of his proposals. The War of the Spanish Succession, which had been raging since 1701, had involved great sacrifices in money and blood, and still seemed to be no nearer its end; it was from this that Bellers derived an argument in favour of his proposal of an international confederation. In a dedication addressed to Queen Anne he points to the sacrifices incurred and the alliance concluded (between England, Holland, and Austria or Germany) in order to secure peace after the end of the war, and how little guarantee after all this alliance afforded, on how many contingencies its maintenance depended, seeing that each one of the allied States had to take other conditions and circumstances into account. In an address to the Powers he further calculates the expenditure in men, money, and economical welfare, incurred through war, directly or indirectly, by European nations since 1688 alone. The method of calculation in this case also is one which is thoroughly original for that period. Finally, he unfolds his proposal. Europe is to be divided into a number of districts (say one hundred) of equal size (cantons or provinces), and each State is to send one member per canton to the Parliament of States, that is to say, each State shall be represented therein in proportion to its size and population. This Parliament, which shall only deal with the external and general relations of States to each other, without interfering with their internal affairs, is to determine how many combatants, or vessels, and how much money each State is to provide per canton, in case a joint action should be required against truce-breakers; and according to the obligations undertaken in this respect by the various States, the number of their votes in the joint Parliament will be proportioned, so that, in addition to their geographical extent, their capabilities will be taken into account. Parliament will then arrange as to the reduction of standing armies and the number of men per canton to be kept under arms in peace-time.

In other respects, too, Bellers shows himself in this essay far ahead of his age. As the title suggests, he reproduces in it a similar project of Henry IV of France. In his comments thereon he remarks that Henry had excluded the "Muscovites" (Russia) and Turkey from his scheme, which, in his opinion, was done only in deference to the Roman See. But, says he, "*The Muscovites are Christians, and the Mahometans men*, and have the same faculties and reason as other men, they only want the same opportunities and applications of their understandings to be the same men: But to beat their Brains out, to put sense into them, is a great Mistake, and w^d leave Europe too much in a state of war; whereas the farther this civil Union is possible to be extended, the greater will be the Peace on earth, and good will among men."

In 1710 it required not only a high degree of intellectual freedom but also no small meed of courage to give expression to this view. The other proposal in this pamphlet, the "*religious Parliament*", which is not to discuss the things that separate religions, meaning dogmas, but is to ascertain what the various religions have in common, which could only be certain ethical maxims, is also a remarkable one for its time, however slender its prospects of success. It breathes a new catholicity. It was an appropriate and dignified reply to the crusade against all denominations not belonging to the Established Church which had been set on foot in the summer of 1709 by Sacheverell, and which, in 1710, was instrumental in raising the Harley–St. John Tory coalition into power.

One of the first acts of the new Government (1711) was to tighten the franchise by establishing a minimum property qualification. This may have prompted Bellers to publish in 1712 an essay in favour of electoral reform, or, as the title says, *An Essay towards the Ease of Elections of Members of Parliament*. It relates chiefly to precautions against bribery, abuse of oaths, etc., at elections. Cases of bribery shall be visited on the bribers, as the seducers, with punishments up to five times as high as the bribed, and the making of oaths shall be replaced by affidavits with legally binding force.

In 1714 he published a larger treatise, in which he anticipates a national health service. This, in fact, is the scope of the essay "*About the Improvement of Physick*, in 12 proposals, By wh. the Lives of many Thousands of the Rich, as well as of the Poor may be saved yearly. With an Essay for Imploying the Able Poor By wh. the Riches of the Kingdom may be greatly Increased. Humbly dedicated to the Parliament of Great Britain." London, 1714.

The most important proposal of this treatise is to establish a systematic connection between the study of medicine and the practice of medical science with the hospital system, which is to be organized and financed everywhere by the public bodies—Parishes, or Hundredths, Counties, or the State. Bellers also enlarges on the equipment and arrangements of hospitals, pleads for the establishment of separate wings or special hospitals for certain diseases, and finally discusses curative methods (as we observed in the Introduction, he was on intimate terms with one of the most eminent physicians of the day), but of course his remarks on this subject are antiquated.

An appendix recapitulates briefly the proposal of the "College", which Bellers never tired of preaching up to his last breath.

Thus as late as in 1723 he published a new essay entitled *An Essay for Employing the Poor to Profit*, with the motto, "If there were no Labourers there would be no Lords; and if the Labourers did not raise more food and manufactures than what did subsist themselves, every Gentleman must be a Labourer, and Idle Man must starve."

The arguments do not differ from those in the former essays, except that those relating to money and foreign trade are put more tersely. Again and again he points to the vicissitudes of life and appeals to "duty and interest" as mighty advocates for stimulating the rich to active provision for the poor. We may refer, as a remarkable feature in this essay, to the attitude adopted by Bellers to the struggle which was proceeding with increasing intensity between the manufacturers and the mechanics over the introduction of technical improvements in manufacturing processes. Bellers, who is so impartial with regard to manufactures as to declare it to be a great mistake to stimulate them without a simultaneous development of agriculture—to be like "placing more Men to a Table without putting more Food there", yet most decidedly opposes all legislation directed against machinery. In this respect his friendliness towards the workers does not blind him for a single moment. Laws against reduction of labour (that is to say against labour-saving machinery and methods) are as unreasonable, he writes, as if one would tie fast one hand of each worker to his back so that two might always be required instead of one. On this topic too he had perfectly modern ideas.

The pamphlet asks for the appointment of a Parliamentary committee to examine its proposals.

In the spring of 1724 Bellers published *An Epistle to Friends of the Yearly, Quarterly, and Monthly Meetings*, that is to say, of the Quaker organizations, wherein he urgently recommends to them active care of the inmates of prisons and hospitals, partly for purposes of propaganda among them, and partly in order to improve their material position as far as possible.

And he sang his swan-song the same year in "An abstract of George Fox's Advice and Warning To the Magistrates of London in the year 1657. Concerning the Poor, with some Observations thereupon, and Recommendations of them to the Sincerely Religious, but more particularly to the Friends of London, and Morning-Meeting of these times." It is a warm-hearted and impressive admonition to his co-religionists not to neglect the cause of the poor, nor to confine themselves to mere almsgiving. It was to the Friends that he first directed his plan for the organization of industrial colleges, and his last word in favour of the creation of methodical arrangements for the useful and profitable employment of the unemployed is again addressed "more particularly to the Friends". In the year 1725 death snatched from his hand the pen which he had indefatigably wielded on behalf of the poor.

What he did by way of direct assistance for the poor and needy is outside the scope of this work; the remark may suffice that he was not simply a benefactor in theory. It would also be beyond the scope of this work to inquire into the effect of Bellers' writings upon the corresponding literature of his and the following ages. In speaking of him we have already gone ahead of the period we had set ourselves to investigate. But this could not be avoided, as not only chronologically, but also as regards the character of his ideas, he stands out as a land-mark between the communism of the seventeenth and the reform movements of the eighteenth century.

CONCLUSION

THE currents of opinion which we have been studying converge in John Bellers. We have seen how the struggle between two sections of the ruling classes for political dominion, in its sequel, brought upon the political stage the most advanced sections of the working classes of the period, and thus led to the formulation of demands which anticipate the programme of modern political democracy. We have also seen how a still lower stratum of the working class produced champions, who, adopting political shibboleths and utilizing religious communistic doctrines imported from other countries, elaborated a system of communism which was more advanced than any similar previous doctrines. We have further seen how the increasing distress of the poorer classes, side by side with the increasing prosperity of the comfortable classes, gave rise to a middle-class school of philanthropism, full of projects of all kinds for providing a remedy by special institutions—suggestions that what was formerly the task of the Church should be performed by the State, by private parishes, or by organized voluntary effort. We have seen too how a new conception of the State gained ground, according to which the State, instead of being an organ of a dominant aristocracy or the tool of a dynasty, should become an instrument for promoting the welfare of all; and we further saw how there developed from the embittered strife of religious parties an advanced anti-clerical, anti-dogmatic school of thought, which led to atheism or deism in one direction, and to the founding of a religion without ritual, viz., Quakerism, in another.

Quakerism is related to atheism as the school of social reform philanthropy is related to communism. Bellers, both as Quaker and social reformer, is an outstanding figure, and in both respects he represents the best tendencies of the movement. In his writings we find reproduced the boldest and clearest ideas of the advanced religious and social reformers of the seventeenth century. Did he receive these ideas from them, or was he acquainted with their writings? It is possible, for it was not then customary to quote references, except when appealing to acknowledged authorities. He may, on the other hand, have received these ideas indirectly through the channels of authors inspired by them, or from his surroundings—we might say they were in the air. He wrote under conditions similar to theirs: at a time of distress, after a political revolution. In 1648 and 1649 it was possible to believe in the feasibility of a democratic revolution, inasmuch as the democratic sections of the nation were then under arms; but in 1688 or 1695 such an expectation was clearly an illusion. On the other hand, it was then possible to launch a sharper criticism of society and its tendencies, not only a moral condemnation of the inequalities pervading society, but also a denunciation of the economic powers that were in the ascendancy and of society's own inability to direct its productive forces in the interests of the whole.

It is the great merit of John Bellers to have perceived at so early a date this aspect of the modern social order, and if it is justifiable to suggest that his schemes and proposals bear the same relation to the Utopia of Winstanley as the Revolution of 1688 did to the Great Rebellion of 1648, we must also admit that his greater insight into the economic structure of society corresponds with the growth in wealth during the intervening fifty years, and that his writings are a refreshing contrast to the eulogies of the contemporary apologists for the middle classes, and constitute the most enlightened plea for the cause of the working classes on the eve of the eighteenth century.

INDEX